International Students Negotiating Higher Education

International students provide an important income to universities, but they also come with their own diverse variety of characteristics and requirements.

This insightful book offers a critical stance on contemporary views of international students and challenges the way those involved address the important issues at hand. To do this, the authors focus specifically on giving voice to the student experience. In particular, they show how the international student experience can be a ready asset from which to glean valuable information, particularly in relation to teaching and learning, academic support and the formal and informal curriculum. In this way, the issues affecting international students can be seen as part of the larger set of difficulties that face all students at university today.

Integrating contributions from academics and student voices from a range of backgrounds, the issues raised include:

- academic writing for international students;
- the internationalization of the curriculum;
- identities: the use of stereotypes and auto-stereotypes;
- international students' perceptions of tutors; and
- the system in reverse: English-speaking learners as 'international students'.

This book will be of interest to education management and administrators, and higher education professionals, especially those working or training to teach large numbers of international students, to which it offers a unique opportunity to understand better the students' point-of-view. Using international case studies including those from the UK, Australia and the USA, *International Students Negotiating Higher Education* is a valuable text for academics in all English-speaking countries that recruit significant numbers of international students as well as the growing number of European and international universities that teach in English.

Silvia Sovic is Senior Research Fellow at the Institute of Historical Research, University of London, and Guest Researcher at the Centre for Learning and Teaching in Art and Design, University of the Arts, London.

Margo Blythman is the former Director of Teaching and Learning at the London College of Communication, University of the Arts, London.

International Students Negotiating Higher Education

Critical perspectives

Edited by
Silvia Sovic and
Margo Blythman

Routledge
Taylor & Francis Group

LONDON AND NEW YORK

First published 2013
by Routledge
2 Park Square, Milton Park, Abingdon, Oxon OX14 4RN

Simultaneously published in the USA and Canada
by Routledge
711 Third Avenue, New York, NY 10017

Routledge is an imprint of the Taylor & Francis Group, an informa business

British Library Cataloguing in Publication Data
A catalogue record for this book is available from the British Library

Library of Congress Cataloging in Publication Data
International students negotiating higher education: critical perspectives/
edited by Silvia Sovic and Margo Blythman
    p. cm.
    1. Foreign study – Great Britain.   2. College student mobility –
Great Britain.   3. Education, Higher – Great Britain.   I. Sovic, Silvia.
II. Blythman, Margo.
    LB2376.6.G72I68 2012
    378.1'9826910941 – dc23
    2012013211

ISBN: 978-0-415-61469-6 (hbk)
ISBN: 978-0-415-61470-2 (pbk)
ISBN: 978-0-203-81748-3 (ebk)

Typeset in Galliard and Gill Sans
by Florence Production Ltd, Stoodleigh, Devon

Printed and bound by CPI Group (UK) Ltd, Croydon, CR0 4YY

Contents

Figures and tables

Figures

Tables

Contributors

Joanna Al-Youssef (EdD, MA ELT) is a lecturer of English for Academic Purposes and a course leader for the Postgraduate Certificate in International Student Advice and Support at Nottingham University. Her research interests include higher education internationalization, and international students' issues.

Carol Bailey has taught English as a foreign language (EFL) in Morocco and China and is Senior Lecturer in EFL at the University of Wolverhampton, UK. Her research interests include the international student experience, academic writing and plagiarism.

Michelle C. Barker is Professor of International Business and Asian Studies, Griffith University. She holds Visiting Fellow appointments at CAPRI, Leeds Metropolitan University, and CACR, University of Victoria, New Zealand. Michelle co-developed the EXCELL Intercultural Skills Program and is internationally recognized for her scholarship in internationalization of the curriculum and intercultural skills training.

Brendan Bartram is Senior Lecturer in Education Studies at the University of Wolverhampton, UK. His research interests include foreign language learning and teaching, pedagogy in higher education and issues in comparative and international education.

Margo Blythman is the former Director of Teaching and Learning at the London College of Communication, University of the Arts, London. Her research interests include student support and student diversity in a context of social justice.

Kelly Coate is based in the Centre for Excellence in Learning and Teaching at NUI Galway and is currently the Vice-Dean for Graduate Studies in the College of Arts, Social Sciences and Celtic Studies. She was previously a researcher at the Institute of Education, University of London.

Weronika Górska is a teaching fellow at Queen Mary, University of London. She teaches academic writing for both taught and research students. Her research interests include academic literacy, internationalization of higher education and computer assisted learning.

Elizabeth Grant is a principal teaching fellow at the Centre for the Advancement of Learning and Teaching, UCL. Between 2007 and 2011, she was responsible for the implementation of the internationalization of the curriculum across the college. She is now focusing her work within the School of the Built Environment, Engineering Sciences and Mathematical and Physical Sciences.

Wendy Green is a lecturer in higher education at the Teaching and Educational Development Institute at the University of Queensland, Australia. Her research interests include internationalizing the curriculum, global mobility of students and academics and continuing professional learning.

Raymond T. Hibbins is Senior Lecturer, Department of Tourism, Hotel, Sport and Leisure Management, Griffith University. His research specialization is migration, gender, ethnicity and sexuality. He has published in journals, books and book chapters concerned with transnationalism, migration, entrepreneurship, leisure and masculinities.

Margaret Kettle is a lecturer at Queensland University of Technology, Australia where she teaches on the MEd TESOL programme. Her research and pedagogical interests include second language teaching and learning, Englishes, internationalization of higher education and critical discourse analysis.

Yu-Ching Kuo is currently a visiting research associate at the Institute of Education, University of London. Her recent research has focused on comparative international student policy regimes, quality assurance in cross-border higher education, and widening participation and fair access policies.

Allan Luke is Professor of Education at Queensland University of Technology. He is currently working on a large-scale evaluation of Australian school reform for Aboriginal and Torres Strait Islander students.

Simon Marginson is a professor of Higher Education at the University of Melbourne, Australia, where he works in the Centre for the Study of Higher Education. His books include *Ideas for Intercultural Education* (with Erlenawati Sawir, Palgrave Macmillan, 2011).

Beatrice Merrick is Director of Services and Research at the UK Council for International Student Affairs (UKCISA). Her research includes international students' experiences of UK education and immigration, international student services in further and higher education and related professional development.

Ganga Rathnayake is a senior lecturer, University of Kelaniya. She has a B.Com. (Special) Degree and an M.Com Degree and is currently reading for a Ph.D. in the Commerce Degree Programme, National University of Ireland, Galway. She has been a university lecturer since 1990. Her interests include human resource management, labour economics and research methodology.

Silvia Sovic is Senior Research Fellow at the Institute of Historical Research, University of London, and Guest Researcher at the Centre for Learning and Teaching in Art and Design, University of the Arts, London. A historical demographer by training, she was Research Co-ordinator for the International Students' Experience Project at UAL.

Ly Tran is a lecturer in the School of Education, RMIT University. She has been involved in various projects including the mutual adaptation of international students and academics, the social security of international students and the internationalization of the curriculum.

Peter Woods is a senior lecturer in the Department of International Business and Asian Studies, Griffith Business School, Griffith University. He was a recipient of the prestigious Australian University Award for Teaching Excellence for Internationalization in 2010.

Acknowledgements

We would like to thank Dr Alison Shreeve who, as Director of the Creative Learning in Practice CETL, gave us considerable support both in initiating and continuing with this project. We also wish to thank Celia Bishop for her thorough and supportive proof-reading of the text and Dr Ros Petelin for her helpful and insightful comments on the draft of this book.

Chapter 1

Introduction

Silvia Sovic and Margo Blythman

This book grew out of the International Students' Experience Project at the Creative Learning in Practice Centre for Excellence in Teaching and Learning (CLIP CETL) at the University of the Arts, London, conducted in 2006–8. The rationale for this was a feeling that there was a dearth of international students' voices in the international pedagogical literature in the UK, especially when it came to discussion about teaching and learning. Many of the 141 international students we interviewed (in their own languages) had never even heard of the term 'teaching and learning' before, but their responses did not square at all with the assumed characteristics of international students as featured in the literature. On the contrary, these students demonstrated plenty of resourcefulness and critical thinking, and they frequently offered solutions to problems that neither pedagogical researchers nor institutions had considered before. Following the publication of the report on this project (Sovic 2008), and with the generous support of Alison Shreeve (then Director of CLIP CETL), in June 2009 Margo Blythman (then Director of Teaching and Learning at the London College of Communication) and Silvia Sovic (the Research Project Co-Ordinator) organized a cross-cultural workshop on 'The Experience of International Students' at the University of the Arts, London. The aim was to bring together other scholars to critically evaluate the current perceptions and to offer alternative views beyond the traditional stereotypes. This book includes contributions from the participants of that workshop as well as several others who had expressed interest but were unable to attend.

This book is divided into four parts. The first consists of five chapters on aspects of policy. Simon Marginson explores the paradigm of globalization and citizenship. Many international students, particularly of non-white origins and from emerging nations, experience various types of discrimination in the country they have chosen for their education. OECD figures of 2010 stated that each year as many as 3.3 million students study outside their country of citizenship. Marginson argues that 'the political and legal Othering of globally mobile students by national governments functions as the master Othering process' (page 10). Marginson calls for a more cosmopolitan approach in international education, and suggests that 'in the interim the enlightened national response is to confer on international students a quasi-citizenship status whereby their rights and entitlements are aligned as closely as possible to those of local students' (page 11). Beatrice Merrick addresses the UK's policies towards international students in recent decades, which she finds to be disjointed because they are spread across government departments. She explores the term 'international students' in various contexts and points out the limitation of this classification; an example would be students from the European Union, who may be categorized as 'home students' in terms of fees, but 'foreign' in terms of nationality. The rhetoric of internationalization is not matched by what is happening in practice. Moreover, financial benefits have led to the prioritization of recruitment, but also to a failure to reward good teaching practice or those who make efforts 'to ensure that those students' experiences are positive' (page 35). At the same time, international students do not fall under the remit of the Quality Assurance Agency, nor are they properly represented by the National Union of Students. Merrick concludes that this heavily constrained environment has necessitated initiatives by students themselves to negotiate UK higher education successfully.

Kelly Coate and Ganga Rathnayake provide a critical overview of the consumerist model of internationalization as currently applied by policy-makers in Irish higher education. They question the ethical commitment of current practices towards less developed countries and discuss the concepts of care, moral responsibility and cosmopolitanism. These values had a prominent role in the history of higher education in this missionary country, and were reflected in more charitable attitudes towards students from 'poorer' countries. The authors take up Rizvi's (2009) call for a 'global humanity' that 'takes primacy over local concerns' and that establishes a 'moral' basis for relationships with international students in an era of economic rationalism in which students are regarded as consumers (page 49). The last two chapters in this section raise more concerns in relation to internationalization. Joanna Al-Youssef takes up the perception of internationalization as understood by different levels of managerial structure at university, while Elizabeth Grant focuses on the current inconsistencies towards an international curriculum and lack of engagement within higher education in the development of such a curriculum.

Part II of the book focuses on teaching and learning. Silvia Sovic addresses creative arts students' perceptions of their tutors and calls for cosmopolitan learning engagement in mixed classrooms, which in a global age will benefit all students. Margaret Kettle and Allan Luke engage with a narrative of two postgraduate students from two major source countries, China and Thailand, in an Australian university. Rather than generalizing about their teaching and learning experiences, the study offers an in-depth insight into 'the complex cultural dynamics and exchanges at work in postgraduate study' (page 105). The evidence presented in the study offers 'new empirical insights into a topic that has been riven with entrenched theoretical position and controversy' (page 106). Ly Tran's chapter investigates 'the theory of transformative learning as a possible explanation for the changes international students make in their journey to negotiate higher education' (page 124). The author's main evidence comes from interviews conducted with Chinese and Vietnamese students about their learning experience at an Australian university. She highlights the contradiction between the transformative environment that universities claim to offer in their promotional literature, and the real situations in which potential transformative learning processes for international students are supposed to take place. In this context, she further problematizes the internationalization of curricula through the spectrum of transformative learning and the positive impact this could present for international and home students alike. Michelle Barker, Ray Hibbins and Peter Woods carried out an exploratory study of masters-level business students with the aim of helping researchers and practitioners to integrate the principle of internationalization into the formal and informal curricula of higher education, to equip university graduates with the knowledge, skills and attributes of a 'global citizen'. Students' own definitions of global citizenship are presented within the framework of cultural intelligence. Part II concludes with Yu-Ching Kuo's chapter, which joins the others in questioning the prevailing view of international students who are seen in the scholarly literature as 'victims' or 'problems', and suggests that many students are much more resilient in entering higher education. She investigates the idea of international students' identity as entrepreneurs, and argues that the identities of customers and entrepreneurs are by no means the same.

In recent years much has been written on the subject of Part III of this book, language issues. It would not be an overstatement to note that language inadequacy, associated with the much-contested concept of 'cultural differences', is far too often offered as a simplistic explanation for the learning deficiency of international students. The two chapters in this part focus instead more specifically on academic writing, which the authors discuss from different angles. Carol Bailey challenges current assessment strategies of academic writing through a critical pedagogical viewpoint, and calls for application of more flexible assessment methods. She argues that 'certain assessment types do disadvantage certain groups of international students', and suggests that higher education should reconsider this issue within the framework of equal opportunities, thus promoting greater inclusivity (page 184). Weronika Górska questions whether students receive sufficient and appropriate guidance and writing support while progressing from generic to subject-specific areas of academic writing. Her study adopts an academic literacies approach, and her findings are based on pre-masters student voices and 'their perspectives on the support they receive, the academic requirements they have to meet and their own engagement in learning to write academically approved texts' (page 190).

The final part of this book addresses the reverse phenomenon: the experience of home students studying abroad, or so-called 'horizontal mobility'. In this context 'home students' are represented by Australian students in the chapter by Wendy Green, and UK students in the chapter by Brendan Bartram. Green points out that there is a vacuum in scholarly research, which focuses on the experience of horizontally mobile students. However, she argues that study abroad is coming to be seen as an important component of an internationalized curriculum. Her study emphasizes that 'if the benefit of studying abroad is to be measured on the basis of levels of immersion in the host culture, universities that send and receive students need to do more to support this intention' (page 223). Bartram reports on his research on UK Study Abroad students' motivations and challenges relating to their sojourn overseas, and concludes that career and academic benefits do not rate as highly as social or personal benefits, such as transformative shifts in self-identity.

The contributors to this book join other recent critical studies that have challenged the widespread notion, usually reached by focusing on a 'deficit model', of international students portrayed as victims. The methodology deployed in these studies is often inadequate, based on anecdotal evidence or with little methodological rigour; many of them fall into the category defined by Holliday as a 'large culture paradigm', an approach that 'imposes a picture of the social world which is divided into "hard", essentially different ethnic, national or international cultures' (Holliday 1999: 240). The contributions to this book show considerable variety in terms of the methodology and techniques they have adopted. Many used semi-structured interviews (Tran, Barker *et al.*, Kuo), in some cases large scale (Marginson, Sovic); others involved a smaller number of in-depth interviews (Al-Youssef) or detailed studies of one or two cases (Coate and Rathnayake, Kettle and Luke). Some have made use of special procedures such as the nominal group technique (Barker *et al.*), positioning interviews (Tran), paradigmatic analysis (Green) and critical discourse analysis (Kettle and Luke). Contributions are also informed by reference to other disciplines such as philosophy (Coate and Rathnayake) and ethnography (Górska).

Throughout this book there are many issues that remain unresolved, but which we hope will stimulate future debate. Who are international students? What do we mean in practice when we talk about internationalization? Most would by now agree that it must entail more than the setting up of an international recruiting office and language centres; but what precisely? What is an international curriculum in practice? Do the so-called 'international' universities have guidance and policy to help their staff create and develop such a beast? Is globalization just for home students? And finally – something that appears repeatedly in the literature – what exactly is meant by 'western learner', 'western education' and 'western pedagogy'?[1] In a recent article on the internationalization of the curriculum, Glynis Cousin debates the concept of westernism and questioned its value-free concept as an explanatory framework in the globalized classroom. In her view,

> the idea of the west 'sets a certain structure of thought and knowledge in motion' that we should be wary of. While we need provisional ideas and concepts to bring to bear on our analytical labour, 'provisional' is the key word here; we need to be open to rival explanations when we examine an issue with a particular frame. A 'tool' that overly frames the direction of our

inquiry in this way presents the danger that we see what we anticipate seeing before we look.

(Cousin 2011: 587)

One could paraphrase this by saying that it is for educationalists to demonstrate critical thinking in practice rather than just brandishing it as a slogan to describe western approaches to learning. Many contributors of this book suggest that the age of globalization should really be the age of cosmopolitanism in the classroom. Institutions and their staff will need to fully engage with these issues, otherwise there is a danger that all students and staff who cherish and value the opportunities of cultural exchanges will come to see internationalism as empty rhetoric.

Given the present climate for higher education, the circumstances and economics of international student migration are set to change, perhaps quite rapidly. The map of migration may look very different in as little as a decade. The economic balance of power, the methods of delivery (with 'local' campuses of 'global' universities), even the ecology of the linguistic map of higher education, may all see fundamental transformation. Much less likely to change are the underlying psychological and social factors at work when students elect for an international dimension to their education and the risks and sacrifices they incur in the process. However much it remains an unfulfilled ideal, a truly cosmopolitan approach, based on premises that are not chained to colonialist or post-colonialist structures and attitudes, is the best hope for a world of genuine international student mobility.

Note

1   A current attempt to explore these issues further is the ESRC Seminar series 'Global Citizenship as a Graduate Attribute'. See www.wlv.ac.uk/globalcitizen (accessed 17 March 2012).

References

Cousin, G. (2011) 'Rethinking the concept of "western"', *Higher Education Research and Development*, 30, 5: 585–94.

Holliday, A. (1999) 'Small cultures', *Applied Linguistics*, 20, 2: 237–64.

Rizvi, F. (2009) 'Towards cosmopolitan learning', *Discourse: Studies in the Cultural Politics of Education*, 30, 3: 253–68.

Sovic, S. (2008) *Lost in Transition? The International Students' Experience Project*, London: CLIP CETL. Online. Available HTTP: http://www.arts.ac.uk/librarylearningand teaching/clipcetl/projects/internationalstudentsexperience/ (accessed 13 February 2012).

Part I

Policy

Chapter 2

Equals or others?

Mobile students in a nationally bordered world

Simon Marginson

Introduction

Across the world, 3.3 million students study outside their country of citizenship each year (OECD 2010: 315).[1] Almost half of them move from Asia and Africa into English-speaking education systems. Another quarter move between countries in the European Higher Education Area. In the UK, Australia and New Zealand international education is a large and growing commercial export industry (Bashir 2007). In the United States international students contribute to the national knowledge economy and American foreign relations. Both the nation of education and the educated international student appear to gain from the exchange. But for international students in general, and more so for non-white students from emerging nations, the exchange is premised on less than equal respect and treatment. Most people in the country of education give this little thought. If it is difficult for international students, the thinking runs, why do 'they' come? Clearly 'our education' is superior to what 'they' have at home. And being supplicants, as it were, 'they' ought to 'adjust' to the country of education to the degree necessary to absorb its bounty.

Leaving behind their country of citizenship and the rights and protections it provides, international students enter a new education system and living setting where they are variously constructed as supplicants, strangers, outsiders, consumers, social isolates and people in learning or linguistic 'deficit'. Without their consent and scarcely with their participation, they are remade into the objects of an inchoate mix of paternalistic pastoral care, well-meaning efforts to culturally connect, neglect, security paranoia and out-and-out discrimination and abuse. They face violations of human security in all domains of public, institutional and private life and cannot access the full range of human rights (Marginson *et al.* 2010; Lee and Rice 2007).

The United Nations' *Universal Declaration of Human Rights* (UN 2010) is the most widely acknowledged definition of human rights. It provides for self-determining personhood in a broad set of domains including personal safety, privacy, access to justice and equal recognition before the law, freedom of movement and expression, 'economic, social and cultural rights' including access to social security and work, 'just and favourable' conditions of work, and rights to education and health. Article 28 states that 'everyone is entitled to a social and international order in which the rights and freedoms set forth in this Declaration can be fully realized'. This comprehensive approach to rights has implications also for the definition of human security. Rights and security are interdependent. The human security of international students rests on their capacity to sustain stable human agency and actively exercise a full set of rights. As Amartya Sen (1985) notes, negative and positive freedoms require each other if each is to be exercised. Both are conditions of agency freedom.

The human rights and security of international students also depend in part on conditions provided by the host government and educational institutions: conditions that allow them to differ from host country nationals within the terms of the law while continuing to access common facilities. But despite the facts that the country of education draws prolonged and direct benefits from these students, they pay the same taxes as local counterparts and they participate in nationally ordered institutions, they are granted less than the full rights, entitlements and protections of local citizens. It is hard for national systems of regulation to encompass cross-border persons. It is harder for the students, at the sharp end of national–global ambiguities and tensions.

The core difficulty for international students is that they are globally mobile persons with plural locations and commitments (Sen 1999), away from national citizenship, in a world where rights and security are organized nationally. While contemporary globalization is in many respects a product of the period of the modern nation state – the two phenomena, globalization and the nation state, emerged simultaneously (Bayly 2004) – there is also a contradiction between global and national. This tension extends beyond formal regulation to include the social domain, where global cultural plurality pushes against bounded national identity in local communities and people variously welcome or resist international students. It will be argued here that the political and legal Othering of globally mobile students by national governments functions as the master Othering process. The duality of citizen/non-citizen shelters, legitimates and amplifies all the other subordinations that international students experience, including the racist Othering, the exclusions, and the abuse and violence.

Included equals or subordinated Others? This is the choice posed by mobile students. The first, liberal impulse is to answer 'included equals, of course'. Yet some who so answer are unreflexively national in outlook – and if international students are to become included on a cosmopolitan basis, then national horizons must open. This chapter focuses on the core problem of international students' lack of citizenship status, and considers a new approach. It begins by reviewing traditional perspectives governing the reception of international students, in the light of the literature and using the particular example of international education in Australia, drawing on interviews with 200 international students in that country (Marginson *et al.* 2010), as outlined immediately below. The chapter then explores the national–global tension in regulation, the dynamics of the official and unofficial Othering of international students and the fallout experienced by the students themselves. The final section canvasses strategic options. It notes the constraints on global approaches, slow to emerge, and argues that in the interim the enlightened national response is to confer on international students a quasi-citizenship status whereby their rights and entitlements are aligned as closely as possible to those of local students.

Engagement with student subjects in the interviews, and the recent experience of targeted assaults of South Asian students in Australia (Marginson 2010), has shaped the normative perspectives underlying the chapter. First, international students are here modelled as most of them already are: as active and self-determining human agents. Second, the ideal international education is cosmopolitan with room for plural cultures. 'Cosmopolitan' implies a relational setting (Rizvi 2005) in which people are grounded in their own given and evolving identities, while they acknowledge and develop a 'flat' interconnectedness and interdependency within the common setting.

Study of international students in Australia

Data on international students' perceptions of their human security and rights were gathered in semi-structured interviews conducted in 2004–2006 with 200 students from 35 nations, enrolled at nine public universities in three of Australia's eight States and Territories.[2] The interviews lasted 30–60 minutes and covered up to 63 questions in 12 areas common to the study. Interviews were voluntary and arranged via emails advertising the study, or via university international offices. A qualitative study of this kind does not constitute a statistically valid sample. But 200 interviews create a large group and it approximated the balances of the actual international student population in gender, fields of study and national origin. Ph.D. students, older students and students from Indonesia were over-represented (Marginson *et al.* 2010). The research was funded by the Australian Research Council and the Monash Institute for the Study of Global Movements at Monash University.

In qualitative work of this kind it is impossible to ensure data are representative, and material must be handled with careful judgement. The quotations used here are consistent with most responses. They are not outliers, mobilized selectively.

Alongside the 200 student interviews were two further inquiries designed to isolate the student experience distinctive to international students: an interview programme involving 20 international and 20 local students; and a comparison in 2007 of the formal rights, entitlements and benefits available to each group of students.

Stereotypes of international students

In English-speaking countries international students are encumbered by stereo-types of themselves that are well entrenched in the host countries and beyond the capacity of the international students themselves to control or modify. These stereotypes have various roots in psychology, education, pastoral care and economics. Each stereotype is widely though not universally influential. They differ in the detail and the 'remedies' they impose, but each stereotype rests on assumptions that the country of education is superior, and each reifies and subordinates the international students.

Cultural 'adjustment'

The dominant approach in counselling psychology models international education as a journey of 'adjustment' in which the student moves from original culture to host country culture. It is assumed that the host country culture normalized by this prescription remains unchanged. The international student 'adjusts' to the host nation but not vice versa. Adjustment is 'successful' to the extent students discard their beliefs and adapt values and behaviours of host country norms. The idea of one-way adjustment implies the host culture is superior, fitting popular prejudices. As Lee and Rice (2007) note:

> We find that most of the literature concerning international student experiences describes their difficulties as issues of adapting or coping, which embodies the assumption that international students bear the responsibility to persist, overcome their discomfort, and integrate into the host society. Some of these studies call for increased sensitivity, but the underlying assumption is that host institutions are impartial and without fault. Few studies consider how institutions and individuals may purposefully or inadvertently marginalize international students.
>
> (Lee and Rice 2007: 388)

The relation between international student and host country is imagined in asymmetrical and ethnocentric terms and as an either/or in which the student must choose between one singular identity or the other. The theory of 'cultural fit' assumes that the closer is the starting position of the student to the host country culture, the happier and more successful the student will be (for example Ward and Chang 1997; Ward *et al.* 2004). Leong and Ward (2000: 765) even claim 'individuals who make cross-cultural transitions are generally expected to conform to the normative values, attitudes and behaviours of their host countries'. This suggests they should suppress their identity; and that discriminatory selection of students on the basis of language and cultural identity would enhance efficiency. But advocates of the 'cultural fit' thesis have failed to ground it empirically despite repeated attempts (Marginson 2009). Students from so-called 'collectivist' Asian cultures (Hofstede 1980) are no less likely to achieve academic success than those from 'individualist' backgrounds.

Of course not all psychology-informed studies are ethnocentric. In Bochner's foundational work on intercultural learning (1972) the task for international students is not to adopt the new culture but instead to learn its characteristics to operate effectively. Both Bochner and Berry imply students can augment their original 'identity and customs' (Berry *et al.* 1989: 186) while shaping new intercultural relations. Reviews of the research on international students by Church (1982) and Pedersen (1991) enable plural perspectives. Kashima and Loh (2006) note dynamic changes in international student identities during the period of education, in which both original and acquired practices are in play. The cosmopolitan student who tolerates a measure of ambiguity, plurality and cultural mixing seems to be the happiest and most successful.

The psychology of cultural fit is paralleled by the educational model of international students as persons in 'deficit'. It is assumed that international students educated in non-European settings have undergone an inferior pedagogical tradition. Again, the response to cultural difference is not to do what the students themselves do, become more plural – that complexity would make life harder for monocultural teachers – but to expect the students to unlearn what they have learned. The deficit stereotype is joined to claims that 'Asian learners' are rote learners who cannot think critically, work creatively or speak up in class (confusing communication difficulties in English with passivity). This denies student agency and identity, blocks intercultural exchange in the classroom and enforces a top-down approach, while stigmatizing the students as prone to domination and lacking agency (see Ninnes and Hellsten 2005).

In student welfare, the equivalent to cultural fit theory and deficit pedagogy are the ideas of international students as weak persons in need of paternalistic care, and persons in social deficit unwilling or unable to integrate with locals. It is assumed that friendship networks with students from the same cultural background block local friendships and integration with the host society, and 'collectivist' Asian students are especially prone to this (e.g. Triandis 1989) – though all evidence suggests that most international students want friendships with local students, and many local students form enclosed networks and self-segregate away from international students (Marginson *et al.* 2010: Chs 13 and 15). The pattern of strong same-culture networking and weak local links (Rosenthal *et al.* 2006) is triggered more by necessity than choice.

International students as consumers

The commercial export nations of the UK, Australia and New Zealand position international students as consumers with consumer protection rights. National governments are more comfortable with the notion of global persons as economic subjects than as plural cultural subjects or extra-national world citizens. This is not because economic life is more intrinsically global than the rest of life. The opposite is the case. Political economy is still nationally bordered. Politics more readily understands globalization as an economic phenomenon and recognizes global actors in the context of economic bargains because politics itself (nation-bound as it is) finds it easier to manage cross-border trade than global cultural flows, and there is a long history of trade regulation.

International education in Australia is regulated by the Education Services for Overseas Students (ESOS) Act and the *National Code of Practice* that governs education providers under ESOS (DEEWR 2007). The ESOS Act and the Code focus mainly on immigration law compliance and consumer protection (DEEWR 2007: Sections A.3.1 and B.4). 'The registered provider must enter into a written agreement with the student' which specifies the programme of study, monies payable and 'information in relation to refunds of course money' (DEEWR 2007: Standard 3, Section 3.1). There is no contract between students and government and no reference to political rights or representation. The notion of student as consumer applies only to international students and is not formalized in the legislation governing the education of local students.[3]

The main protections for the consumer are information, prohibition of fraud and safeguarding of monies in the event of market failure. Prior to enrolment institutions must provide 'clear and unambiguous' marketing and 'information about the course, fees, facilities, services and resources offered'. They must not offer 'false or misleading information or advice' in areas like 'employment outcomes associated with a course', 'automatic acceptance into another course' or 'possible migration outcomes' (DEEWR 2007: Section D, Preamble to Standards 1–4, 10–11; Standard 1, Section 1.2; Standard 2, Section 2.1). The Act and the Code touch only briefly on rights and security in other domains. The main thrust is to specify mandatory information on welfare and housing rather than actual services. The notion of student as consumer ensures the claims students make on authority are primarily legal and economic. It also shifts the locus of claims from government to provider (the 'firms' in the market). Student agency is confined by the marked information asymmetry between provider and consumer in international education. Questions of social, industrial, civil and political rights, which are ultimately claims on governments rather than providers, are off the agenda.

The notion of student as a consumer engaged in business transactions is a regression from ideas of self-determining democratic agency that have evolved since the French Revolution. It is also a slippage from the stronger norm in higher education itself: students as knowledge producers co-shaping their own development. Likewise it is something less than the welfare state promise of a universal right to high-quality common services. The welfare regime was paternalistic. It underplayed personal empowerment. But it was more generous and equitable than the consumption regime.

Yet the notion of student as consumer does not altogether eliminate agency. And it promises a global right – though one more limited than is provided by, say, global citizenship. 'The market' cuts across differences of nation, culture, gender, age and social status. It is nested in a national legal regime but offers students from anywhere a common presence. Yet the ESOS Act and its counterparts in other nations also set out to claw back this global agent under their control. The international student as consumer is a global subject ordered and subordinated within a national political economy. Thus national power strives (ultimately in vain) to contain the global, which is subversive of national authority and habitually breaks through its limits.

The students and the stereotypes

How do the students see it? The 200 interviews indicate that many students were critical of these stereotypes. Some proposed counter-models of themselves. A few interviewees used the notion of student as consumer as a basis for claims, but on government rather than providers. Other interviewees just rejected the idea.

> We're basically seen as 'cash cows'. And that's something that should change.
> (male, 33, Ph.D. in medicine, Spain)

The interviewees repeatedly showed they were strong rather than weak agents, open to the new, adapting rapidly and remaking themselves in passage. None saw it as necessary to displace their old selves in doing so, though inevitably some elements became changed and pluralized, and doubts and dilemmas could arise.

> There's hell a lot of differences between living there and living here. The advantage of living out here is it teaches you how to be independent, the survival of the fittest. How to do things, manage your entire life. Back home, you have your parents to support you, back up. Out here, there is no back up; you're on your own. There are crucial decisions, and the decisions have to be taken by you, not by your parents. You learn a lot.
> (male, 27, business, India)

Interviewees resented or were upset by notions that they were in educational deficit and rejected the idea of social deficit. What they lacked was information and local experience, not capacity or empathy. Most emphasized that they wanted to befriend local students. Many were disappointed that they had not achieved this. The main reason they gave was local student indifference. This confirms other studies. A large-scale survey of both international and local student populations in 2006 (AEI 2007) found 81 per cent of international students wanted more local friends, and 67 per cent had tried actively to make them. But only 46 per cent of local students wanted more international friends and only 37 per cent had attempted this. Half the international students (48 per cent) thought locals were not interested in having international friends; only 24 per cent disagreed (AEI 2007). Just 58 per cent stated that local students were even 'friendly'.

> When I was living in China I thought that it would be difficult to make friends with the locals [in Australia]. But provided that I was talking – I have an active attitude and I'm an outgoing and friendly person – I would be able to make local friends. But it was much more difficult than I imagined.
> (female, 25, business, China)

Cultural stereotyping and the student as consumer are methods (formal and informal) of regulating and ordering the international student population. Much is invested in these methods. Despite a lack of foundation the cultural and educational stereotypes are difficult to shift – after all, they provide locals with the priceless asset of a sense of superiority – and the consumer notion is continually restated by policy and management. Both kinds of ordering are sustained by the national border itself and the non-citizen identity of international students in the country of education. The citizen/non-citizen divide is the essential dualism. This is the master Othering that shelters all the other forms of Othering, from deficit pedagogies to racist abuse.

Nation-boundedness and Othering

Nation states naturally tend to Other cross-border students. They have no ready method of imagining and managing mobile persons except to treat them as outsiders.

Despite partial global integration and convergence (Held *et al.* 1999), and awareness of global interdependence, it is a nation-state world. There is no global state or other comprehensive system of governance. There is a sketchy system of international law resting on voluntary multilateral engagement. There are cross-border agencies with roots in and outside nations and a thickening global civil society beyond regulation. But in law and policy, persons are managed by national governments on the basis of 1) where they are active and 2) where they are citizens. National authority is constituted by sovereign control over a legally, and mostly geographically, bound territory. This fits poorly with globally mobile persons such as international students.

Most international students are citizens of one state but present within the jurisdiction of another. (Dual citizenship is provided by some countries but rarely accessed by cross-border students and other temporary migrants such as tourists, workers and business executives.) This framework has three implications for mobile students. First, they are affected by two national regimes, to a differing extent, and by the political and legal relation between them. Second, notwithstanding this, persons who are citizens of one nation while on the territory of another fall into a gap between the two states. They are present in two jurisdictions. But in the sense of full agency they are present in neither. They cannot exercise full citizenship in either place and this weakens their claim to human rights and security. They are citizens in the home country but cannot access its legal, welfare and political systems. Yet in the country of education their different and inferior status as aliens debars them from participation in at least some of its institutions and programmes. Third, they have ambiguous meanings for the country of education. They seem to offer both benefits and threats.

From time to time home country governments take up individual and collective issues with the nation of education, though it varies. China and the USA are busier than most governments on behalf of offshore students. In the last decade China has actively pursued issues of student security within Australia and New Zealand. At one point it issued a website advisory against study in New Zealand, triggering a sharp drop in numbers from China (Marginson *et al.* 2010). But home country governments have only a limited capacity for instrumental effects. Embassies and consulates can handle few individual cases. The home country depends on host government cooperation. The nation of education has the practical power.

But in the nation of education, international students are subordinated. Exactly what this means is variable. It depends on the nation of education. All mobile persons are affected by laws and programmes concerning aliens and citizenship, and students are affected by laws and programmes pertaining to them, like ESOS in Australia. Further, the nation of education may discriminate by country of origin. In the European Union (EU) other EU students pay lower tuition than non-EU students. Australia confers a quasi-citizen status on New Zealanders for some purposes. Australia also imposes more stringent visa requirements on persons from countries whose nationals are reckoned as most likely to overstay their visas, based on probabilistic data.

Struggling to manage global people flows they never fully control, national governments flip between the benefits and the dangers (as they see them) constituted by international students. The students are managed within two conflicting normative frameworks. In both frameworks they are Othered, but one is more benign than the other. On one hand international education is a global market where the student is nominally valued, welcomed and sovereign and might become a future citizen. Education officials emphasize the revenues, research labour, international goodwill and cross-border cultural and economic integration. On the other hand international education triggers border anxiety and old style bureaucratic force. Officials from immigration or homeland security, often reflecting anti-migration sensitivities in the host population, worry about the absorption of scarce national resources in education, health, welfare and housing, and the dangers to property, life and national character. International students overstay their student visas and attempt backdoor migration, it is said. Some are criminals. All are potential terrorists. In threat mode the nation state focuses on its own welfare and security, asserts its own interests as a right and models the students as outsiders threatening *its* national security. It is difficult for that same nation state to conceive of international students as (temporary) insiders with legitimate issues of *their* human security and rights.

Some of those who attacked New York and Washington in September 2001 had entered the USA as students. After 9/11 the Bush government established the SEVIS surveillance system, which positioned international students as potentially dangerous aliens, infringed their liberties and imposed a regulatory burden on universities (Rosser *et al.* 2007). Meanwhile, Australia cancelled the visas of international students for often-minor breaches of the rules governing student work, placing many in prison-like detention. The students had no recourse except protracted expensive appeals – often from within detention – against the visa cancellations. Yet a third of the cancellations were overturned (Marginson *et al.* 2010: 247–50). These failures to treat international students humanely point to the connections between borders and fear, and the nation's customary use of pre-emptive violence to protect its arbitrarily defined territory. Imposed by force in the past, borders are always remade (Vaughan-Williams 2008). Nations that have signed the Universal Declaration of Human Rights ignore it. The duality between citizen and non-citizen is more potent. This highlights the weak point in multilateralism: its universal principles are regulated by sectional interests.

The inferior status of mobile non-citizens removes their power, rendering them vulnerable compared to national citizens. This is less important for short-term visitors like tourists. It is more problematic for students resident for several years to complete degrees. These persons are Othered as aliens yet must deal with housing and employment markets and subject themselves to police, the legal system and public bureaucracies, just as local citizens. Many pay the same taxes as locals.

Formal Othering in Australia

The 200 student interviews in Australia included questions about dealings with the federal immigration department. The department was a compulsory call for visa renewals, changes in institution or study programme and permission to work. No other domain of questioning elicited such an outpouring of emotion. A large majority of the students reported negative experiences (some who reported neutral or positive experiences said they were surprised by this). At immigration the students were subordinated. They were made to feel like supplicants, outsiders, marginal to Australia. Their dignity was undermined. Their bona fides seemed in question. Their lives were devalued. In short, as non-citizens they were spectacularly Othered by the officials.

> Dealing with Immigration is pretty hard. Extending a visa, it was a big process. It's not easy. You go to the counter there and pick up this ticket number and you have to wait for ages. And people there are not friendly. They never smile, as if we are thieves or have a criminal offence. You go there, you're really tense and nervous. You can't be yourself.
>
> (male, 27, computing, Sri Lanka)

> I hate the Immigration Department. It really freaks me out, seriously. What I feel is that the people in the Immigration Department, they just want to find some reason to send a student back to their place. That's what I feel. Other international students feel the same.
>
> (male, 23, business, India)

As noted, in the study associated with the 200 student interviews there was a comparison of the formal rights, entitlements and benefits available to international and local students (Marginson *et al.* 2010). The position of international students was inferior in 28 policy domains. Nearly all forms of public financial support, including welfare and housing, were inaccessible. In the two largest Australian states, they paid full fares on public transport. Local students paid concession rates. Public schooling was free for local families but most international students paid full-cost fees for their children. International students received less financial support from universities, though they paid higher tuition fees. Some postgraduate research scholarships were unavailable to them, as were certain bank services. Both groups had access to health cover but international students were excluded from the public Medicare scheme and had to take out private insurance, which was more costly than the Medicare levy that locals paid via taxation. During semesters international students could work for only 20 hours per week. Local students had an unrestricted right to work. Moreover, international students from certain countries faced implied restrictions on political activity. Their visas included condition 8303: 'You must not become involved in any activities that are disruptive to, or in violence threaten harm to, the Australian community or a group within the Australian community'.

The cultural factor

The same study included parallel interviews with 20 local and 20 international students. This research plus the main 200 interviews and the work on comparative entitlements suggest that four related factors distinguish the international student experience (Marginson *et al.* 2010). First, international students are outsiders, temporary residents without citizen status, and always seen as such. Overall their lives are more marginal and lonelier. Outsider status is reinforced by communication problems, immigration department hostility, bad experiences in the housing market and open discrimination and abuse. It reinforces loneliness and isolation and difficulties in making local friends. Second, most international students experience an information gap, though it diminishes over time. The interviews show that this problem plays out in many areas including housing, dealings with university administration, lack of local cultural knowledge in communication and unfamiliarity with the education system. Third, most international students are from countries where English is not in daily use, and experience communication difficulties. These also diminish over time, but affect both academic progress and daily life, especially cross-cultural relations, inhibiting the potential for local friendships. Fourth, most international students experience cultural difference, for example in politeness regimes, private values, religion and expectations of institutions. The effects of cultural differences diminish over time, and become easier to navigate, but rarely disappear.

The four factors intersect. Recentness of arrival, information gaps and outsider status emphasize perceived cultural difference. Communication problems, lack of knowledge and perceived cultural difference magnify outsiderness. Difference becomes separation and stigma. 'Not only do international students need to adapt to a foreign education system and a foreign language and culture, like migrants, they also need to adjust to being part of a social minority . . . they encounter difficulties associated with being different' (Forbes-Mewett and Nyland 2008: 185). Even when they are not:

> Often white people are surprised when I open my mouth and start speaking English to them. They can't believe I can speak English. And I say to them, do you believe I just got here six months ago . . .! [laughs].
>
> (female, 26 years, medicine, Malaysia)

> Some people don't make an effort to understand what you are saying when you speak with a different accent. It can be in a shop or it can even be in the university . . . they are probably not aware but it is a racist prejudice that this person is not able to communicate with me. It sounds trivial but it's actually very important when it happens systemically.
>
> (male, 28, sociology, Cyprus)

The *National Code* addresses only one of the four issues, the information gap. Regulation ignores cultural difference. It makes the implicit presumption that Anglo-Australian culture is neutral and normal. So cultural difference mostly plays out as an unacknowledged factor. Yet it is more than 'background' or 'context', intersecting continually with formal laws, regulations and social structures both inside the campus and out in the general community. The federal department's own student surveys show the international student experience is most fraught when cultural identity is at play (DEEWR 2007). This affects mostly non-white students and especially East and Southeast Asian students (Marginson *et al.* 2010: Chs 9 and 12–15).

The differences between local and international students are less obvious in areas such as finances, work and health. Nevertheless even where the statistical incidence of problems is similar for international and local students, the experience of those problems can be different, being articulated through lack of knowledge, cultural factors and outsider status. For example, students from both groups experience ultra exploitation and other problems at work, such as rates of pay below the legal minimum wage, unpaid work, and forms of coercion and sexual harassment. What makes the international student experience distinct – aside from less knowledge of labour markets – is immigration status. Despite the limit of 20 hours' work a week during semesters, international students often work for longer to make ends meet. But students working outside their visa conditions are scarcely in a position to complain to public authorities about low rates of pay, demands for excessive hours or sexual harassment in the workplace.

Informal Othering in the community

In the 200 interviews there were numerous instances in which international students were subordinated, marginalized or abused. Either their outsider status was at play, or the perpetrator positioned them as outsiders. Some of this happened on campus. One student had been abused by a uniformed member of the university security staff.

> It happened just two days after September 11 . . . He just yelled at me with very rude words, and said 'fucking Muslims', and 'go back to your country'.
>
> (female, 30, science, Indonesia)

A 2006 survey of international students in one Australian university found that more than half the respondents agreed with the statement 'I don't really feel I belong here at the university' (Rosenthal *et al.* 2006: 28). But research finds that most sharply negative experiences – acts of profound Othering – occur in the general community. In the 200 interviews 99 students, just under 50 per cent, had experienced cultural hostility or prejudice. The rate was especially high for students from Singapore and Malaysia and above average for students from China, and higher among women than men. Muslim students faced particular difficulties in the wake of the 'War on Terror' in Iraq and the Bali bombings in 2002, when 88 Australians died, and 2005.

> *Q:* Have you experienced hostility or prejudice while in Australia?
> *A:* Yes, many times.
>
> (male, 37, Ph.D. in mathematics, Indonesia)

Many interviewees had been abused on the street or public transport. It could also happen in shops, and at work when dealing with local customers (and sometimes when dealing with the boss). Several students had suffered unprovoked incidents that greatly distressed them. They were profoundly Othered with lasting effect. There was no process whereby they could claim rights and reassert their dignity and agency and their sense of belonging. They found themselves pushed in the other direction.

> There was one incident that I'll never forget. It happened to me when I was up in Melbourne, in my first six months here. I was at the South Yarra train station. I was standing next to this woman, and she turned round to me and started abusing me. 'Why don't you just go back where you came from, we don't want you here!' It really took me aback. It was the last thing I expected . . . I was blind. I was walking into town . . . I just carried on walking. It was so embarrassing. Ever since that, I've been more conscious about being different, about my colour, my nationality.
>
> (female, 22, business, Zimbabwe)

In sum, the lives of international students are framed by an asymmetry of rights and conditions, as shown by the legal forms and practical entitlements. In turn, non-citizen status enables not only official discrimination but also unofficial

Othering by hostile elements in the local population (and the hostility can creep into official regulation as well). Recurring problems of stereotyping, discrimination and abuse affect not just international students in Australia but in all English-speaking provider nations (e.g., of many, UKCISA 2004; Spencer-Rodgers 2001; Spencer-Rodgers and McGovern 2002). In turn, inequality and Othering block more fruitful relations between local and international students (e.g., of many, Lee and Rice 2007; Volet and Ang 1998). Research suggests that the dynamics of cultural segregation shift in a sustained manner for large numbers only when local and international students live together for a year or more in student residences (Marginson *et al.* 2010: Chs 7 and 16).

In the Othering process non-white appearance and communication barriers are often the triggers. Non-white appearance can also play against local citizens of non-European background. But for international students the two forms of binarism, cultural difference and outsider status, reinforce each other. Here the national border is the most important single element. By no means all local citizens are prejudiced towards the foreign students in their midst. Many are welcoming. A smaller number are culturally engaged. But nearly all see them as outsiders with weak claims to the common weal, and something less than equality of respect. Thus governments genuinely committed to formal non-discrimination police a relational structure that isolates and marginalizes international students. Uncorrected, the binary structure of citizen/outsider opens international students to more brutal forms of marginalization in the community. It gives perpetual comfort to the perpetuators of abuse and violence – who are in no doubt that *they* belong and are superior to the outsiders.

Renorming international education

The book *International Student Security* concludes with proposals for improving international student security and rights (Marginson *et al.* 2010). A strong contribution governments can make is to subsidize affordable student housing, for a mix of local and international students, in areas where students study and work. An infrastructure programme in student housing would lead to improved safety: international students would no longer be attacked on public transport when returning home at night. As noted, it could also foster closer intercultural relations. In relation to communications, competence in English should be made a formal requirement for degree status, alongside competence in the academic and professional content. This would oblige providers to offer foundation, remedial and support English to both international and local students. For many international students acquiring English language competence is as important as completing the degree, and it is central to living in an English-speaking country. Student safety would be advanced by supervised transport, especially at night; targeted policing of places where violence is occurring; community education to facilitate inclusion and tolerance and pathologize cultural hostility; rental housing inspections; and better information on arrival.

However, the larger problem is the nationally structured lacuna in the rights of the globally mobile. If present international education is essentially asymmetrical, and nation-state regulation is the primary Othering, all remedial strategies are limited. It remains a nation-state world for the foreseeable future. International students will remain non-citizens in the country of education. What then is the way forward?

There are two kinds of potential for change. The first is what enlightened national governments can do, severally and through bilateral and multilateral negotiation, to renorm international education. The second potential, scarcely visible, is global regulation by an extra-national agency able to intervene in national matters.

A more cosmopolitan approach

A renorming of international education at national level would include the following:

- To ensure the common freedom and security of international students it is necessary to regulate and, where necessary, override the economic market.
- International students are not weak or in 'deficit'. They are strong self-determining human agents, engaged in complex self-formation through education and global mobility (Marginson 2009). Their challenges and achievements mostly exceed those of native-speaking local students.
- If international students are worthy of equal respect with local students this does not mean their need for particularized services and supports vanishes, especially in the early months of their stay.
- International students are bearers of the full range of acknowledged human rights, as the principle of universal humanism suggests.
- Human rights apply in all domains, regulated or unregulated, in education institutions and the general community. Human rights include protections, freedom of association and movement, freedom from discrimination and abuse, and personal capacity in areas such as communications or housing.
- As far as possible, nations should extend to non-citizen international students the same rights and entitlements as apply to citizen students. (There may be exceptions in a small number of designated areas where national treatment is warranted, such as voting in national elections.) This norm of equivalence with locals minimizes the *outsider* element, the primary limit on security and rights.

Nations whose students study abroad (sending nations) could negotiate, with nations that receive international students, a protocol providing for the rights and entitlements of the students of the sending nation. Using the *Universal Declaration of Human Rights*, the protocol would include specifications in domains of activity of international students such as education, housing, crisis support and intercultural relations. If enough such agreements are reached on a bilateral basis, this creates momentum for an informal global standard subject to widespread policy imitation. The regime of international student security and rights would be thereby constructed by an incremental process of voluntary agreement, whereby each nation makes its education system into a globally responsible space.

Global agencies

In turn, this would create favourable conditions for the development of a universal global standard for multilateral consideration and/or monitoring and regulation by a global agency, whether existing or purpose-built. Here international education could also lead the development of global approaches to other, more difficult areas of cross-border people movement – not just labour and business migration, but political refugees, and people displaced by global climate change. In principle the need for global agency involvement is obvious. The welfare and rights of mobile persons should be seen primarily as a matter of *global public good*, not a matter of national private or public good, or global private good created in global markets. Everyone has a common interest in the freedom and security of cross-border movement.

But the problem in providing global public goods is that there is no global state. Global civil society is emerging, but cannot provide universal rights and protections. It would be a radical innovation for global agencies to assume obligations of this kind in relation to individual national citizens such as international students. Perhaps this is why existing global agencies are largely indifferent to international students. The International Labour Organization discusses migrant workers but does not admit international students as migrant workers, though they are temporary migrants.

Cross-border agencies are more active in relation to stateless persons and refugees. No national government has jurisdiction over such persons. Nations readily accept the need for supranational intervention. However, the case of international students is not qualitatively different. In both cases the core problem is absence (full or partial) of nation-state coverage. Though international students are partly regulated by both nations, regulation by either and both is incomplete.

Conclusion

Global mobility demands adjustment by mobile persons. On the face of it, it also demands adjustments by the institutions and systems that mobile persons encounter, especially when there are many such persons. But institutions and systems in the country of education rarely adjust much to the 'strangers'. They would be more willing to adjust if international students were no longer defined as 'strangers'.

International students are investors in geographical and social mobility. They face many difficulties. Some have good personal, institutional and governmental backup. Others do not. Nevertheless, most will enter the top socio-economic status quintile at home or somewhere in the world. International students are not proletarian subjects. But they are at the cutting edge of two problems of global governance, or rather its absence. One is the extent to which regulation should modify market forces. The other is the disjunction between mobile populations and national regulation.

Global mobility will increase. The number of international students is expanding. And in future there will be a marked increase in displaced persons, including those affected by climate change. Ultimately cross-border people movement will have to be managed via a multilateral and/or global approach. No one nation can solve it. So why focus on students? Refugees are more in need of immediate assistance, and there are more of them. The answer is that for many receiving nations international students are economically desired, because they create revenues and/or become skilled migrants. Nations have incentives to improve the conditions of international students, especially once better norms are established. And getting the global protocol right on international students helps to advance the position of refugees.

Ultimately it will be necessary to de-nationalize, globalize and humanize international education. The bedrock of a student rights regime is not national interest, but a global humanism in which every person is a self-determining subject with equal respect.

Notes

1   Data for 2008, students abroad for one year or more.
2   The institutions were the Universities of Ballarat, Melbourne, New South Wales and Sydney; and RMIT, Swinburne, Victoria, Deakin and Central Queensland (Rockhampton and Melbourne campuses) Universities. All interviews were conducted with permission of the universities concerned and the project received ethics clearance at Monash University where all of the researchers were then based.
3   'Overseas students differ from domestic students in that they are subject to migration controls and face different needs for consumer protection' (DEEWR 2007: Section 6.1).

References

AEI (Australian Education International) (2007) *2006 International Student Survey: Higher Education Summary Report*, Department of Education, Employment and Workplace Relations (DEEWR), Canberra: AEI.

Bashir, S. (2007) 'Trends in international trade in education: Implications and options for developing countries', *Education Working Paper Series*, 6, Washington: World Bank.

Bayly, C. (2004) *The Birth of the Modern World 1780–1914: Global Connections and Comparisons*, Oxford: Blackwell.

Berry, J., Kim, U., Power, S., Young, M. and Bujaki, M. (1989) 'Acculturation attitudes in plural societies', *Applied Psychology*, 38: 185–206.

Bochner, S. (1972) 'Problems in culture learning', in S. Bochner and P. Wicks (eds) *Overseas Students in Australia*, Sydney: University of New South Wales Press.

Church, A. (1982) 'Sojourner adjustment', *Psychological Bulletin*, 91, 3: 540–72.

DEEWR (Department of Education, Employment and Workplace Relations) (2007) *National Code of Practice for Registration Authorities and Providers of Education and Training to Overseas Students*, Australian Government. Online. Available HTTP: http://aei.dest.gov.au/AEI/ESOS/NationalCodeOfPractice2007/Default.htm (accessed 5 February 2008).

Forbes-Mewett, H. and Nyland, C. (2008) 'Cultural diversity, relocation, and the security of international students at an internationalised university', *Journal of Studies in International Education*, 12, 2: 181–203.

Held, D., McLew, A., Goldblatt, D. and Perraton, J. (1999) *Global Transformations: Politics, Economics and Culture*, Stanford: Stanford University Press.

Hofstede, G. (1980) *Culture's Consequences: International Differences in Work-related Values*, Beverly Hills: Sage.

Kashima, E. and Loh, E. (2006) 'International students' acculturation: effects of international, conational, and local ties and need for closure', *International Journal of Intercultural Relations*, 30, 4: 471–85.

Lee, J. and Rice, C. (2007) 'Welcome to America? International student perceptions of discrimination', *Higher Education*, 53, 3: 381–409.

Leong, C.-H. and Ward, C. (2000) 'Identity conflict in sojourners', *International Journal of Intercultural Relations*, 24, 6: 763–76.

Marginson, S. (2009) 'Sojourning students and creative cosmopolitans', in M. Peters, S. Marginson and P. Murphy (eds) *Creativity and the Global Knowledge Economy*, New York: Peter Lang.

—— (2010) 'International student security: globalization, state, university', *Journal of the World Universities Forum*, 3, 3: 49–58.

Marginson, S., Nyland, C., Sawir, E and Forbes-Mewett, H. (2010) *International Student Security*, Cambridge: Cambridge University Press.

Ninnes, P. and Hellsten, M. (eds) (2005) *Internationalizing Higher Education: Critical Explorations of Pedagogy and Policy*, Dordrecht: Springer.

OECD (Organisation for Economic Cooperation and Development) (2010) *Education at a Glance, 2010*, Paris: OECD.

Pedersen, P. (1991) 'Counselling international students', *The Counseling Psychologist*, 19, 10: 10–58.

Rizvi, F. (2005) 'Identity, culture and cosmopolitan futures', *Higher Education Policy*, 18: 331–9.

Rosenthal, D., Russell, V. and Thomson, G. (2006) *A Growing Experience: The Health and the Well-being of International Students at the University of Melbourne*, Melbourne: The University of Melbourne.

Rosser, V., Hermsen, J., Mamiseishvili, K. and Wood, M. (2007) 'A national study examining the impact of SEVIS on international student and scholar advisers', *Higher Education*, 54, 4: 525–42.

Sen, A. (1985) 'Well-being, agency and freedom: the Dewey Lectures 1984', *Journal of Philosophy*, 82, 4: 169–221.

—— (1999) 'Global justice: beyond international equity', in I. Kaul, I. Grunberg and M. Stern (eds) *Global Public Goods: International Cooperation in the 21st Century*, New York: Oxford University Press.

Spencer-Rodgers, J. (2001) 'Consensual and individual stereotypic beliefs about international students among American host nationals', *International Journal of Intercultural Relations*, 25: 639–57.

Spencer-Rodgers, J. and McGovern, T. (2002) 'Attitudes towards the culturally different: the role of intercultural communication barriers, affective responses, consensual stereotypes, and perceived threats', *International Journal of Intercultural Relations*, 26, 6: 609–31.

Triandis, H. (1989) 'Cross-cultural studies of individualism and collectivism', in J. Berman (ed.), *Nebraska Symposium on Motivation*, Lincoln: University of Nebraska Press.

UKCISA (UK Council for International Student Affairs) (2004) *International Students in UK Universities and Colleges, Broadening our Horizons: Report of the UKCISA Survey*, London: UKCISA.

UN (United Nations) (2010) *The Universal Declaration of Human Rights*. Online. Available HTTP: http://www.un.org/en/documents/udhr/index.shtml (accessed 20 October 2010).

Vaughan-Williams, N. (2008) 'Borders, territory, law', *International Political Sociology*, 4, 2: 322–38.

Verbik, L. and Lasanowski, V. (2007) *International Student Mobility: Patterns and Trends*, London: Observatory on Borderless Higher Education (OBHE).

Volet, S. and Ang, G. (1998) 'Culturally mixed groups on international campus: an opportunity for inter-cultural learning', *Higher Education Research and Development*, 17, 1: 5–24.

Ward, C. and Chang, W. (1997) ' "Cultural fit": a new perspective on personality and sojourner adjustment', *International Journal of Intercultural Relations*, 21, 4: 525–33.

Ward, C., Leong, C-H. and Low, M. (2004) 'Personality and sojourner adjustment: an exploration of the Big Five and the cultural fit proposition', *Journal of Cross-Cultural Psychology*, 35, 2: 137–51.

Chapter 3

Whose initiative?

International student policy in the UK

Beatrice Merrick

Introduction

This chapter considers how the UK government has tended to view international students in recent decades, and how its policies have affected international students, both directly and indirectly. It suggests that rather than a unified international student policy, international students are affected by a number of larger agendas, resulting in a disparate, and occasionally conflicting, set of policies which include them, but in which they are not the main players. This creates a framework that constrains more than it enables the individual international student in their experience of UK higher education. It is then left to students themselves to negotiate this landscape successfully.

Government policy

Between 1998 and 2011, the UK government ran a programme, launched by Tony Blair, called the Prime Minister's Initiative for International Education (PMI). This began as a response to Blair encountering the Mayor of Shanghai, discovering he was an alumnus of a UK university and realizing the potential benefits of international students. The programme continued under the 'PMI' banner through two changes of Prime Minister and one change of party, although the aims of the programme became increasingly disconnected from other elements of government policy.

While, in the early stages of the initiative, real efforts were made to provide 'joined-up government' on international student issues, in reality the policies of different government departments were often pulling in different directions – immigration policy increasingly out of step with international education policy – which meant that, over the longer term, there was no unitary international student policy, merely an interweaving of agendas that acted in complex ways to shape the environment into which international students came. Even where agendas coincided, government still sometimes failed to join up: for example the Science and Engineering Graduate Scheme to allow international students to stay and work in the UK after their studies was announced by the Treasury (HM Treasury 2003) with no reference to PMI or the department then responsible for it. This has been typical of how policy towards international students has developed piecemeal over time.

As we will see below, government has variously viewed international students as sources of soft power, bearers of cultural diversity, good ('highly skilled') or bad ('bogus') migrants, recipients of aid, sources of export earnings or even threats to national security. Rarely if ever has government policy constructed international students as agents determining their own fate – with the possible exception of the 'bogus student', who is portrayed as trying to find loopholes and abuse systems of control, or perhaps (although rarely in the UK) as consumers.

As a consequence, this chapter might seem out of place in a book focusing on international students negotiating their own identities within higher education. Yet each student is acting within the constraints of the UK government's international education policy. For example, as Marginson *et al.* (2010) point out, mobile students do not have equivalent rights to citizens and residents within a country, but only a partial and often grudging set of concessions, limiting their ability to participate and function on equal footing to other students. This chapter will therefore focus on the constructions and constraints that governments (in this case in the UK) apply to international students, directly through their own policies or indirectly when policies determine how colleges and universities in turn behave towards their students.

Who is an international student?

The most immediate sense in which 'international students' are constructed is, of course, in the definition which determines that a particular set of criteria – be it nationality, visa status or educational history – defines one group of students as 'home' and another as 'international'. As has often been pointed out (for example King *et al.* 2010), there is no consistent definition or use of the term, either internationally or nationally. Within the UK, it is sometimes used to distinguish between UK and non-UK nationals or residents; and sometimes to distinguish between EU (or EEA) and non-EU (or EEA) nationals or residents. Perhaps most frequently it is used to describe students who pay full-cost fees, a category that largely corresponds, but is not identical, to the category of students who require a visa to come to study in the UK.

This leads to some fluidity in terms of who is perceived as an 'international student' by institutions or government (quite apart from whether students perceive themselves as 'international'). A liminal category exists of those who fall within some of the definitions but not others; for instance, European students from countries other than the UK may be 'home' in terms of fees but 'foreign' in terms of nationality. Others in this category include British nationals whose residence status has led to overseas-fee classification, and nationals of other countries who have spent many years in education in the UK, which is not counted as residence for the purposes of fee classification, but may have influenced their sense of their own identity.

For the purposes of government policy, the definition of international student will depend on whether the context is immigration (visa status), economics (fee status) or, for example, soft power (nationality). For the rest of this chapter, the definition is kept open and fluid.

National policy: from aid to trade to internationalization . . . to migration

The history of international student policy in the UK and Australia (both countries having shared a similar trajectory) is sometimes described as moving from 'aid' to 'trade' to 'internationalization' (Smart and Ang 1993).

Starting with the colonial period, when universities were seen as a method of developing a trained cadre of trusted 'native' civil servants to run the Empire, to a post-colonial, cold-war rationale of influence through the provision of aid in the form of scholarships, international student policy, even in its 'aid' phase, developed largely with the interests of the host country in mind.

The introduction of full-cost fees for international students in 1980 (and slightly later in other major English-speaking destinations such as Australia, New Zealand and Canada) signalled the shift from the 'aid' to the 'trade' phase of international education, where underfunded UK universities suddenly acquired a new, unconstrained source of additional revenue in the form of overseas student fees and became remarkably business-like in pursuing it.

The 'trade' phase also saw students increasingly cast as 'consumers' – a trend also within the domestic student arena, but more pronounced for students paying full-cost overseas fees. Official government recognition of this can be seen in countries such as Australia and New Zealand where the Education Services for Overseas Students (ESOS) Act (2000) and the New Zealand Code of Practice for the Pastoral Care of International Students (arising from the Education Act 1989) purposely provide consumer protection for international students. It has been argued (Marginson *et al.* 2010) that the protection is in fact for the benefit of the educational institutions and the country rather than for students, as consumer protection of this type is relatively weak. Either way, UK government policy has yet to extend to any specific protection of the consumer rights of international students.

In subsequent decades, while the 'trade' aspects of international education remained active, a new rhetoric developed about broader benefits and partnerships. 'Internationalization' was taken to benefit the mobile student by providing a more relevant experience, rather than fitting a round international student into a square British education hole. Moreover, home students, it was claimed, benefited from internationalization (and international students) bringing global perspectives, intercultural skills and knowledge of other parts of the world. Institutions were deemed to become higher quality and more competitive if they were 'internationalized'. Many of these claims are contested or at least unproven (see, for example, Turner and Robson 2007, Morgan 2010).

Activities corresponding to 'aid', 'trade' and 'internationalization' continue, but government policy in many of the main host countries is now more explicitly driven by another issue, taking us into what we may call the 'migration' phase.

In the positive spin on the migration phase, countries with a strong history of inward migration have increasingly seen international students as a ready pool of highly educated and ready-socialized immigrants whose prior experience of living in the country is seen to ease their transition. They are also an extraordinarily cheap source of skilled labour, given that all the costs of their school and university education, both in the home country and in the receiving country, have usually been met by the migrant themselves or their home country government.

In the negative aspect of migration debates, student visa routes are sometimes perceived as (and sometimes are) an alternative route for economic migration, and one which may be open to 'abuse' (i.e. that migrants may use them for their own ends rather than for the ends specified by governments).

Moreover, the immigration agenda has, since the terrorist attacks of 11 September 2001, sometimes been linked to national security issues, although more so in the US than in the UK. Even prior to those events, some postgraduate students in the UK were subject to a vetting regime to prevent countries on the UK's watch list from gaining access to technologies with a potential for use in nuclear, chemical or biological weapons development (initially through the Voluntary Vetting Scheme, then the Academic Technology Approval Scheme). These schemes have been run by the Foreign and Commonwealth Office, but linked to the visa approval process, with greater or lesser degree of involvement by institutions. By virtue of the involvement of the security services, these processes are opaque to both institutions and students, but the implications are inescapable: some (potential) students are viewed as a threat to national security, and subject to restrictions as to what, or even whether, they can study in the UK.

Over the last decade the UK government has been shifting uneasily between viewing international students as welcome and unwelcome migrants, and frequently holding both views at once (perhaps in relation to different sub-groups of students). On the one hand, in 1999 the visa requirement to prove 'intention to leave' at the end of studies was abolished, and several routes allowed students to switch into work visas after graduation (namely the Fresh Talent Working in Scotland Scheme, the Science and Engineering Scheme, International Graduate Scheme and finally Post Study Work). It thus seemed as though the UK was looking to capitalize on international student migration. However, in parallel with these moves, increasing political and press references to 'bogus colleges' and 'bogus students' (for example Home Affairs Committee 2009) led to clamp-downs on both institutions and individual students who were perceived to be using student visas for economic migration rather than study.

In April 2011 the Lib-Con coalition government reduced further the possibilities for international students to stay in the UK through abolishing Post Study Work, restricting work rights during study and setting limits on the number of years for which students could study (UKBA 2011). Earlier in the year, Australia had moved in a similar direction by cutting down the possible routes from study to permanent residence. Yet this was by no means a unanimous international trend: at the same time there were calls in countries such as Canada and Germany to view international students as a useful source of highly skilled labour (for example Workpermit.com 2010, Chakma 2010).

These characterizations of 'aid', 'trade', 'internationalization' and 'migration' should not be taken to be exclusive phases. 'Aid' retains a significant role even now (for example through UK government funding of Commonwealth Scholarships and Fellowships). 'Trade' in the form of international student recruitment remains the major driving force behind most UK universities' international strategies. 'Internationalization' was taking place long before the term was coined. 'Migration' of students was controlled throughout the period. To the extent to which we can claim these to be separate phases, it is mainly a shift of which issues are foregrounded in the current discourses about international students.

These four aspects of international student policy not only co-exist, but also mirror the divisions in the organization of government, which perhaps explains why international student policy, far from being unified, is a reflection of the current preoccupations of separate government departments.

The UK Department for International Development (DfID) has, since the 1990s, seen international student mobility, particularly to expensive developed-country universities, as a relatively low priority for delivering aid – and of course does not wish to see it lead to the kind of migration often characterized as 'brain drain'.

Under the current arrangement of UK government departments, trade (in the form of UKTI, the UK's trade promotion organization) and higher education both sit within the Department for Business, Innovation and Skills. Yet even so, the UK's desire to promote education as an export industry is not an aim that is well-integrated with the UK's higher (or further) education policy, or vice versa, as higher education policy has continued to focus on the UK student. Following the PMI, government seems to be stepping back from any active support for marketing 'Education UK', leaving this once more to universities themselves.

Government engagement with 'internationalization' as an aim has been relatively low-key, at least for higher education, with PMI phase 1 being primarily about exports and even PMI phase 2 promoting wider ideas of internationalization in a somewhat piecemeal way.

While Home Office policy towards students pays lip service towards the value of international students as sources of revenue, and their educational and cultural benefits (for example UKBA 2010), the political imperative to reduce migration usually appears to trump these in terms of policy as enacted. In this context it is interesting to note the repeated use of the phrase 'brightest and best' in relation to immigration policy on international students (UKBA 2010). It is unclear whether this is supposed to relate to academic merit, potential as future migrants or some other unspecified definition.

Thus government policies affect international students by controlling their access to the UK through immigration policy, limiting their right to work and access state benefits and by determining who has subsidized education through home fees or state scholarships. Beyond that, government policy influences institutions to behave in certain ways towards international students; we shall consider these next.

Institutional views of international students

Despite the rhetoric of 'internationalization' as an intentional process, if one was to start from scratch and design an internationalized university, it is unlikely that it would look much like any actual university. In practice, the demographics of the student population are hugely skewed by history, politics and economics reflecting former colonial links, spheres of influence, established migration routes and supply and demand factors in the availability and affordability of international education (CEC/UKCISA 2000). Institutions proudly trumpet from how many countries their international students come, but in reality all are dominated by large numbers from a small number of sending countries and only very small numbers from each of the rest. The effect of policy on the demographics is clearly illustrated by the shift from subsidized to full-cost fees in 1980 for non-EU students. This (at least initially) reduced the numbers of students from some of the traditional non-EU sending countries (for example Iran and many Commonwealth countries such as Nigeria) while numbers of (home-fee paying) students from other EU states increased steadily.

In addition to these broader political, economic and geographical factors, recent government policies have continued to influence institutional internationalization policies.

One driver has been financial: the removal of the subsidy for non-EU students in 1980 and the introduction of full-cost fees made it impossible for home-fee paying and overseas-fee paying students to be treated the same. The former were subject to government regulation in terms of numbers of funded (or unfunded) student places, while institutions could recruit as many of the latter as they chose, in a free market. Institutions had to accept the funding and fees set by government for the former, but could charge what they liked to the latter. This has also had the effect of introducing a market discourse about international students (as has subsequently happened for home students, following the introduction of domestic student fees). As such, one of the key characterizations of international students has become as customers or consumers (or more pejoratively, 'cash cows'). We will consider this further later in this chapter.

A second driver was strategic: where insufficient UK students were available who were willing or able to follow certain subjects such as mathematics, engineering and economics, the gaps could be filled with non-UK students. The increasing concentration of research funding on 'internationally excellent' departments encouraged the recruitment of high-quality international students, particularly at doctoral level.

A third was that the government as funder has influenced the product delivered by institutions. The policies it sets and the funding it delivers are designed to provide for UK interests. Little work has been done to examine the extent to which this skews the content or delivery of courses away from the needs of the international students who also take them and who have no advocate to represent their (diverse) interests. For example, reforms to research degrees following the Roberts Review (Roberts 2002) have not been examined to see whether they are equally appropriate for students whose career paths after graduation may be quite different to a UK Ph.D. graduate, ranging from teaching in a developing-country university (perhaps with little or no opportunity for research), to applying research in an environment with very little research infrastructure, to tackling local or regional issues which require a different approach or knowledge base to that offered in the UK. This is therefore one example where the discourse of international student as consumer seems flawed (see Brown 2009). Asymmetries of power and constrained access to knowledge and channels of communication make it hard for international students individually or as a group to influence such policies.

Other government policies have periodically influenced institutional internationalization policies. Some direct support for marketing UK education overseas has come from the PMI and the inclusion of an education-promotion role in the remit of the British Council, but with a nationally set list of 'priority countries', which might not accord with institutions' own.

Since the introduction of the Points Based System for visas in 2008, in order to bring in international students on visas, institutions had to become 'sponsors', responsible to the UK Border Agency for assessing the 'bona fides' of their would-be students, monitoring and reporting on their students (and on those who failed to become their students), even to the extent of a requirement to report suspicions of those who might be flouting the conditions of their visas, for example by working more than their permitted number of hours. This has introduced a requirement for institutions to differentiate between their students (defined on the basis of visa status).

There are also some areas where there is a lack of direction from the UK government compared to some other countries. There is relatively little encouragement for UK universities to be involved in aid and capacity-building projects with developing countries, at least compared to some Northern European and Scandinavian countries for whom this is a significant area of universities' international work.

The UK government has also put very little resource into encouraging internationalization of UK students' experiences in terms of language or intercultural skills, global awareness or employability. For many other European countries, policies encouraging teaching in another global language (usually English) and internationalization of the curriculum have been much more directly supported and encouraged by governments (cf. Wächter 2004).

One of the starkest differences for international students as compared to their domestic counterparts, however, is the complete absence of a discourse about 'widening participation' for international students. The difference can be most starkly seen in some UK further education colleges where UK students may be from lower socio-economic groups, but international students are almost exclusively from wealthy backgrounds. Discourses about aid relate only to countries, not to seeking to provide equality of opportunity to individuals. Whatever the merits and practicalities of the argument, it is very noticeable by its absence even as an aspiration.

Drivers of staff behaviour

Just as national policies have determined the general direction of institutional policies, the latter lay down the parameters within which staff operate, and provide constraints to contexts in which they interact with their students.

Research performance, rather than teaching excellence or administrative competence, continues to be the overriding criterion for promotion in the majority of UK universities, driven by the funding and prestige elements determined at national level. Inevitably this skews the willingness of staff to engage with non-research activities that are seen as time consuming or difficult. Unfortunately, teaching international students is often characterized that way. Thus, although the system may prioritize the recruitment of international students, it fails to reward those who work to ensure that those students' experiences are positive.

That is not to say that institutions are unconcerned about the experiences of international students. The large numbers who pay for expensive market research such as the i-Graduate International Student Barometer demonstrate this. But this is concern based on business effectiveness (customer satisfaction) rather than ethics. The Students Without Borders project (Sparqs *et al.* 2010) is a rare example of a more collegiate way of involving international students in improving the quality of their experience. It is of note that this originates not from institutions themselves, but from students and funders.

Individual teaching staff may (and frequently do) invest large amounts of time and effort into transforming teaching and learning for an international (including UK) student group (for example Madge *et al.* 2009). But they are unlikely to be rewarded by the organizational structures within which they work. And few institutions, departments or programmes regularly critique their curriculum's relevance and appropriateness for international students of varying backgrounds, interests and future intentions. This is time consuming, and no external drivers encourage it. For example, the Quality Assurance Agency, although currently developing best practice guidance on international student issues, does not consider teaching methods or curriculum to fall within its remit.

Students as agents in context

International students are, as we have seen, only a group in so much as others label them as such, and there are multiple, sometimes overlapping, definitions. Even within any defined group, the individuals are extremely heterogeneous in terms of personal characteristics such as nationality, age, gender and educational background. The paths they choose and the ways in which they construct themselves will be equally varied. All, however, will do so in the context we have considered above, where – as far as government is concerned – the aspirations and intentions of individual students are secondary to their utility to the state in achieving certain ends in relation to immigration, security, finance, or social or cultural capital.

Government policies distinguish 'international' from 'home' students in terms of some or all of these factors:

- immigration restrictions limiting length of stay and imposing conditions for example on what and where they may study, the type and extent of employment they may undertake, whether they may be accompanied by dependants, and access to public funds;
- the fees they are required to pay for their courses;
- whether they have access to grants or loans for fees, living expenses, hardship or support for disability-related needs.

It then neglects international students entirely, and focuses solely on domestic students, when considering the impact of domestic higher education reforms and agendas.

In addition, international students may be disadvantaged compared to UK residents in both social integration and access to resources, from banking facilities to the legal system, not to mention restrictions on their access to the democratic process (see for example Pharoah *et al.* 2009 for consideration of the issues that Chinese migrants, including both students and non-students, face). Both at institutional and national level, the voice of international students is somewhat muted. The National Union of Students, which might be expected to speak out for this group of its members, has only had an International Student Officer post for a few years, initially only in a part-time capacity, and this post is elected by a small number of self-selected delegates. International students may therefore need to call on alternative resources, either from home or from informal networks, to counteract their disenfranchisement, if minded to try to influence government policy.

If international students are not accorded the rights of citizens, are they at least given those of consumers? Marginson *et al.* (2010) write critically of the very limited notion of 'consumer rights' compared to fully fledged human rights: contracts with institutions, even when regulated by government, are often weighted against the student, and heavily constrained, for example by students being subject to immigration control, and unable to access benefits such as subsidized access to legal aid.

The environment created by government, therefore, is one that constrains more than it enables the individual student. To return to the title of this chapter, it would seem that it is the initiative taken by students themselves, more than the initiatives of government or universities, that is key to their successful negotiation of UK higher education.

References

Brown, R. (2009) *The Role of the Market in Higher Education*, Oxford: Higher Education Policy Institute.

CEC/UKCISA (Council for Education in the Commonwealth/UK Council for International Student Affairs) (2000) *Student Mobility on the Map: Tertiary Education Interchange in the Commonwealth on the Threshold of the 21st Century. Report of a Joint Working Group of the Council for Education in the Commonwealth and UKCOSA*, London: UKCOSA, the Council for International Education.

Chakma, A. (2010) 'Why international student scholarships are good for Canada', in *Western News*, 11 November 2010. Online. Available HTTP: http://communications. uwo.ca/com/western_news/stories/why_international_student_scholarships_are_good_for_canada_20101111447078/ (accessed 4 January 2010.)

HM Treasury (2003) *Pre Budget Report 2003: The Strength to Take the Long-term Decisions for Britain: Seizing the Opportunities of the Global Recovery*, London: HM Treasury. Online. Available HTTP: http://webarchive.nationalarchives.gov.uk/20081230012 706/http://www.hm-treasury.gov.uk/d/pbr03chap3_197.pdf (accessed 21 February 2011).

Home Affairs Committee (2009) *Bogus Colleges: Eleventh Report of Session 2008–09*, London: House of Commons. Online. Available HTTP: http://www.publications. parliament.uk/pa/cm200809/cmselect/cmhaff/595/595.pdf (accessed 20 December 2010).

King, R., Findlay, A. and Ahrens, J. (2010) *International Student Mobility Literature Review*, Bristol: HEFCE.

Madge, C., Raghuram, P. and Noxolo, P. (2009) 'Engaged pedagogy and responsibility: a postcolonial analysis of international students', *Geoforum*, 40, 1, 34–45.

Marginson, S., Nyland, C., Sawir, E. and Forbes-Mewett, H. (2010) *International Student Security*, Melbourne: Cambridge University Press.

Morgan, J. (2010) 'Warning: developing regions may fall off the world map', in *Times Higher Education*, 28 October 2010. Online. Available HTTP: http://www.timeshigher education.co.uk/story.asp?sectioncode=26&storycode=413986&c=1 (accessed 4 January 2011).

Pharoah, R., Bell, E., Zhang, H. and Fan, Y. (2009) *Migration, Integration, Cohesion: New Chinese Migrants to London*, London: The Chinese in Britain Forum.

Roberts, G. (2002) *SET for Success: The Supply of People with Science, Technology, Engineering and Mathematics Skills.* The report of Sir Gareth Roberts' Review, London: HM Treasury. Online. Available HTTP: http://webarchive.nationalarchives.gov.uk/+/http://www. hm-treasury.gov.uk/d/robertsreview_introch1.pdf (accessed 4 January 2011).

Smart, D. and Ang, G. (1993) 'The origins and evolution of the Commonwealth full-fee paying overseas student policy 1975–1992', in A. Peachment and J. Williamsson (eds) *Case Studies in Public Policy*, Perth: Public Sector Research Unit, Curtin University, 111–127.

Sparqs, NUS Scotland and Scottish Government (2010) *Beyond Borders: A Mapping Project of International Students' Engagement in the Scottish Higher Education Learning Experience*, Edinburgh: NUS Scotland. Online. Available HTTP: http://www.nus. org.uk/PageFiles/12238/Beyond%20Borders.pdf (accessed 25 February 2011)

Turner, Y. and Robson, S. (2007) 'Competitive and cooperative impulses to internationalization: reflecting on the interplay between management intentions and the experience of academics in a British university', *Education, Knowledge and Economy*, 1, 1: 65–82.

UKBA (UK Border Agency) (2011) *Government Outlines Overhaul of Student Visas*, London: UK Border Agency. Online. Available HTTP: http://www.ukba.home

office.gov.uk/sitecontent/newsarticles/2011/march/54-student-visas (accessed 21 July 2011).

Wächter, B. (ed.) (2004) *Higher Education in a Changing Environment: Internationalisation of Higher Education Policy in Europe*, Bonn: Lemmens.

Workpermit.com (2010) 'German education organization calls for more foreign students'. Online. Available HTTP: http://www.workpermit.com/news/2010-11-22/germany/german-education-organization-calls-more-foreign-students.htm (accessed 20 December 2010).

Chapter 4

An ethical commitment

Responsibility, care and
cosmopolitanism in the
internationalized university

Kelly Coate and Ganga Rathnayake

Introduction

The internationalization of higher education has decisively moved from being a scholarly tradition of mobility across borders to an almost purely economic concern. This is a trend that is most pronounced in countries such as England, Australia and the USA in particular, which have become the dominant exporters of the higher education business or, as Allan Luke suggests, the global 'edubusiness' (Luke 2010). Alongside the growth of this edubusiness has developed a growing literature theorizing the implications of the shift to the student as consumer model of higher education (e.g. Kuo 2007; Lambert *et al.* 2007; Maringe 2011). For those of us working in international classrooms, particularly in the developed countries that are the main exporters of higher education globally, our relationships with international students are formed against a backdrop of an increasingly predominant consumerist model of higher education. In this chapter we will take a critical view of the shift towards a consumerist model of internationalized higher education, through a consideration of how this shift has eroded the moral basis for relationships with international students. However, there are signs of hope, and in the second part of the chapter we will be offering a philosophical approach based around the concepts of care, responsibility and cosmopolitanism. We will argue that these commitments, taken together, have the potential to re-establish an ethical commitment to students.

The foundations for this chapter reside in previous research by one author (Kelly) into internationalization in English higher education, which led to a critical view of the higher education export business that turns students into customers (Wende *et al.* 2005; Coate 2009). As an indirect beneficiary of internationalization, however, Kelly was also privileged to work closely with a number of international students in the UK who were themselves researching various aspects of internationalization in higher education (see for example Kuo 2007; Welikala 2008; Takagi 2009). After leaving England for Ireland, Kelly's interests in international student mobility continued through a project with Ganga on internationalization in Irish higher education (Coate and Rathnayake 2008).

Working together across cultural differences highlights the often uneasy, challenging and rewarding aspects of the internationalization of higher education.

These aspects are brought to the fore in intercultural relationships between students and staff. Perhaps more so than with relations with students from the dominant culture of the 'host' country, these intercultural encounters highlight how necessary it is for successful pedagogical relationships to be based on trust (Curzon-Hobson 2002). A key concern, then, is that currently the driver behind these intercultural encounters is the market. Market relationships are based on trust only to the extent that the service being bought is satisfactorily delivered. Therefore, in the absence of any clear guidance as to how pedagogical relationships with international students are to be formed, apart from on the basis of a consumer relationship, questions can be raised about the ethics of the international education business. This is particularly the case when the product being 'sold' does not deliver the value that might reasonably be expected.

The Irish higher education context, which is the subject of this chapter, has opened up new avenues for exploration in relation to the global 'edubusiness' of higher education. Although Ireland is an English-speaking country (an advantage in the market-place), it has a small higher education system, with about 180,000 registered students of which 10 per cent are international students. Ireland is therefore not a dominant exporter of higher education globally; however, there are signs that attention is turning in this direction. The economic drivers for international student recruitment are recently but noticeably entering the official discourse. For example, a report on international students in Irish higher education acknowledges that Ireland is not a 'significant player': a type of language that firmly establishes the economic rather than academic agenda (Enterprise Ireland 2010). Even more telling was the recent closure of the International Education Board Ireland (an organization that played a somewhat similar role to the British Council's international education division) and the relocation of staff to the offices of Enterprise Ireland, the government organization responsible for helping Irish businesses to achieve global success. One of the first tasks in the new International Strategy, now being managed by Enterprise Ireland, is the development of the Education Ireland 'brand' in an attempt to capture a greater market share of international students (DES 2010).

Internationalization strategies in export countries are, as Marginson and van der Wende (2006) note, bound up in the new public management reforms that have swept across European, North American and Australian higher education systems. The modelling of higher education on business practices, with a drive towards efficiency, income generation, transparency and increased competition, has become a familiar 'template' that universities around the world are copying. While the response to these global trends remains largely undocumented in the Irish case, it is clear that the template is being used to push through quite fundamental reforms. The new international strategy for Irish higher education encourages a 50 per cent increase in international student numbers by 2015, for instance, in the stated effort to catch up with global competitors.

As many commentators have pointed out, however, the templates may be the same all over the world but the local contexts vary. Irish higher education has a long way to go before it becomes a global 'player', and until then patterns of recruitment will be somewhat ad hoc. Ireland's history as a missionary country also gives a local flavour to some of the attitudes towards international students, particularly students from developing countries. This 'charitable' view of the value of Irish higher education in relation to 'poorer' or less developed countries was expressed to us on a number of occasions during interviews with academics and managers. Whilst it may be difficult to object to a charitable, rather than profit-driven, view of the value of internationalization, it unfortunately positions the students who travel to Ireland from the developing world as being in need of 'help' or aid, and can also shade into somewhat anxious feelings about the 'burden' such charity imposes, as we will go on to discuss. This type of asymmetrical power relationship is not the typical student–teacher relationship. It is instead an unequal relationship between those who are deemed to 'have' and those who 'have not'. Again, it seems necessary to question the ethics of a relationship with students that starts from such a peculiar position of inequality. Therefore, in order to explore some of the possibly unwelcome side effects inherent in the international-ization templates that higher education institutions are adapting to all over the developed world, we will relate some of the challenges faced by international students in Ireland.

This chapter will therefore proceed by moving between a macro analysis of global trends to a micro analysis of the experiences of international students before turning to philosophy as a way of making sense of the phenomenon of international education. These philosophical arguments call for an ethical commitment to our educational practices. Here we will explore the concepts of care, responsibility and cosmopolitanism as potential means of offering a moral framework for our relationships. The global picture supports our experiences and research at a much more local level. At the same time, the emergence of particular philosophical arguments within this contemporary climate offers alternative perspectives to the value of international student mobility that delegitimizes the dominant, economic drivers.

Exploring the experiences of international students in Ireland

Ireland offers almost a blank slate in terms of generating an account of recent developments in international student recruitment and the experiences of international students. Both quantitative and qualitative data are thin on the ground. Higher education institutions do not collect data in a uniform manner, leading to acknowledged difficulties of reporting statistics and trends accurately (Enterprise Ireland 2010). More qualitative studies may begin to emerge, but their absence is notable particularly in relation to the wealth of research on the experiences of international students in the UK and Australia. However, there are a few studies that give some insight into the student and staff experiences. Dunne (2009), for example, explores home students' perceptions of international students in a university in Dublin, and Keane (2009) touches on the issue of international students in her research on diversity, but there seems to be little else.

In 2008–9, with the funding of a small grant from the National University of Ireland, Galway, we conducted a research project on international student recruitment, focusing on our institution and conducting interviews with staff and students. At the time, Kelly was a lecturer in Teaching and Learning in Higher Education at NUIG and Ganga was a doctoral student from Sri Lanka. We worked closely together in order to gain insights into many of the daily challenges that international students faced. Researching the category of 'international students' as one group is fraught with the danger that they will be portrayed largely as a homogenous group who are passive recipients of an education in developed countries (or the 'global north'). Madge *et al.* (2009) suggest that it is more helpful to recast 'international students' (and arguably the staff who work with them) as 'globalized agents', emphasizing both individuality and agency, or free choice. Both Kelly and Ganga had arrived in Ireland as willing participants in the higher education marketplace: Kelly from the UK for employment opportunities, and Ganga as an internationally mobile postgraduate student. The prospect of global agency is now a possibility available to many of us in contemporary higher education, although the patterns of mobility follow particular historic, economic, post-colonial and geographical trends. In particular, the patterns of mobility into Ireland follow trends that deserve much more attention than they have received in the past.

For example, one Sri Lankan student we encountered through this research received an aid scholarship in order to register for a doctoral degree in Ireland. These types of scholarships are a significant, and possibly under-researched, aspect of international student mobility (Adnett 2010). At first glance they seem to eschew the concerns of the student as consumer model, given that their underlying rationale is development: the donor is assisting the recipient through the provision of higher education. Scholarships such as these are, however, a form of 'tied aid' that requires the recipient to purchase from donating countries, and these bilateral agreements ensure an outflow of students from the global south to the global north. The various imbalances that this one-way traffic has engendered, such as lack of capacity in some countries to develop their own national education systems, are now receiving critical examination (Bashir 2007; Adnett 2010). Altbach, for instance, has drawn attention to the 'unprecedented flow of academic talent – particularly from poor to wealthy countries' (2007: xiv). Khadria (2001: 62) calls it the 'repatriation of remittances' as money flows from poor to rich countries through international student fees. It therefore is likely that these forms of 'aid' are exacerbating rather than relieving global inequalities, leading Adnett (2010: 631) to describe them as 'beggar thy (poor) neighbour' policies.

By situating an individual case within this global context we recognize there is a danger of seeming to privilege structural inequalities over individual choices and agency, which again reinforces the need to think more about globalized agency alongside a recognition of structural inequalities. At the individual level the global patterns of economic flows from the south to the north recede from view, and in their place emerges a complex picture of individual histories, difficult choices, opportunities and varying degrees of simultaneously empowering and disempowering experiences. Sidhu (2006) also helps us to see how these histories, experiences and choices are often bound up in post-colonial patterns of international relations. International students are individually taking advantage of the opportunities they have been afforded: collectively they are potentially adding up to an outflow of revenue from the poorest to the richest. These trends could be described as a Sheriff of Nottingham funding model writ large, to borrow the terminology being used to describe the pumping of funding into elite universities (Currie 2009).

The case we are presenting is a Sri Lankan student who we will call Devni. The award of a prestigious scholarship enabled her to embark on a doctorate in Ireland and she brought her husband and teenage son with her. She and her husband both had a leave of absence from their professional posts and intended to enrol their son into a school in Ireland. Shortly after arriving, visa and immigration changes meant that they could no longer avail themselves of publicly funded education but would have had to pay private fees. They sent their son back to live with close family in Sri Lanka, thereby splitting their tight knit family and exacerbating the homesickness and culture shock they were both experiencing. Their encounter with the rather harsh rules of the immigration services is not unique and highlights a tension that many export countries have faced: they want the 'business' of higher education trade, but the flow of non-national students across borders brings into action the immigration rules largely designed to keep non-nationals out. The populist 'fear' of immigrants that characterizes discourses in many developed countries is also strong in Ireland, thereby tainting the experiences of international students with racism. They are 'othered' from the very start within the dominant national culture.

During the course of our research the student visa issue received national attention when a North American student was threatened with deportation after the police discovered she had been sending her son to a state-funded primary school. When we interviewed a staff member in the international office of the university, she admitted that the 'problem' of increased immigration to Ireland in recent years had resulted in a concern about the state provision of education to immigrants and had led to the policy of prohibiting student visa holders to avail themselves of state-funded education. That the 'immigration problem' (whether real or imagined) could be applied to international students shows a convenient disregard for the fact that students are not immigrants but are temporary residents, and that they generate a large amount of revenue for Ireland rather than being a drain on resources. A further challenge is that it is the police – the Garda National Immigration Bureau – who deal with student visa registrations and renewals in Ireland, thereby causing distress for some international students who have never had to respond to police interrogations and feel highly intimidated when doing so. Indeed, the biggest complaint from the international students we interviewed was about their experiences of the visa system.

Another salient feature of Devni's experience as an international student, which may be particularly pronounced for female students from certain cultural backgrounds, was her reluctance to live on her own without her husband. The lack of appropriate postgraduate accommodation for mature international students is a problem that Irish universities will need to tackle if they are to become, as the intention seems to be, global players. In common with many other post-graduate students in Ireland, Devni and her husband rented a room in a shared house with other students. Their lack of familiarity with other cultures created some anxieties, and in common with what research elsewhere has shown (Dunne 2009) Devni was not comfortable with the drinking and partying culture that is a predominant feature of Irish student life. Devni found the student partying culture very disruptive, with frequent late-night disturbances from loud, inebriated students returning home from the clubs. Even perhaps more subtly, but no less importantly, she was reluctant to cook curries in the house in case her housemates were not used to the smell of Asian spices. When her husband was required to return to his job in Sri Lanka at the end of his leave (desperately wanting to work again, having not been allowed to gain employment under immigration regulations in Ireland), they both decided he should stay. He was as reluctant to leave Devni in Ireland as she was anxious about the prospect of being on her own. This resulted in her husband losing his job in Sri Lanka.

The economic costs to Devni's family through taking advantage of this 'aid' were high. These types of scholarship, whilst prestigious and therefore a significant long-term investment, arguably bring more immediate advantages to the Irish universities who can 'market' this international initiative with pride. Again, however, the discourse of charity positions the scholarship receivers as the needy and deserving poor: the World Bank Scholarship website notes that two-thirds of its scholarship holders are from 'humble and poor backgrounds'. We were surprised to find this discourse also used at the International Student Induction day in our university, which we both attended in September 2008. We were sitting with several Sri Lankan students as different presenters from the university spoke to about 800 international students, and learned a number of important characteristics of the Irish higher education market.

What was striking about sitting in a large sports hall with 800 international students was the extent to which the Sri Lankan students were already 'othered' on this occasion. Almost all of the students were young, white and North American. Irish universities have capitalized on the historical connections between Ireland and the USA and, even though US higher education is much more of an export country than an import country, undergraduate students have proven willing to study abroad for a semester in Ireland. Their motivation to come to Ireland is often to take advantage of a type of 'educational tourism' (Nielson 2011). The impact they have on Irish universities is perhaps not the type of 'internationalization' of higher education that is discussed in the literature: the potential benefits of intercultural exchanges are somewhat diminished by the fact that these international students are in Ireland only for a few months and do not have the opportunities or motivation to benefit from cross-cultural exchange. The potential for Irish students to benefit from their presence is also diminished by the fact that US students come from a hegemonic and dominant cultural background. Yet their presence generates much revenue and therefore much attention from the international office. Those who have travelled from further afield on aid scholarships are positioned quite differently within this student market.

Throughout the day as we listened to presentations from various offices of the university it became clear just how much effort was focused directly on the young, white, North American students rather than mature postgraduate students from Asian or other backgrounds. The advice given to the students by the Health Centre, for example, was to avoid 'getting laid' and going home pregnant. For a mother who had just sent her son home, this advice was particularly misguided and painful. We need, as Luke (2010: 61) reminds us, to engage with 'difference within difference'. The differences within differences, however, go well beyond easy distinctions between the students from the developed world and those from less developed countries. The international officer welcomed the few scholarship recipients from 'less developed countries' such as Sri Lanka and Ethiopia, and one of the Sri Lankans sitting next to us expressed her annoyance at Sri Lanka being placed in the same category as Ethiopia on the development continuum. She whispered 'Sri Lanka is more developed than that'. Exploring this 'difference within difference' may raise difficult questions, but those in the developed educational system need to engage with these differences if the aim is to achieve better intercultural understandings. The tendency to categorize all international students as somehow similar may leave the international students from less well-represented countries feeling alienated.

For those of us who find ourselves working in the export edubusiness (Luke 2010) of higher education, the chaotic, complex and often contradictory nature of the whole enterprise can be bewildering. Although we might imagine the responsibility of universities to be education, the explicit endorsement of internationalization becomes complicated when that strategy is based on the one hand, for example, on exploiting a rich market of transient young Americans who want to party for a few months, and on the other by offering aid through a third party to those from poor countries who are perceived to be worthy beneficiaries of an education in the global north. A greater awareness of these drivers behind the strategy to recruit more students can go some way towards enabling a better understanding of whether these drivers provide a moral foundation for educational relationships, or not.

The strategy in Ireland to increase international student numbers by 2015 (DES 2010) comes at a time of change in Irish higher education. As global rankings of universities have become accepted as a 'plausible' measure of a higher education system's global positioning (Hazelkorn 2009; Marginson and van der Wende 2006), institutional processes are adapted and geared towards setting targets and improving outcomes within the parameters of the ranking systems. Internationalization is seen as a key indicator of success, because 'national pre-eminence is no longer enough' (University of Warwick 2007, cited by Hazelkorn 2009: 18). The imperative to compete globally strips away the moral values of our relationships within universities, as higher education becomes less of a public good and more of a status good, bought and sold through international markets or donated to those deemed to be the deserving poor.

The enterprise of this global edubusiness provokes an internal logic within higher education institutions that focuses on performance, outcomes and the never-ending pursuit of excellence. Certainly the rise of managerialism within universities in the last few decades has been well documented in the higher education literature. What we will now turn to in the second part of this chapter is a philosophical argument for a different set of parameters to measure the 'worth' of higher education. A critical view of the predominant drivers shaping the competitive international 'arms race' of higher education systems (Hazelkorn 2009) highlights some of the values we are neglecting. If a sense of higher education as a public good is to be preserved, and even further developed as a greater global good, we need to be more explicit about the ethical commitments we can make in terms of placing a higher value on humanity than the market.

On being careless

Difficult questions arise once the ethical dilemmas of the international student market are exposed. One of the key questions is of complicity. At what point do those working in the global edubusiness become complicit in supporting the economic and competitive drivers of the international student marketplace? It might be easy to establish that those working in the frontlines of international student recruitment, such as the recruiting agents whose job it is to find high fee-paying students for the dominant export institutions, are complicit. Yet what about the academics who find increasing numbers of international students in their classrooms? Berg (2006) suggests that academics often occupy the paradoxical position of contesting and reinforcing neo-liberal practices (cited in Madge *et al.* 2009). Understanding better the global pattern of the movement of resources from the south to the north through the 'gift' of western scholarships might, for example, enable us to reconsider whether to encourage a future scholarship holder from a developing country to come to Ireland. Not to question the value of this 'gift' would entail the suppression of ethical considerations, an activity that Zipin and Brennan (2003) suggest has become commonplace amongst academics in contemporary higher education.

Accepting some level of complicity in the global phenomenon of the higher education edubusiness necessitates a rethinking of what we are doing as educators. An alternative approach might be to ignore change: one academic we spoke to about our research admitted to simply not knowing whether she had international students in her classroom. If there is, however, a will to respond to increased internationalization and to question the relentless drive towards a market-driven higher education system, there are a number of conceptual frameworks that can help re-cast the role of educators. The first question to pose in order to open up this more philosophical discussion is deceptively simple: *who cares?*

The philosophical concept of care in education has a long history, perhaps most well known recently through the work of Noddings (1992, 2003). The idea that educators begin the process of educating through a commitment to care for the individuals they are working with is subtly profound. It involves, as Noddings (2003) suggests, a sense of oneself as the 'I' who cares but also a commitment to the 'you' who is cared for. As she argues, in this conceptualization of care, the ' "one-caring" and the "cared-for" are reciprocally dependent' (Noddings 2003: xiii). Furthermore, caring in education involves developing relationships of trust, openness and inclusiveness (O'Brien 2010), in an explicit commitment to the improvement of human relations.

Accepting a duty of care might seem to be a tall order in the contemporary university. Arguments against inducements to care include the notion that care is better provided by the counsellors and support services for students than the teachers themselves. Whilst there may be a rationale for separating pastoral and academic responsibilities, this might cause anxiety for some students whose previous experience with teachers was one which privileged their pastoral, care-giving role. Students who encounter personal difficulties and approach their tutors might find it disappointing and confusing to be referred to the student counselling service, for example. For those academics who do take on pastoral roles, research suggests that in Anglo-European universities they are more likely to be women (e.g. Morley 1998). Care is therefore a gendered concept in higher education, given the acknowledged imbalance between women and men educators in relation to care-giving duties. Yet before we dismiss the duty of care as an inappropriate burden placed largely on women, it is worthwhile considering that engendering a general ethos of care within the university might offer an alternative vision to the unequal relations that tend to be reproduced in higher education. A commitment to care can be fostered as a moral virtue rather than seen as a duty that needs to be fulfilled.

The work of Kathleen Lynch and colleagues (Lynch 2010; Grummell *et al.* 2009) has brought new insights into the concept of care in higher education. They argue that the performance-driven culture of contemporary entrepreneurial universities is a care-*less* culture. The imperative for universities to be engines of economic growth has taken precedence over the desire for many within universities to contribute to the development of humanity. They illustrate this through their research on senior managers in Irish higher education institutions who acknowledge the difficulty of rising up the hierarchy of management roles if duties of care are required to be given outside the home. The performance-driven culture of higher education necessitates a commitment to sacrificing home lives for the demands of the organization, and those in senior management positions in universities are now quite explicit about the extraordinary demands that work places on them.

Lynch (2010) draws a useful analogy between a culture of work in which care responsibilities are not valued outside the home, and a general culture of care-lessness inside the organization. In other words, there is a fundamental lack of humanity in an organization that does not recognize that many people have responsibilities as care-givers. A care-less ethos is one in which values become skewed towards the needs of the organization, over and above the needs of the people within it.

Masschelein and Simons (2002) pose a similar concern but describe it in different terms: they write about the pressures of the international university as exerting an immunization against 'being together'. In other words, the knowledge workers in entrepreneurial universities are compelled to act on an individually competitive basis rather than acting in the interests of the community. For Masschelein and Simons (2002), the subjectivities of contemporary education workers are interpellated, through a focus on outputs and performance, as entrepreneurial selves. The processes that enact this interpellation operate in disregard to the concept of community, in which the subjects are united by common obligations rather than individual interests. As the authors go on to suggest, these obligations are about what we owe to each other, rather than what is owed to us through our actions. Again, echoing Noddings' insistence (2003) on the interdependence between the 'one-caring' and the 'cared-for', this particular view of 'being together' recognizes that 'we are irreducibly connected with others' (Masschelein and Simons 2002: 602). We accept responsibility for others without knowing what that responsibility will entail and, in accepting that responsibility, we lose some of our own autonomy.

The lack of care in the contemporary university, then, will not be redressed by, for instance, identifying specific tasks that need to be done to support international students. The concepts of care and community that are being proposed above are about the responsibility to others as a fundamental mechanism of accounting for ourselves (Butler 2005). We would not know, for instance, how to 'care' for someone in Devni's position prior to meeting her. The university cannot have all the necessary support structures in place to ensure that all of the challenges she faced were mitigated or relieved in some way, and this holds true for our encounters with students from any other country. The issue here is not about identifying the needs of a group called 'international students', or defining the 'lack' of capabilities that international students might display when living and studying in a different country (as they are often perceived to be 'deficient' in some way or other in the literature). If we reduce 'care' to fulfilling others' needs, we refuse to address the lack within ourselves: our lack of willingness to discover what others will offer to us and what we will offer in return. The concept of care that we are drawing out here, therefore, is more about the recognition that we, and others in the university, are committed to an openness in our relationships with each other. We are open to the possibility that international students (and indeed other 'globalized agents') will ask of us things that we cannot predict, and we are open to the richness that this relationship offers to us.

The heart of the criticisms that are being made about the contemporary university, then, are that the managerial focus on outputs rather than processes, and individual competition rather than community and humanity, is developing a culture of distrust between individuals at the expense of the trusting relations that are essential to successful pedagogical relationships. Particularly in a globalized higher education system, a careless and distrustful culture is a disastrous one from which to invite others to join us. Therefore some of the theorists and philosophers who are writing about globalization and higher education are promoting a fundamental shift away from increased marketization, towards a vision of a cosmopolitan ethos that starts from a foundation of improving humanity rather than the economy (e.g. Rizvi and Lingard 2010; Rizvi 2009). Cosmopolitanism entails an ethical commitment to responsibility for others, and these are the final, related concepts we wish to consider.

Committing oneself

The history of cosmopolitanism is sometimes traced back to the Greek philosophers, who understood the term to mean 'citizens of the world' committed to global humanity over and above the local (Nussbaum 1997; Rizvi 2009). There have been more recent formulations of cosmopolitanism within the literature on globalization (e.g. Appiah 2006) in which new, ethical relationships are imagined that cross national boundaries. For political and social theorists, cosmopolitanism offers a potential reshaping of the forces of globalization that cause global inequalities and injustices. For educational philosophers, such as Todd (2009) and Rizvi (2009), cosmopolitanism offers the potential to open new educational spaces in which global connectivity is the predominant ethos. Rizvi (2009) in particular elucidates an educational agenda in which global humanity takes primacy over local concerns. He argues for a development of 'epistemic virtues' that recognize the situatedness of students within a globalized world, and our interconnectedness with others on a global scale.

Looking through this lens of cosmopolitanism by way of the work of the philosopher Emmanuel Levinas (2006) brings a new understanding to these ethical commitments and epistemic virtues. Levinas proposes that all individuals have a responsibility towards the Other, and that all individuals are Others to us. For Levinas, the Other is always an unknown and is unknowable, but it is our responsibility to accept this unknowability. Any attempts we might make to 'know' the Other before we meet is an act of injustice, or symbolic violence, to the Other. As argued previously (Coate 2009), much of the literature on international students in western higher education attempts to 'know' who these students are in order to define their needs. Whilst much of that work is valuable and necessary, the philosophical argument that all Others are unknown is quite a powerful way of reframing the debate. Particularly in a globalized world, in which more of us are mobile, we must accept that easy categorizations of the Other are increasingly hard to sustain. Devni, for instance, initially assumed that Kelly was Irish, in the same way that many of us teaching in higher education have made assumptions in the past about whether certain students are international or 'home' students that proved to be incorrect. The students may also make assumptions about each other: an Irish student informed us that she sometimes worries about the challenges of working in groups with international students and has concerns about the work being slowed down due to language difficulties. We therefore need to find ways of encouraging students, as globalized agents, to open up to each other as well.

The consequences of opening ourselves to the Other are profound. As Levinas (2006: 29–30) says: 'The relationship with Others challenges me, empties me of myself and keeps on emptying me by showing me ever new resources. I did not know I was so rich.' What is accepted within this commitment to the Other is an acknowledgement of interdependence. Our selves are inextricably bound to the Other. This, then, is the type of epistemic virtue that theorists such as Rizvi (2009) are advocating as appropriate for a globalized world, and that we are suggesting can form the basis of an ethical commitment as educators. Our interconnectivity as citizens of the world then becomes the new backdrop for international student mobility and our relations with each other.

Conclusion

As policy-makers and managers in Irish higher education institutions set new targets for international student recruitment in the hopes of generating more income for a beleaguered system, it may be that we are setting our hopes too high. Suggesting that we make ethical commitments in our relationships with those who enter our institutions is not likely to be high on the agenda of the decision-makers. The prevailing performance-driven, outputs-focused culture is also difficult to challenge, particularly now that a national concern with the efficient spending of public funds has become firmly entrenched.

However, accepting an ethical commitment and a moral responsibility within education is a starting point. Otherwise we are left feeling and being complicit within unethical relationships, as Zipin and Brennan (2003) warn can happen as a consequence of working within the norms and the 'habitus' of the managerial university. At a certain point our own actions become unethical, and surely there is merit in deciding at what stage we begin to resist and reformulate an alternative vision. The work of Rizvi is valuable in this regard, as he clearly elucidates an alternative 'imaginary' in which we help students (and each other) to:

> examine the ways in which global processes are creating conditions of economic and cultural exchange that are transforming our identities and communities; and that, unreflexively, we may be contributing to the production and reproduction of those conditions, through our uncritical acceptance of the dominant ways of thinking about global connectivity.
>
> (Rizvi 2009: 266)

It is perhaps all too easy to rely on an uncritical acceptance of the perceived impact of globalization and far harder to critically reflect on our interconnectivity with others in the world.

There is, after all, an Irish tradition of taking pride in international connections: for example by maintaining strong relations with North America which absorbed a large part of the Irish diaspora, but also by the portrayal of Ireland as welcoming to others. The Irish tourism agency is called 'Fáilte Ireland', or 'Welcome' in Irish. Indeed, the new Education in Ireland 'brand' is a shamrock with the tagline 'warmest of welcomes'. The warm welcome might be a celebrated symbol of Irish culture, but the reality for international students suggests a slightly different experience. The demands to make repeated visits to the Garda (police) stations for registrations and visa renewals; the strict requirements of student visa holders that make it nearly impossible for them to bring dependent family members with them; the lack of appropriate accommodation for postgraduate students with families; the lack of understanding or willingness of some academic staff to familiarize themselves with the needs of international students; and the generally very busy nature of academic life, which results in limited time to meet with students, all add up to an experience that can feel quite unwelcoming. Obviously these challenges are not unique to Irish higher education, but portraying the Irish experience as warmly welcoming might give international students certain expectations that will not always be met.

Having said all of that, the indirect benefits of globalized agency are powerful incentives to work towards a more ethical future for international higher education. The friendship that we are now trying to maintain between the distance that stretches from Ireland to Sri Lanka is well worth the challenges of intermittent email access and demanding working lives. The strength of intercultural friendships, pedagogical encounters and working relationships arguably begins when two people bridge cultural differences and decide that they do, emphatically, *care*.

References

Adnett, N. (2010) 'The growth of international students and economic development: friends or foes?', *Journal of Education Policy*, 25, 5: 625–37.

Altbach, P. (2007) *Tradition and Transition: The International Imperative in Higher Education*, Boston: Centre for International Higher Education.

Appiah, K.A. (2006) *Cosmopolitanism: Ethics in a World of Strangers*, London: Penguin.

Bashir, S. (2007) 'Trends in international trade in higher education: implications and options for developing countries', *World Bank Education Working Paper Series*, no. 6, Washington DC: World Bank.

Butler, J. (2005) *Giving an Account of Oneself*, New York: Fordham University Press.

Coate, K. (2009) 'Exploring the unknown: Levinas and international student recruitment in higher education', *Journal of Education Policy*, 24, 3: 271–82.

Coate, K. and Rathnayake, G. (2008) 'Irish higher education in a global marketplace', paper presented at the SRHE Annual Conference 2008, Liverpool, England.

Currie, D. (2009) 'Funding on "Sheriff of Nottingham model" could cut productivity', *Nature*, 461: 1198.

Curzon-Hobson, A. (2002) 'A pedagogy of trust in higher learning', *Teaching in Higher Education*, 7, 3: 265–76.

DES (Department of Education and Skills) (2010) *Investing in Global Relationships: Ireland's International Education Strategy 2010–2015*, Dublin: Department of Education and Skills.

Dunne, C. (2009) 'Host students' perspectives of intercultural contact in an Irish university', *Journal of Studies in International Education*, 13, 2: 222–39.

Enterprise Ireland (2010) *International Students in Higher Education in Ireland 2009–2010*, Dublin: Enterprise Ireland.

Grummell, B., Devine, D. and Lynch, K. (2009) 'The care-less manager: gender, care and new managerialism in higher education', *Gender and Education*, 21, 2: 191–208.

Hazelkorn, E. (2009) 'Rankings and the battle for world-class excellence', *Higher Education Management and Policy*, 21, 1: 1–22.

Keane, E. (2009) '"Frictional" relationships . . . tensions in the camp: focusing on the relational in under-represented students' experiences in higher education', *Irish Educational Studies*, 28, 1: 85–102.

Khadria, B. (2001) 'Shifting paradigms of globalization: the twenty-first century transition towards generics in skilled migration from India', *International Migration*, 39, 5: 45–71.

Kuo, Y.-C. (2007) 'Fluctuating identities: overseas students in an age of entrepreneurialism', paper presented at the Learning Together Conference, July 22–24 2007, Institute of Education, London.

Lambert, C., Parker, A., and Neary, M. (2007) 'Entrepreneurialism and critical pedagogy: reinventing the higher education curriculum', *Teaching in Higher Education*, 12, 4: 525–37.

Levinas, E. (2006) *Humanism of the Other*, Champaign, IL: University of Illinois Press.

Luke, A. (2010) 'Educating the other: standpoint and theory in the "internationalization" of higher education', in E. Unterhalter and V. Carpentier (eds) *Global Inequalities and Higher Education: Whose Interests are we Serving?*, Basingstoke: Palgrave Macmillan.

Lynch, K. (2010) 'Carelessness: a hidden doxa of higher education', *Arts and Humanities in Higher Education*, 9, 1: 54–67.

Madge, C., Raghuram, P. and Noxolo, P. (2009) 'Engaged pedagogy and responsibility: postcolonial analysis of international students', *Geoforum*, 40: 34–45.

Marginson, S. and van der Wende, M. (2006) *Globalisation and Higher Education*, Paris: OECD.

Maringe, F. (2011) 'The student as consumer: affordances and constraints in a transforming higher education system', in M. Molesworth, R. Scullion and E. Nixon (eds) *The Marketisation of Higher Education and the Student as Consumer*, London: Routledge.

Masschelein, J. and Simons, M. (2002) 'An adequate education in a globalised world? A note on immunization against being-together', *Journal of Philosophy of Education*, 36, 4: 589–608.

Morley, L. (1998) 'All you need is love: feminist pedagogy for empowerment and emotional labour in the academy', *International Journal of Inclusive Education*, 2, 1: 15–27.

Nielson, K. (2011) '"This place is not at all what I had expected": student demand for authentic Irish experiences in Irish studies programmes', in M. Molesworth, R. Scullion and E. Nixon (eds) *The Marketisation of Higher Education and the Student as Consumer*, London: Routledge.

Noddings, N. (1992) *The Challenge to Care in Schools*, New York: Teachers College Press.

—— (2003) *Caring: a Feminine Approach to Ethics and Moral Education*, 2nd edn, Berkeley: University of California Press.

Nussbaum, M. (1997) 'Kant and Stoic cosmopolitanism', *Journal of Political Philosophy*, 5, 1: 1–25.

O'Brien, L. (2010) 'Caring in the ivory tower', *Teaching in Higher Education*, 15, 1: 109–15.

Rizvi, F. (2009) 'Towards cosmopolitan learning', *Discourse: Studies in the Cultural Politics of Education*, 30, 3: 253–68.

Rizvi, F. and Lingard, B. (2010) *Globalizing Education Policy*, London: Routledge.

Sidhu, R. K. (2006) *Universities and Globalization: to Market, to Market*, Mahwah, NJ: Lawrence Erlbaum.

Takagi, H. (2009) 'Internationalisation of undergraduate curricula in Japan: the gap between ideas and practice in Japan', *London Review of Education*, 7, 1: 31–9.

Todd, S. (2009) 'Towards an imperfect education: the task of facing human pluralism', Invited Distinguished Lecture, American Education Research Association Annual Conference, 15 April 2009, San Diego, California.

Welikala, T. (2008) 'Disempowering and dislocating: how learners from diverse cultures read the role of the English language in UK higher education', *London Review of Education*, 6, 2: 159–69.

Wende, van der M., Coate, K., Kontigiannopoulou-Polydorides, G., Luitjen-Lub, A., Papadiamantaki, Y., Stamelos, G. and Williams, G. (2005) 'International comparative analysis', in J. Huisman and M. van der Wende (eds) *On Cooperation and Competition II: Institutional Responses to Internationalisation, Europeanisation and Globalisation*, Bonn: Lemmens.

Zipin, L. and Brennan, M. (2003) 'The suppression of ethical dispositions through managerial governmentality: a habitus crisis in Australian higher education', *International Journal of Leadership in Education*, 6, 4: 351–70.

Chapter 5

An international approach to teaching and learning from a UK university management perspective

Implications for international students' experience on campus

Joanna Al-Youssef

Introduction

The main focus of this chapter is on interpretations of internationalization by a UK university's management team as well as their views of international students and their experience, especially their academic experience. This is thought to have significant implications for all members of the UK higher education institutions (HEIs), especially the group labelled 'international students' in relation to integration and academic success.

A changing higher education global context has resulted in greater numbers of international students in the UK. The need for international students in UK universities as both a significant source of income and an important element necessary for a cultural mix was articulated by university management and enhanced by government initiatives such as the Prime Minister's Initiatives PMI 1 and PMI 2, which encouraged more recruitment of international students into UK universities. As a result, a more strategic approach to internationalization emerged and it has become a priority target and an important instrument for HEIs for the development and planning of their international activities.

With the increasing attention to internationalization worldwide, research has been done to understand the term, and several themes have been associated with it such as the internationalization of learning, teaching and research, and internationalization strategies (Kehm and Teichler 2007). However, the international role of higher education has always been highlighted and seen as a positive force throughout the history of the university in Europe in the sense that student mobility has led to exchange of cultural knowledge, thus contributing to an increased sensitivity to foreign cultures and an appreciation and an understanding of other ways of life (De Ridder-Symoens 1992).

As internationalization is seen to affect all members of HEIs (Kehm and Teichler 2007), research into the term has been conducted on several fronts and with focus on different elements of internationalization and the different stakeholders.

Focusing on international students' experience of internationalization, for example, research shows that internationalization is seen as a way to understand the world, respecting differences between cultures and, perhaps from a more job-oriented view, to be able to work in different cultural contexts (Leask 2010). Students' views of their higher education experience also included reference to the gaining of knowledge of their own 'selves' through raised awareness of their own values and attitudes through their encounters with 'Others' in the HEI (Leask 2010).

International students' views and experience at universities outside their home countries have been used by HEIs for services development and other purposes. An example is the International Student Barometer (ISB) (I-graduate Online n.d.), which is adopted by HEIs worldwide and is used as a feedback tool that also gives HEIs a competitive advantage. This chapter examines representations of international students and their experience through reporting on views by university management, collected in case study research that shows how international students are perceived and the implications this has for their experience on campus. First, a brief description of the research is given with the main aim, an overview of the relevant literature and the methodology. Then, data relating to meanings of internationalization, international students, and reference to teaching and learning, are presented, followed by a final discussion and concluding remarks.

The study: previous research

Internationalization in the literature is seen in relation to universities' global function (Bolsmann and Miller 2008). In this sense, it is also seen as a response to globalization through university policies as defined, for example, by Altbach and Knight (2007: 290) as 'the economic, political, and societal forces pushing 21st-century higher education toward greater international involvement'. The relationship between internationalization and globalization is, however, not so succinctly or convincingly explained. This is perhaps due to the complex interaction between the two, the thing that makes any attempt to define the role of HEIs within the frame of either internationalization or globalization unattainable. Nevertheless the two terms have, on occasions, been used interchangeably (Sanderson 2004). However, responding to globalization is not the only rationale for the internationalization of higher education mentioned in the literature. Other rationales for the internationalization of HEIs, such as social transformative, educational and cultural ones, have also been presented as in Knight (1995), de Wit (1995) and Qiang (2003). For HEIs the ambiguity surrounding the term, and the different rationales attributed to it, have led to an implicit or explicit conflict between the economic and the educational rationales of universities themselves (Stier 2004).

The empirical literature underlying the research comprised studies on internationalization in different university and national contexts (Davies 1992; Rudzki

1995a and 1995b; Knight 1995; Van Dijk and Meijer 1997). Each of the studies concluded by drawing a model of what internationalization processes and policies looked like in the environment concerned. The models are largely descriptive and very much context-bound. The above models fail to address three main issues regarding internationalization research (Al-Youssef 2010). First, being context-bound, these models reflect data collected within that particular context only; thus the interpretations of the data gathered in that context are restricted to its particularities. Second, the above studies do not provide insight into possible meanings of internationalization based on their findings or the models. Third, the models represent internationalization as a linear process, moving the institution from 'here' to 'there' without acknowledging the interaction between the various actors and elements involved. The 'social' aspect of the process and the role of actors are also ignored in the internationalization models, as well as what Trowler (2002) refers to as the agentic approach to internationalization which takes into account the actors' perceptions and contributions in reconstructing both the policy and its discourse. Within a university context, those actors can also be seen as Cultural Others who stand outside the policy-making circle. 'True' inter-nationalization is seen in the interaction with the Cultural Other at an individual level (Sanderson 2004), and is also seen to lie on a continuum between symbolic and transformative internationalization (Turner and Robson 2008), which reflects a multidimensional, complex view, in contrast with the linear view represented by the models above.

The study presented in this chapter was inspired by the gap in the studies mentioned above and by the local changes within the university towards more attention to internationalization and the desire to generate a document reflecting the university's stand on internationalization. These local changes were not, however, isolated from a broader national emphasis on the importance of internationalization for HEIs represented, for example, by the Prime Minister's Initiatives PMI 1 and PMI 2 as seen above (NASES 2008).

The study: methods

The case study aims broadly at exploring perceptions of internationalization in a UK HEI. More specifically, the main aim of the study is to investigate how internationalization is understood by middle and senior management at the university as it was in the process of creating its international strategy. Senior management at the institution concerned refers to central management and senior lines reporting directly to the Vice-Chancellor. As the strategy was mainly devised within the university's central management, senior managers who were going to manage the process were chosen as participants in the study. Individuals with middle management responsibilities who were involved in the dissemination of the strategy in their departments and faculties were also approached. The case study was largely inductive, and in-depth semi-structured interviews were carried out in order to explore participants' interpretations of internationalization, going beyond the practices of the institution and into the accounts of the individuals who manage internationalization.

Prior to the interviews, data were collected from five university documents relating to the international strategy or the concept of internationalization. The documents provided direction to the research question and were also used in the interviews asking participants to comment on them. These documents are the university's international strategy document, a discussion paper leading to the formulation of that international strategy, an international operational plan to follow the international strategy, the university's mission statement and a document reporting a study on international students' experiences at that university. The documents were analysed using basic textual analysis to examine both their manifest as well as latent content (Sarantakos 2005). In the international strategy document, internationalization is seen as a target and a goal reflecting a desired end-state. The international strategy appears to be a response to external factors such as the global market, advocating an increase in the level of inter-national activities including recruiting more international students. However, it is not clear how this new strategy will bring about change in the HEI concerned, especially with regard to developing an international culture, one of the objectives in the international strategy document.

Following the analysis of the five documents in which no deep elaborations on meanings of internationalization were present, twenty-one interviews were conducted to address this issue. Interviewees were from various university depart-ments and covered a wide range of roles and positions. There were three pro-vice chancellors, three faculty deans, three academic staff involved in international activities and with management positions, heads of services of accommodation, catering, human resources, the international office (and two international officers), the library, marketing and communication, security, sports, students support services and the students' union. Interview transcripts were stored and organized in NVivo software for qualitative research. The software was initially used mainly as a database since there were no predetermined categories or codes due to the nature of the context-bound inductive study. Main themes and codes in relation to internationalization issues or the international strategy were then identified and analysed within NVivo as and when there was reference to such areas in the interview data.

The interview data can be divided into three main areas. The first area covers interviewees' perceptions of the international strategy and their views on whether or how the strategy is thought to bring about change to the institution. The participants talk about the different motives behind creating the strategy, and these can be divided into external factors, such as government and competition pressure, and internal influences such as the financial need to recruit international students and regulating resources. In both cases, the strategy is seen to be a response. Regardless of the factors behind it, the newly created international strategy is interpreted differently by the interviewees whose views are influenced by their roles and worldviews. Some see it as a policy mind shift that leads to major changes on the university campus; others do not see it changing anything at all but merely reflecting what is already taking place at the institution. The second area covered in the interviews is to do with barriers to the international strategy and internationalization at the institution concerned. The barriers are thought to include resistance to the strategy by individuals at the institution, the devolved structure of the university management, lack of agreement on what internationalization means, lack of a culture that supports internationalization, limited resources, lack of integration between people of different nationalities and lack of a clear follow-up plan to the strategy document. The third area of interview data covered in the interviews is participants' understandings of internationalization. This area is explored further later in this chapter in relation to participants' views, with particular reference to learning and teaching.

Study results: meanings of internationalization

As mentioned earlier, the main aim of the research was to explore how internationalization was interpreted by senior and middle managers of the HEI. The data from the interviews show a lack of shared understanding. Generally, however, internationalization was seen in terms of numbers of international students and staff. Some senior managers see it as 'having a suitable proportion of international students', and see the HEI as being already international 'in terms of the student population as one measure'.

The views of internationalization reflect individuals' roles at the university. There appears to be, perhaps understandably, a clear divide in terms of individuals' priorities as far as internationalization is concerned. This divide is in itself not necessarily inappropriate, but it simply means that a central internationalization strategy to be implemented across the institution is doomed to face some challenges and resistance due to the different priorities. The data as a whole show that internationalization is predominantly viewed as a target which the institution aspires to reach. One senior manager, for example, believes that in order to reach the institution's targets, 'there is all manner of activities that suddenly become a lot more important; collaborative research, knowledge transfer, commercial activities, staff and students exchange'.

Numbers of international students and staff are thought to be two indicators of internationalization at the institution. Other indicators are international links, international curriculum, international recognition and international research. These six indicators are seen – presumably – to lead to the creation of an international ethos at the HEI.

At a deeper level, internationalization is viewed from two main perspectives. The first regards internationalization as a financial strategy that is of paramount importance for the present and future work of a university that is operating very much like a business. This view is expressed by one senior manager and head of service who believes that 'it is a business at the end of the day, it is a business of educating people and like any other business, it is competitive'. In this senior manager's view, attracting international students and projecting an institutional image that embraces internationalization are necessary parts of that business, and that is important for achieving top world ranking.

This view gives weight to marketing, the university's reputation on a world stage, and also its place on the league tables. It sees the world as a global economy in which the university's major goal is financial survival. On the other hand, looking at the world as a multicultural community leads to the view that internationalization is about cooperation and mutual understanding, in which case the creation of a multicultural university campus becomes a priority. Another senior manager and head of service thinks that it is 'very much looking at focusing as much as you can do on the whole community and . . . recognize that in everything you do'. To this senior manager, 'internationalization is actually looking at the whole university holistically . . . not too many international offices in the university or international student recruitment offices'.

According to the research data, a multicultural campus can be achieved through research links, but more importantly through recruiting international students. The question here remains whether having students from different nationalities together within the boundaries of campus does naturally lead to a guaranteed state of multiculturalism. This view does not seem to take into account cultural conflicts and clashes that might also occur with the mix. The line dividing the two views is not, however, that straightforward, as even within the 'multicultural' view participants also believe that recruiting international students is helpful in generating essential income, a view that is more about marketing, although indirectly. There seems to be a causal link somehow between the international strategy and the international community, although the latter is not clearly defined. The international strategy is seen to attract international students, thus an international community is to emerge, which consequently positively influences the university's international reputation.

The two views of internationalization mentioned above can be seen to resemble those of Sanderson (2004) of strong and weak internationalization, where weak internationalization is seen as a result of global forces that affect the HEI and push it to meet certain targets, and strong internationalization is about engaging with Otherness in a multicultural community. The two views can also be seen to parallel a model referred to by Turner and Robson (2008) in which internationalization is seen to be positioned on a continuum from symbolic (weak) to transformative (strong). Symbolic internationalization is temporary as it responds to changing external factors. Here, the focus of strategic management is on student recruitment and marketing. Transformative internationalization, on the other hand, is about having a long-term commitment to internationalization issues, and the concern of strategic management would be with cooperation and knowledge sharing. Turner and Robson's model presents a more dynamic interpretation of the multifaceted concept of internationalization.

Study results: international students, teaching and learning

In addition to the differing views of internationalization, other related issues emerge in the data. The HEI is seen mainly as being a UK institution at its core in which international students are labelled as a group and are put in opposition to the group labelled 'home students'. A number of areas of comparison are referred to by participants. One area is to do with attitudes to academic studies and learning styles. Respondents generally believe that there are certain characteristics associated with international students' preferences for learning. One senior manager thinks that 'arguing or debating with a member of staff, to them, may show disrespect – you do not question what you are being told'. Another senior manager refers particularly to the issue of plagiarism and explains that the problem occurs with international students 'because they are used to just having to quote what people have said, that is how they learn'. A sub-group of international students is even thought to have its own qualities, as is believed by another senior manager: 'a Chinese student might appear really shy in a personal seminar or a tutorial where there is a small group' – a rather stereotypical generalized view.

Another area of comparison between home or UK students and international students is the amount of effort made to adapt to the British way of life, and British versus international 'ways' of socializing. UK students are seen to 'have a far more relaxed attitude towards "their" academic studies' by one senior manager and head of service, and 'it is just local for them or the norm is to come away and spend three years [away from home]'. On the other hand, this senior manager thinks that international students 'feel this huge pressure to perform because it has cost them so much money to come to university', and that 'it is such a big thing for some of them to have come half way across the world'. Another senior manager believes that home students 'do not socialize with parents or grandparents' and they have a 'far more independent lifestyle'. International students are, however, thought to have 'a far closer family life'. Therefore, this senior manager thinks, it is more difficult for international students to be away from home as 'they are expected to make a huge effort to adapt to our British way of life and to how things are done over here'.

As can be seen in the quotes above, the discourse surrounding views of international students' learning styles and attitudes to academic studies and social life is packed with references to 'us' and 'them', clearly emphasizing the differences. International students are seen to avoid confrontations in academic contexts as this is thought to be disrespectful in 'their' view. Plagiarism is thought to be one major problem for international students as there is the view that 'they' are used to quoting others. One reason given by respondents for the issue of plagiarism by international students is thought to do with the fact that 'they' are educated outside the English education system. This view ignores the fact that home students new to the university environment might also have little awareness of the issue of plagiarism (Barret and Malcolm 2006).

On a more positive note, the 'international' tag on international students is removed for some participants. One middle manager and academic believes that individuals differ not necessarily by nationality but by their personal learning preferences and that 'we are now thinking much more about the internationalization of the university community as a whole. It has become much more [about] how do different groups of students originating from different countries actually learn from each other?' This seems to further the division down into groups of countries rather than treating all international students as a single group. Although this view acknowledges the influence of the cultural and social context on education and on learning (Savin-Baden *et al.* 2008), it does not offer ways in which students who come from different cultural and national contexts can become aware of their context's inherent restraints on their learning and how they can use this awareness in their mutual learning from each other.

Some participants believe that international students need learning support in areas related to their academic studies at the UK HEI. These areas include English language and IT, as well as areas that are thought to be indirectly affecting international students' ability to learn, such as catering, and having support workers who are sensitive and interested in students from different backgrounds. A senior manager and head of service states: 'my staff have to be very conscious about multiculturalism and diversity within the university. We understand what happens in Britain but we do not necessarily understand what happens on the other side of the world.' According to this senior manager, it is important to train staff on these issues in order to 'understand and break down some of the barriers'. A number of participants also think that it is the faculty's responsibility to guide international students and to become 'aware of difficulties that international students have, and which our faculty think they have, about adapting to the UK system', as another senior manager puts it. In this regard, some challenges are seen to face academics teaching international students, especially with the change in the nature of the students' cohort. One middle manager believes that academics who 'have been used to, they understand, British students and how to teach them and suddenly they have got a class that is the majority international students, they are not coping very well with that kind of change'. On the other hand, some see learning as a mutual process to which international students can contribute. A senior manager at central management thinks that 'a lot of the learning process is to do with what the students bring to it as much as what the tutors bring to it, and it is the interaction of those things, that mutual learning'. As for the curriculum, views on choice and design differ to a large degree. On the one hand the curriculum is thought to be mostly Eurocentric and does not allow for input from international students to be incorporated into the university's teaching. One middle manager and academic observes that 'we are not often taking their experience of their countries and incorporating it into our teaching and learning here'. On the other hand, there is the view, expressed by a senior manager and faculty dean, that 'it is more useful, to be honest, having international staff who know how something works in a different country, this is of more benefit in terms of designing an international curriculum than asking the students'. In general, there is a concern that because the HEI in this study developed incrementally, change in terms of practice in particular is going to be difficult, as a senior manager and head of service reflects on the institution's processes and practices and thinks that they 'have not really adapted enough to embrace the wider diversity agenda and so it is quite a struggle for people to actually find a way in, whether that be on their academic programme or on the social life'.

In order to facilitate a change in practices, some respondents argue for a change in attitude through reflections on current policies and practices. One senior manager and head of service believes that 'projects [are] needed to give individuals more time to think and to reflect on what we do and give us even small ways, some concrete ways forward, modest changes that will lead to a different practice'.

Discussion: a way in or a way out

Many of the above views reflect an understanding of internationalization as a 'good' thing for the university to have, and with it international students as Cultural Others will be given the academic and other support required for the duration of their studies to help them adapt to the UK HEI system, achieve success and help the HEI achieve its high reputation by providing this service. Internationalization is largely seen as a response to factors inside and outside the institution; it is a response for change, but it is not clear how it might bring about change except by increasing the volume of activities and the numbers of international students. Internationalization is not seen as an agent for change (Knight 1999) beyond this 'quantitative' view, which only considers numbers. However, a few participants emphasized the need for change at the institution through reflections on practice, as in the quote above, leading eventually to major changes and a more inclusive practice. As far as learning and teaching are concerned, Turner and Robson (2008) offer a way forward. They suggest adopting a 'reciprocal learning approach' as a way towards more cultural inclusiveness by making adjustments to different aspects of teaching and learning practices through reflective discussions that would lead to major conceptual changes regarding teaching, learning and the curriculum, a view that is expressed by some participants as illustrated above.

As mentioned earlier, the discourse in the literature surrounding the internationalization of higher education institutions is influenced by market discourse and values of profit and profile (Haigh 2008; Bolsmann and Miller 2008; Toyoshima 2007). This is being achieved as one method by increasing the numbers of international students at HEIs and, consequently, affecting the nature of services provided by those HEIs and influencing their practices. However, the influence of the rising numbers of international students is short-lived, as the strategies that are devised to respond to that rise have a temporary nature since they are a response to external factors which are in themselves likely to change. What is missing is the creative engagement with the Cultural Other through internationalization (Stohl 2007), and that engagement can only be achieved by creating space for reflections. One way to achieve this is to move away from the aspirational 'quantitative' view of internationalization, seeing it as a quantified target, into a more non-material micro-approach which sees HEIs as places where individuals from diverse backgrounds meet, rather than structures that contain large numbers of isolated groups, some labelled 'international'. The move leads to what Sanderson (2004) calls existential internationalization, which is the internationalization of the self; building a bridge to the Cultural Other through reflexivity and the elimination of the fear of the unknown. This fear of the unknown is what Otherizes it and leads to emphasizing differences rather than similarities. However, the difficulty in the HEI in point is that that fear of the threat posed by the Cultural Other is seen as an opportunity to satisfy certain criteria such as high ranking or reputation. Therefore, it is not possible to see through the disguise of opportunity into the real feelings of distance and detachment from the Cultural Other. In other words, this Cultural Other, in the form of international students, is only seen as a guest who is requiring attention without genuine engagement or the creation of a true opportunity for mutual learning and a more sustainable form of internationalization. In the research data, a genuine desire to go beyond this superficial view is expressed by some participants, as for example in the view of a senior manager at central management, who thinks that there is the emerging realization that 'it is much more helpful to see that as part of a much bigger issue which is about making the strange familiar'.

A first step towards a more constructive engagement with Cultural Others might be to break through the barrier of the discourse of 'us' and 'them', and celebrate cultural differences without emphasizing them. It is about describing how individuals learn, rather than how students of certain nationalities learn. It is about the co-creation of internationalization at HEIs by members of those institutions regardless of their nationalities. It is about changing mindsets that tend to see stereotypes rather than individuals, thus providing a framework for the creation of a positive international community, and the creation of an all-institution environment that does not define borders based on nationalities, group traits or ownership of space.

One implication of the views mentioned above for international students – and indeed all students – on campus is not only the reproduction of an age-old rift between groups, but also a more pronounced form of that divide in which boundaries are distinctly emphasized. The consequences of such an approach may not be visible for faculty insiders in management positions who plough their way through obstacles and pressures imposed on them through regulations, targets and competition. The main consequence for students is a study environment in which there is more to celebrate than simply talent and educational excellence. The 'Otherizing' of international students as a group could potentially lead to creating more obstacles and barriers that might affect their academic performance and, therefore, academic success, and this would influence the university's reputation in the long term. In the research data, the academic aspect of international students' life in the HEI concerned is implicitly and inadvertently portrayed as a form of academic alienation or difference. One senior manager at central management, for instance, thinks that it is 'more about academic orientation to what it is like to be in the UK, a UK setting and in a UK university', thus implying a distinct UK academic environment to which some adjustment on the part of outsiders is required in order to fit in. The question remains of whether those international student Others actually like to be or benefit from being treated differently and made to feel special or ostracized.

Conclusion

This chapter presented a case study exploring the interpretations of internationalization at a UK HEI by middle and senior managers involved, directly or indirectly, in the creation and implementation of an international strategy. International students are considered to be of particular significance to the strategy in the sense that it aims at increasing their numbers. Participants in the study also see international students as an important group for the university for various reasons including generating income and contributing to the cultural mix. They are also seen as a main indicator of internationalization at the university. However, referring back to the research data and the quotes above, international students are Cultural Others who are labelled and described as a group and are ascribed certain learning styles. This view of international students leads to a divide in the university community of which they are a vital part. It also leads to a superficial engagement with international students based on their nationality and the 'benefit' they bring to the university.

One way forward towards a more sustainable internationalization seems to be by reconsidering the viewpoint in which international students are seen as estranged Others, and by creating opportunities for a deeper engagement with issues relating to internationalization. With this in mind, a strong form of internationalization can be seen as a way to engage with the Cultural Other through continuous reflexivity of the self. Giving all students an opportunity to engage in such reflexivity through creating space for dialogue and reflective discussions on issues of direct significance to them could possibly encourage such a practice. Some of the above views do not completely negate the importance of such an environment of the co-creation of values. However, at the moment, and taking the data as a whole, it would appear that attempts to provide such opportunities of engagement are still isolated efforts that do not constitute the norm at the HEI concerned.

In addition, the above views of internationalization and international students have implications for the role of universities and higher education in general. The conflict between the economic and educational rationales for higher education is evident in the data. On the one hand, there is an aspiration to achieve high profile and reputation through marketing. On the other hand, there is an emphasis on creating an inclusive academic and social environment, as shown in the quotes above. The result is a clear divide within the university structure with regard to this opposition of rationales. Although the conflict is not articulated as such at any level of the institution, the economic rationale is most emphasized at the level of senior and central management with concerns for recruitment and income generation, for example. On the other hand, the educational rationale is clearly accentuated at the level of individuals with teaching responsibilities who are in more direct contact with students.

As a response, internationalization puts HEIs at the mercy of changing national policies and global forces that only partially define the role of those institutions. The model of internationalization that emerges in the case study and is supported by participants' views is, therefore, reactive following an ad hoc path in the sense that internationalization and the international strategy are a reaction to internal and external factors affecting the HEI's policy direction. Within this model, the international strategy is seen as regularizing activities and extending power and control over what is already happening, and therefore any change accomplished would be broad but not deep in the sense that change would affect more aspects and more members of the HEI concerned, but no major changes in attitudes, values or discourse are foreseeable in the near future. Ways for the integration of a more sustainable internationalization and reflexivity into the university's culture, as well as ways for utilizing international students' views of the above issues to improve institutional practices, remain areas for further research and study.

References

Altbach, P.G. and Knight, J. (2007) 'The internationalization of higher education: motivations and realities', *Journal of Studies in International Education*, 11, 3/4: 290–305.

Al-Youssef, J. (2010) *The Internationalization of Higher Education Institutions: Meanings, Policy and Practice*, Saarbrücken, Germany: VDM.

Barret, R. and Malcolm, J. (2006) 'Embedding plagiarism education in the assessment process', *International Journal for Educational Integrity*, 2, 1: 38–45.

Bolsmann, C. and Miller, H. (2008) 'International student recruitment to universities in England: discourse, rationales and globalization', *Globalization, Societies and Education*, 6, 1: 75–88.

Davies, J.L. (1992) 'Developing a strategy for internationalization in universities: towards a conceptual framework', in C.B. Klasek (ed.) *Bridges To The Future: Strategies For Internationalizing Higher Education*, Carbondale: Association of International Education Administrators.

De Ridder-Symoens, H. (1992) 'Mobility', in H. De Ridder-Symoens (ed.) *A History of the University in Europe*, vol. 1, Ch. 9, Cambridge: Cambridge University Press.

De Wit, H. (1995) *Strategies for Internationalization of Higher Education: A Comparative Study of Australia, Canada, Europe and the United States of America*, The Netherlands: European Association for International Education.

Haigh, M. (2008) 'Internationalization, planetary citizenship and Higher Education Inc.', *Compare*, 38, 4: 427–40.

I-graduate Online. Available HTTP: http://www.i-graduate.org/services/student_insight–student_barometer.html (accessed 16 January 2011).

Kehm, B.M. and Teichler, U. (2007) 'Research on internationalization in higher education', *Journal of Studies in International Education*, 113/4: 260–73.

Knight, J. (1995) *Internationalization at Canadian Universities: The Changing Landscape*, Ottawa, Canada: Association of Universities and Colleges of Canada.

—— (1999) 'Internationalization of higher education', in J. Knight and H. de Wit (eds) *Quality and Internationalization in Higher Education*, 13–28, Paris: Organisation for Economic Co-operation and Development.

Leask, B. (2010). 'Beside me is an empty chair: The student experience of internationalization', in E. Jones (ed.) *Internationalization and the Student Voice*, London: Routledge.

NASES (National Association of Student Employment Services) (2008) *PMI2*. Online. Available HTTP: http://www.nases.org.uk/content/index.php?page=22962 (accessed 31 December 2010).

Qiang, Z. (2003) 'Internationalization of higher education: towards a conceptual framework', *Policy Futures in Education*, 1, 2: 248–70.

Rudzki, R. (1995a) 'The application of a strategic management model to the internationalization of higher education institutions', *Higher Education* 29, 4: 421–41.

—— (1995b) 'Internationalization of UK business schools: findings of a national survey', in P. Blok (ed.) *Policy and Policy Implementation in Internationalization of Higher Education*, Amsterdam: EAIE.

Sanderson, G. (2004) 'Existentialism, globalization and the Cultural Other', *International Education Journal*, 4, 4: 1–20.

Sarantakos, S. (2005) *Social Research*. Basingstoke: Palgrave Macmillan.

Savin-Baden, M., McFarland, L. and Savin-Baden, J. (2008) 'Learning spaces, agency and notions of improvement: what influences thinking and practices about teaching and learning in higher education? An interpretive meta-ethnography', *London Review of Education*, 6, 3: 211–27.

Stier, J. (2004) 'Taking a critical stance toward internationalization ideologies in higher education: idealism, instrumentalism and educationalism', *Globalization, Societies and Education*, 2, 1: 83–97.

Stohl, M. (2007) 'We have met the enemy and he is us: the role of the faculty in the internationalization of higher education in the coming decade', *Journal of Studies in International Education*, 11, 3/4: 359–72.

Toyoshima, M. (2007) 'International strategies of universities in England', *London Review of Education*, 5, 3: 265–80.

Trowler, P. (2002) *Higher Education Policy and Institutional Change: Intentions and Outcomes in Turbulent Environments*, Buckingham: Society for Research into Higher Education and Open University Press.

Turner, Y. and Robson, S. (2008) *Internationalising the University*, London: Continuum International Publishing Group.

Van Dijk, H. and Meijer, K. (1997) 'The internationalization cube: a tentative model for the study of organisational designs and the results of internationalization in higher education', *Higher Education Management*, 9, 1: 157–67.

Chapter 6

Inheriting the earth

Competencies and competition within the internationalized curriculum

Elizabeth Grant

Internationalization: institutional interpretations

There have been many developments within higher education over recent years that are directly attributable to effective internationalization reforms. Strategies and mission statements abound, committees have been established and in many institutions the 'international strategy' primarily focusing upon international student recruitment has been replaced by 'internationalization strategies' covering every service within the university. However, despite these developments and the helpful reviews of provision that such change encourages, questions remain about the consequences of conflating the 'internationalization' of 'higher education' with 'curriculum' and the epistemological implications of that.

To understand these issues it is necessary to understand internationalization at national policy level. One of the most frequently cited definitions of internationalization used within institutional strategies is that it is 'the process of integrating an international, intercultural and/or global dimension in to the purpose, functions and delivery of post-secondary education' (Knight 2003a: 2). This definition recognizes a plurality of interpretation; and it is cognizant of national and local context, institutional identity and regional and demographic characteristics. For a number of institutions, internationalization is perceived as offering opportunities for commercial presence within other countries and forms a central strand within institutional strategy. Some see international student recruitment as a key priority; yet others emphasize the encouragement of student 'global' mobility through, for example, initiatives associated with the European Higher Education Area.

There are also differences in national needs which influence how internationalization is promoted and implemented. For example, the rapid expansion or reconstitution of higher education provision, exemplified by India's Innovation Universities (Mishra 2010, cited in Eastman 2011: 6), or the ambitious massification of HE programme across Ethiopia (World Bank 2003: vi) are two national reforms that demonstrate the purpose, value and expectations placed upon national higher education systems that lead to specific internationalization missions and strategies.

Yet, regardless of individual institutional and/or national emphasis, the need to respond to economic, political, academic and socio-cultural drivers of internationalization (De Wit 2002: 83–102) is shared by universities across the globe. At their 2006 summit, the UK Leadership Foundation for Higher Education made it clear that if higher education institutions are to survive they must take internationalization seriously.

Prioritizing responses to the drivers of internationalization is complex, involving institutional, national and international agencies at a variety of levels; and when it comes to the internationalized curriculum there is no general consensus as to what should be included within its parameters and what should not. From terms used within the updated Internationalization Quality Review Process (Knight 2004), procedures designed to self-evaluate the extent of institutional progress developed originally by Knight and de Wit (1999), the following provisions were included as indicators of internationalization relating to student learning:

> Student exchange programmes, foreign language study, internationalized curricula, area or thematic studies, work/study abroad, international students, teaching and learning process, joint double degree programmes, cross-cultural training, faculty/staff mobility programs, visiting lectures and scholars [and] link between academic programmes and other strategies.
>
> (Knight 2004: 14)

These terms suggest that any review should have a clear idea about what a curriculum is. It denotes curriculum as an aspect of learning provision that is based upon an agreed definition; that it is an educational 'component' that can be isolated and subjected to an external referent along with a range of other educational processes and programmes. However, 'curriculum' requires some interrogation. Barnett and Coate (2005: 24) argue that there is a real need for substantial debate on 'curriculum' in higher education – within the UK in particular. Without this debate, they suggest, it is 'likely to lead to curriculum approaches that run counter to the understandings and practices that are necessary if higher education is to be in any way adequate in the contemporary world' (Barnett and Coate 2005: 25). 'Curriculum', then, is problematic, as is the internationalization of it. Caruana (2010: 30) proposes that 'internationalization' [of the curriculum] is not a clearly defined, absolute set of "best practices", but rather a nuanced construct which is highly context specific'. Thus, if there is no consensus on what curriculum embraces, and the internationalization of it cannot be made clear, how do we 'integrate an international, intercultural and/or global dimension' into it?

Curriculum

There is little in the way of curriculum theory studies represented on the UK Higher Education Academy website, which perhaps suggests too that little has changed since Barnett (2000: 255) made his earlier observation that curricula have not been systematically studied in higher education. The observation is shared by Smith (1996, 2000), who makes reference to studies that stem from the school system, and from ideas such as 'subject' and 'lesson'. Despite this lack of engagement of the term within higher education in many publications on the internationalization of the curriculum, there appears to be a suggestion that curriculum as a concept has what semiologists would term a 'denotative signification'. In other words there is an agreed cultural meaning associated with the term, whereas there appears to be no consensus on the concept.

Examples of internationalization of the curriculum variously promote a competency-based approach to learning; whilst others suggest an integrated holistic 'process'. In outlining the problems of each of these models of curriculum, Smith (1996, 2000) suggests that the former can be criticized because learning is reduced to a list of competencies to be ticked off, competencies that cannot adequately ever really be measurable; whilst the latter incorporates everything within the student experience to such an extent that the word 'curriculum' is redundant. Barnett suggests a review of the concept of curriculum within higher education and proposes that 'we need to situate curricula [itself] amid the wider social and even global context' (Barnett 2000: 257), if we are to prepare students for what he describes as a 'supercomplex' world. Thus if we are to develop a theory of curriculum that acknowledges the total context within which learning is placed, we need to consider the numerous meanings attributed to and approaches of the concept of curriculum. Moreover, since higher education is increasingly internationally market driven, will 'curriculum' need to be negotiated and understood by all stakeholders? Could this lead, in part at least, to a theory of curriculum driven by global trade?

Curriculum as a tradable global commodity

Since 1995 and the creation of the World Trade Organization's General Agreement of Trade in Services (GATS), which perceives higher education as a service trade, the UK higher education sector has engaged in numerous transnational activities. Trade liberalization is influencing the activities of universities across the world and provision can now, depending upon the extent of national agreement, be developed for one of four 'modes of supply' (World Trade Organization, Final Act, 1986–94). A theory of curriculum that is internationalized would have to take account of each mode of supply:

- cross-border: provision that is developed within one country to be delivered in another (e.g. distance or online learning);
- consumption abroad: consumers travelling to another country to receive a service (e.g. 'international students' – incoming or outgoing);
- commercial presence: territorial presence in another country (e.g. campus abroad);

- presence of national persons: persons entering another country to supply a service (e.g. teachers/researchers).

Adapted from General Agreement of Trade in Services
(Knight 2003b: 3)

There are, however, many potential barriers to overcome when considering the 'curriculum' for such modes of supply, since such learning is situated within unique contexts. Barriers to the development and/or delivery of learning appropriate for each mode have already been experienced. These include restrictions based on discipline or area of study deemed to be against national interest, restrictions on electronic material, visa and entry requirements, and difficulty in approval of joint ventures and accreditation procedures – amongst others (Knight, cited in UK Higher Education Europe Unit 2006). As many of these barriers are related to consensus over what should be included in the 'curriculum', it can be inferred that issues of power and control are clearly relevant in seeking an understanding of 'curriculum' appropriate for internationalization. If an internationalized curriculum offers the opportunity to develop the kind of curriculum needed for the 'supercomplex' world that Barnett proposes, then acknowledging cultural constructions, and recognizing national ideologies, would seem to be essential in building a theory of such a curriculum. So too, then, is the recognition of the increasing financial motivations offered through trade liberalization and the extent that such development will influence theories of curriculum and their congruence with the socio-cultural and academic rationales underpinning reforms within higher education.

Curriculum and competition

Resources on the UK Higher Education Academy 'Internationalization' website indicate that the interest in the Consumption Abroad 'mode' has remained a focus for learning and teaching development. Interestingly, whether stimulated by the need for revenue that international students bring to the HE economy, or by the national need to produce graduates who can 'move seamlessly between different nations, cultures and languages' (American Council on Education, cited in Fielden 2006: 3), Consumption Abroad is driven by economic competitiveness in some form. Graduates that have international attributes 'will be positioned to capitalize on the next scientific, technological or information revolution' (ibid.).

This aim of developing students to be able to interact effectively within the world is both a new and an old concept. The significance of this is the extent to which these ideals are part of a developmental continuum that has, at its core, a European epistemology that all students, whether labelled 'home' or 'international', will experience and normalize.

Curriculum promoting the ideals of the European university 'at home'

Domestic students, and the need to internationalize them, have been the focus of Internationalization at Home (IaH). This intervention is described as 'aimed at the 90 per cent of university students that do not go abroad for study or placements' (European Association for International Education, n.d.). Based on an original idea by Nilsson who defines internationalization of the curriculum as 'preparing students for performing (professionally, socially, emotionally) in an international and multicultural context' (Nilsson 2000: 22), there seems to be a similarity between the purpose of this 'curriculum' and Humboldtian Bildungsideal. Humboldt's idea is of a university that is concerned with personal transformation through 'a process of acquiring the world, and to connect it with the person, and thus to interact with the world' (Wilhelm von Humboldt, c.1792–99). According to Elton (2005: 35), this Humboldtian idea has considerably influenced the modern research university for over 200 years, although it is only relatively recently that Humboldt's ideas have been influencing British higher education in terms of teaching and learning (Elton: ibid.).

Could IaH be the vehicle or 'process' through which this European concept of the university continues to be promoted? The idea of internationalization as an inherent part of a continuum based upon accepted norms of the university has received little attention in the literature. Internationalization of the curriculum is often portrayed as a 'new' initiative requiring new teaching and learning approaches, rather than a manifestation of the need to attend to the issue of 'curriculum' itself.

Curriculum, equality and meaningful learning

As far as 'consumption abroad' is concerned, and specifically in relation to the international/intercultural classroom, after the many praiseworthy developments in recent years there are two quintessential questions that remain unanswered: first, have these activities been a helpful 'Trojan horse', igniting an interest in issues of equality and meaningful learning and an inherent part of a continuum based upon accepted indicators of 'good' teaching and learning within liberal, industrialized countries? Or, more pessimistically, could some of these activities be promoting a deficit model of learning that has the potential, at least, to encourage counter-productive cultural stereotyping and elitism? This second concern is perhaps further augmented as, despite reference by Knight (2004: 7) to one of the many drivers of internationalization being the development of a knowledge society – characteristically considering networked societies, indigenous knowledge, social [and global?] equality and considerations of the knowledge and digital divide – there seems to be an incongruity with current thinking on the internationalization as it relates to student learning across the development gap. For example, the UK Higher Education Academy asserts that intercultural competencies are necessary because 'graduates today will need the resilience and competencies to communicate and *compete* in a rapidly changing, complex global workforce and world' (Higher Education Academy 2012) (my emphasis). This, however, begs the following questions:

1   Who is competing with whom and for what?
2   How level is the global playing field?
3   Why is a competency and reductionist approach to curriculum (apparently) being promoted?
4   Who has access to these competencies?
5   Do such competencies include local interpretations – if so, are they based on divisions of labour?
6   If we can articulate intercultural competence, how do we understand intercultural 'incompetence'?

Finally, could the competencies approach, with its apparent focus upon economic competition, merely conceal and reinforce economic and social divides between and within countries?

Curriculum and the promotion of transnational inequality

In addressing these questions, it is necessary to recognize the role of the national education schooling system and the nexus of societal agencies that are the 'apparatus' through which individuals come to know their 'place' in the state. The type of school attended, the socio-economic class (and cultural capital) of the family, the interplay between religious, media, political and other apparatus will determine the career and life chances of the individual. In other words young people are 'provided with the ideology which suits the role [they have] to fulfil in class society' (Althusser 1970: 155). This reproduction of social inequality as perceived by Althusser in the 1970s through such state apparatus, according to Liodakis, continues in the globalized world of today. Referring to the work of Robinson and Harris (2000), Burnham (2001) and Sklair (2001), he asserts that 'the formation of social classes is considered as an increasingly *transnational process*' (Liodakis 2003: 7) (my emphasis). Thus, whether a domestic or international student, the type and location of the educational institution attended will have been largely pre-determined by birth.

Breaking this cycle of social inequality at national level within the UK has generated interventions that aim to widen participation in higher education on the basis of socio-economic class, disability and ethnic group ever since the publication of the Dearing Report (NCIHE 1997).[1] Despite this, it is sobering that Karen Dunnell, author of the UK National Statisticians Annual Article on Society (2007), reported that inequality in income distribution has increased over the last twenty years. Her findings show that children from Pakistani or Bangladeshi backgrounds are more likely to be living in poverty; and that children, generally, who live in poverty are more likely to suffer mental illnesses. Even within economically developed countries such as the UK, then, and with interventions that aim to encourage participation, fair access to university education remains an issue. Moreover, for those from under-represented groups who do progress into higher education, achieving an equitable and fulfilling engagement is still problematic. For example, Greenbank found that, in some cases, going to university had alienated students from their friends at home, causing them to disengage themselves 'from the working class environment they were once part of' (2009: 162).

In terms of the 'massification' of higher education, then, equality of life chances and the well-being of certain socio-ethnic groups remain unresolved. These inequalities are reflected more starkly as Mohamedbhai (2008) reports in his study on the massification of African universities. He found that 'students [in Africa] usually complete higher education without having gained the necessary skills to make them employable. They spend most of their time just trying to survive and pass their exams and therefore do not have much time for self-development' (2008: 12). These students, although representative of the minority of young people from countries within Africa who access higher education at all, are also the majority of students who cannot access learning 'abroad' or the self-development integral to the 'at home' mission – the mission that will help them to perform 'professionally, socially and emotionally' as Nilsson suggests (2000: 22). If these students are representative of many of the world's university students, who then do (for example) the majority of our African international students actually represent?

Strategic cosmopolitans

To understand internationalization as it is applied to student learning, then, it is necessary to understand the interplay between all apparatus; and to acknowledge how education systems at all socio-economic levels differ *within* and *between* national frameworks, their differing purposes and how they are connected. This seems fundamental if we are to develop learning that is not focused upon the development of graduates who become professionals who merely reproduce values of a tiny elite who 'criss-cross the globe as representatives of powerful, transnational firms' (Obadare and Adebanwi 2009: 511). Such global mobility has been made possible through de-territorialization that has, according to Mitchell, created a move toward 'strategic cosmopolitanism' (2003: 387). Strategic cosmopolitans are able to move between territories and across borders (spatial or ideological) and can strategically adapt to new global contexts. The cosmopolitan 'citizen', however, will experience these new contexts differently dependent upon whether such mobility was created through either personal choice and privilege or a fear of redundancy and compulsion (ibid.: 388). The former are 'global players [who] can demand concessions and protection from states, tax holidays, disciplined labor, macro-economic stability' (Hansen and Stepputat 2005, cited in Obadare and Abedanwi 2009: 511); the latter are disenfranchised, disappointed and unwelcome. In an interview for the *New York Times* (5 June 2011), a Gambian science teacher enticed to Spain for better prospects shares his frustration and disappointment: 'you [Europeans] think you are civilised. But this is how we live here. We suffer here' (Daley 2011). If, then, our 'curricula' are being developed to enable students to become global players, how do we perceive the relevance of the strategic cosmopolitans who move because they have no real choice?

Curriculum for multiculturalism or cosmopolitanism?

Mitchell's article (op cit.) makes an interesting observation about the relevance of 'multi-cultural' education within democratizing nations. She argues that movements towards cosmopolitanism are perhaps only really possible in industrialized countries where national identity is already defined by cultural diversity. In countries where national cohesion has yet to be achieved, multi-cultural education, she suggests, is more appropriate. Additionally, Obadare and Adebanwi (2009: 499), in their article exploring the implications of migration from remittance-dependent countries posit that migration may be 'unwittingly weakening the nation-state as a form of (socio-political) solidarity'. Such concerns reveal the complexity of curricula that aim to promote cosmopolitanism in an intertwined world – one in which such approaches may not be in the national interest for all countries.

Thus, national contexts influence the interpretation of rationale and process of the internationalization of higher education. Internationalization can only be understood in relation to national context and in turn the relationship between nations – 'inter-nations'. How programmes of study are chosen and teaching and learning methodologies developed must by implication also be highly contextualized and differentiated depending upon the nature and status of the institution, and cognizant of the extent of national economic development and democratization. These factors in turn have considerable consequences for the development of appropriate theory for curriculum, for student learning and for graduate attributes associated with both national and global citizenship.

The global citizen and the purpose of university

The United Kingdom has emphasized the importance of developing 'global citizens' and that these citizens would be 'globally employable', have 'international experience' and should be 'international citizens', 'able to move seamlessly between different nations, cultures and languages' (American Council on Education, 2002, cited in Fielden 2006: 19). Citing Universities UK, they reinforced the benefits of international student recruitment because international students provide 'opportunity to educate citizens of other countries', and concluded that 'this provides the UK with significant geopolitical and cultural benefits as well as broadening the educational experience of UK students and ensuring the diversity of the student body' (UUK 2005, cited in ibid.: 4). Interestingly, despite reference to Global Citizenship, the benefits are focused upon the UK student body. International students are seen as a resource to enable the development of UK domestic students. International, multicultural classrooms and study abroad were seen as the learning environments through which students could be internationalized. However, as international students, especially those who are not EU or government funded, are likely to be of a privileged social class, to what extent are these students the legitimate representatives of other countries, able to provide geopolitical and cultural knowledge that will enable such a 'global citizen' to emerge? How do students within the non-elite institutions from countries across the development gap view the purpose of a university education?

Discussions with domestic students from universities within Ethiopia, India and the United Kingdom

Ethiopia: Gondar, Amarha

In 2007 a project, funded by the Department of International Development, to strengthen links between a newly established university in Ethiopia and a UK university was part of an initiative responding to the Ethiopian Government's mandate to expand higher education 'in order to realign [Ethiopia's] higher education system in order to contribute more directly to national strategy for economic growth and poverty reduction' (World Bank 2003: 6). A small team travelled to Ethiopia to work with Ethiopian colleagues as they developed the pedagogic infrastructure. Whilst there, three of the team met with undergraduate students to begin to scope the needs of the institution and to identify potential learning opportunities that could be offered by transnational links between students at both institutions.

The students' initial responses included perfunctory information about the difficulties caused by lack of resources, and descriptions of what they felt their institution did well. These responses were helpful in understanding the context, and thus the material and academic needs of students and staff. However, it was the subsequent discussion about the value of the link between the two universities, and more particularly student links, that provided an insight into these students' perceptions of themselves, their national identity and their perceptions of a kind of misplaced voyeurism with which they felt the 'rest of the developed world' were guilty. They reported their frustration with representations of drought, of famine and the victim status with which they felt their nation was labelled. They proposed that the UK students should help to promote a positive image of Ethiopia – its runners, as the birthplace of humankind, its history and as a great coffee producer (Grant 2008). These students could see a purpose in a relationship between UK and Ethiopian students, but the purpose appeared tied with the values of a collectivist socio-political framework that promotes a form of citizenship tied to national identity, patriotism, national pride and loyalty (Nelson and Kerr 2006: 13).

India: Aligarh, Uttar Pradesh

The characteristics of the students from Ethiopia appeared in a similar discussion that focused on motivations and aspirations of a group of Indian students studying at a Muslim University in Uttar Pradesh (Grant 2010). Here students felt an obligation to contribute to, and promote, India as a powerful nation. They reported a sense of privilege from being given the opportunity to participate in higher education – and as a consequence they felt a responsibility to the nation. One student explained that he had been given the opportunity to represent his local community, a privilege that would be repaid by his hard work and achievements, as he was the first from his community to be accepted into a university. An emphasis on regional and national loyalty appeared to be suggested, although aspirations to become a global human being were also expressed.

According to Nelson and Kerr (2006: 15) such characteristics are common in Asian cultures where 'the development of active citizenship [within the curriculum] is underpinned by a desire to nurture a sense of belonging to nation, and a moral obligation to contribute to society and the building of the nation's future' (ibid.: 16). These secular perspectives on higher education were augmented by the Muslim students who articulated the relationship between religion and their own learning. Personal and spiritual development, learning and the search for truth – which they explained to be a Muslim duty – and the achievement of a 'sense of being' were all considered to be factors in their participation in higher education.

United Kingdom: Leicester and London

In contrast, responses from domestic students at two UK universities (Grant 2008, 2010) appeared to imply a different and 'economic' model of citizenship, consistent with individualist frameworks. Responses centred on career opportunities, the transition between school and work – a rite of passage, a time to meet others, to learn life skills and a place to have fun. Purposes for working 'transnationally' were given as 'learning from others and sharing knowledge' (Grant 2008: 4). These students then appeared to value the university experience because it would aid them in 'becoming financially self-supporting, becoming a self-directed learner, becoming a creative problem solver and adopting entrepreneurial values' (Nelson and Kerr 2006).

Citizenship, multiple identities and the student voice

Kennedy's models of citizenship are used in a comparative study conducted by Nelson and Kerr (2006) and published by the International Curriculum and

Assessment Archive (INCA) to describe models of citizenship education promoted within national (school) curricula. Although India and Ethiopia are not INCA participating countries, the student groups in this study appeared to display characteristics that did accord with Kennedy's national educational citizenship classification.

However, although these characteristics may be identified within particular national school curricula, and although the students represented here suggest compliance to type, it would be naive to suggest national homogeneity. Indeed, Banks (2008: 133) refers to the theoretical and empirical work of multicultural scholars who 'indicate that identity is multiple, changing and contextual, rather than fixed and static'. Thus these students cannot be considered representative of all students from any one country, despite displaying apparently typical characteristics of collectivist and individualist societies. However, their comments do emphasize contexts and histories that contribute to shaping their beliefs and behaviours through the interplay between apparatus. In India, for example, collectivist and individualist behaviours – and a combination of both – will be exhibited depending upon the context and the education of the individual (Sinha et al. 2001:144). The national school curriculum, then, as an integral part of that Ideological State Apparatus, promotes and recreates societal norms and as such is central to the values, beliefs and behaviours of individuals.

The Ethiopian and Indian students in particular are from socio-economic backgrounds unlikely to predispose them to become the kind of fee-paying 'international students' that UK institutions aim to attract. It is precisely because of this that these students and their teachers are crucial in the reform of higher education, to theories of curricula and in the development of the conceptions of the 'global citizen'.

The UK international student body

International students are significant not because they are international, but because they are students. Indeed, many international undergraduates will have previously been educated within the UK – a substantial number at UCL come from British public schools and international colleges within the UK (private communication, UCL admissions, 7 March 2010); some will have been educated within educational frameworks based upon that of the UK (e.g. Hong Kong and Singapore); and some will have been educated in international schools within their own countries. From the use of Received Pronunciation English within presentations given by an international, multicultural group of medical students at my own institution, prior exposure to elite British institutions appears evident. Some international students may be studying within British institutions through the aid of bursaries or governments' sponsorships, but whatever the economic status, domestic or international, many students will struggle with their learning for a variety of reasons that may, or may not, be related to cultural 'difference'. As Davidson (2009: 3) points out, '[cultural] stereotypes . . . entrench difficulties.

Such stereotypes may relate to passivity, criticality, plagiarism, and rote learning to name a few. At the very least perceptions of academic difference should be treated with caution.'

International students may already possess a disposition and motivation to travel for learning, whether or not they have been educated in the host country. Decisions to travel abroad to study according to student choice theory are made in specific situated contexts and shaped by home and educational background (McDonough 1997; St John and Asker 2001 cited in Salisbury *et al.* 2009). Thus, international students by definition cannot represent concerns and worldviews of the many students who remain 'at home' as these latter students may have economic and socio-cultural barriers that prohibit them becoming 'international' in the first place. Such students are 'chained to place' (Beilharz 2001, cited in Roman 2003: 275), whatever side of the development gap their nations occupy. Moreover, as the quality of learning and of student attainment, according to Study Abroad researchers, is considerably improved for those who are able to participate in learning within another country (Salisbury *et al.* 2009: 124), the opportunity to learn abroad provides educational and ultimately economic advantage that could be perceived as actually widening poverty gaps – inconsistent with any HE internationalization teaching and learning missions.

It is unsurprising that opportunities for international and intercultural dialogue through study abroad were a concern of the Directorate General for Education and Culture of the European Commission. In a survey into the socio-economic background of Erasmus students they concluded that the 'question of how to decrease the bias towards students from the advantaged socio-cultural groups [studying abroad] is in fact very problematic' (Directorate General for Education and Culture 2000: 4). This challenge appears to be being addressed by pedagogic interventions under 'Internationalization-at-Home', but if international students are not nationally representative and we are exploring something other than the European Humboldtian idea of *Bildung*, then it may be important to review what, why and where international and intercultural knowledge should be generated and to devise some kind of internationally accepted curriculum theory that does justice to all universities and their students.

The development of an internationalized curriculum is not then justified by the presence of international students, nor is the need to prepare students to be globally mobile. The apparent preoccupation with identity described by the 'economic label' of the 'international' student deflects from the complexity of internationalization and its significance for learning and teaching and for understanding the world. Labelling students 'international', 'home' or 'EU' is not helpful in achieving a truly international/intercultural or global experience. If we are concerned with ensuring that we offer such learning then we need to look both further afield and closer to home, and not to the students who are already globally mobile and who can 'inhabit the globe' (Beilharz 2001, cited in Roman 2003: 275). If, as human capital theorists argue, our worldviews, educational attainment and life chances are consequent upon our histories, experiences and interpretation of our individual realities, then it could be concluded that only those with the financial and cultural capital to become international students in the first place will also be those who will be globally mobile.

Our students may well be studying abroad (either as incoming international or outgoing domestic students) and choose to do this because they have the opportunity to do so. They become 'intellectual tourists' (Bauman 1998, cited in Roman 2003: 272) and ultimately they may seek employment outside of their home countries. However, many people with a university education from the new universities being established across the development gap may also travel to seek work outside of their home countries after they have completed their studies, but for very different reasons. Bauman makes a distinction between 'tourists' and 'vagabonds' to describe the difference between the motivations to travel. Tourists, he suggests, move because they choose to, whilst the vagabonds move because they have no real choice (ibid.: 275).

There have been initiatives that aim to establish partnerships through projects between institutions from across the development gap.[2] Similarly, study abroad initiatives such as those associated with the European Higher Education Arena validate the need to reach out and learn with others. Yet there is still much to learn about our relationship with those whose lives are connected to our own but are chained to place. Indeed, the majority of higher educational curricula (however it is defined) continue to ignore this silent majority and with the current economic uncertainty and inevitable increase in institutional competitiveness, the drivers of internationalization could well be re-prioritized, with international student recruitment gaining even more momentum, and global citizenship becoming a privilege for those who are already destined to 'inherit the earth'.

Higher education continues to change rapidly. However, approaches to learning and teaching continue to be driven through national, institutional and student need underpinned primarily by economic gain. If our higher education institutions are genuine about preparing students for their interconnected futures, they must listen to the voices of staff and students from all university sectors on both sides of the development gap. How else will it be possible for our students to work together on the global problems facing them all? We need to engage with colleagues and students representative of the range of university sectors across the world to debate and discuss what it really means to have an 'internationalized curriculum'. In short, we need a system of higher learning within inclusively agreed educational frameworks that do not unintentionally promote and reinforce inequalities.

Acknowledgements

With very many thanks for the kind support in the gathering of student views from the four universities referred to within this chapter: Professor A.R. Kidwai, Academic Staff College, Aligarh Muslim University; staff and students at Aligarh Muslim University, Uttar Pradesh, India; Mr Craig Daraz and Ms Moira Wright,

Centre for the Advancement of Learning and Teaching, UCL, London, UK; Professor Yigsaw Kebedee and Professor Mike Silverman, Gondar–Leicester Link; Professor Brenda Smith, Higher Education Academy; Ms Lynnette Mathews, University of Leicester; Ato Worku Negash Mihret, Gondar University; staff and students at Gondar University, Ethiopia and the University of Leicester, UK.

Notes

1   Although not the focus of this chapter, it is interesting to note that according to National Statistics the highest numbers of unemployed within the UK are ethnic Chinese. There is also a strong correlation between ethnic group, low income and disability.
2   For example, the UK Department for International Development, 'Developing Learning Partnerships in Higher Education (DELPHE)' http://www.british council.org/delphe.htm (accessed 5 August 2011).

References

Althusser, L. (1970) ' "Lenin and philosophy" and other essays ideology and ideological state apparatuses (notes towards an investigation)'. First published in *La Pensée*, 1970; translated from the French by Ben Brewster; source: *Lenin and Philosophy and Other Essays*, Monthly Review Press 1971; transcribed by Andy Blunden.

American Council on Education (2006) cited in J. Fielden, 'Internationalisation and leadership – what are the issues?', in Leadership Foundation for Higher Education (2006) *The Leadership and Development Challenges of Globalisation and Internationalisation*, London: Leadership Foundation for Higher Education. Online. Available HTTP: http://www.lfhe.ac.uk/publications/leadershipsummit2006.pdf (accessed 20 June 2011).

Banks, J. (2008) 'Diversity, group identity, and citizenship education in a global age', *Educational Researcher*, 37, 3: 129–39.

Barnett, R. (2000) 'Supercomplexity and the curriculum', *Studies in Higher Education*, 25, 3: 255–65.

Barnett, R. and Coate, K. (2005) *Engaging the Curriculum in Higher Education*, Maidenhead: Open University Press.

Bauman, Z. (1998) *Globalization: Human Consequences*, New York: Columbia University Press, cited in L.G. Roman (2003) 'Education and the contested meanings of "global citizenship"', *Journal of Educational Change*, 4, 3: 269–93.

Beilharz, P. (ed.) (2001) *The Bauman Reader*, Oxford: Blackwell Publishing Inc.; cited in L.G. Roman (2003) 'Education and the contested meanings of "global citizenship"', *Journal of Educational Change*, 4, 3: 269–93.

Burnham. P. (2001) 'Marx, international political economy and globalisation', *Capital and Class*, n.75; cited in G. Liodakis (2003) 'The new stage of capitalist development and the prospects of globalisation'. Paper prepared for the conference: Economics for the Future, Cambridge, UK, 2003. Online. Available HTTP: http://www.econ.cam.ac.uk/cjeconf/delegates/liodakis.pdf (accessed 3 August 2011).

Caruana, V. (2010) 'The relevance of the internationalised curriculum to graduate capability: the role of new lecturers' attitudes in shaping the "student voice"', in E. Jones (ed.) *Internationalisation and the Student Voice*, London: Routledge.

Daley, S. (2011) 'Chasing riches from Africa to Europe and finding only squalor', *The New York Times Supplement* of the *Observer* (UK), 5 June.

Davidson, M. (2009) 'The culture of critical thinking', University of Nottingham. Online. Available: www.nottingham.ac.uk/pesl/internationalisation (accessed 20 May 2012).

De Wit, H. (2002) *Internationalisation of Higher Education in the United States of America and Europe: A Historical, Comparative, and Conceptual Analysis*, Westport, CT: Greenwood Press.

Directorate General for Education and Culture (2000) *Survey into the Socio-economic Background of ERASMUS Students*, European Commission. Online. Available HTTP: http://ec.europa.eu/education/erasmus/doc/publ/survey_en.pdf (accessed 3 August 2011).

Dunnell, K. (2007) *Diversity and Different Experiences in the UK: National Statisticians Annual Article on Society*. Online. Available HTTP: http://www.statistics.gov.uk/articles/nojournal/NSA_article.pdf (accessed 6 June 2011).

Eastman, J. (2011) *Notes on Higher Education in India: Current Status and Issues*, Association of Universities and Colleges in Canada. Online. Available HTTP: http://www.aucc.ca/policy/documents/higher-education-in-india-status-issues-julia-eastman-e.pdf (accessed 2 August 2011).

Elton, L. (2005). *Recent Developments in Student Learning in Britain and their Relationship to the Bologna Declaration*. Online. Available HTTP: http://www.raco.cat/index.php/papers/article/viewFile/25816/25650 (accessed 4 December 2011).

European Association for International Education (EAIE) (n.d.) 'Internationalisation at home'. Available HTTP: http://www.eaie.org/home/about-EAIE/expert-communities/special-interests/iah.html (accessed 17 March 2012).

Fielden, J. (2006) 'Internationalisation and leadership – what are the issues?', in Leadership Foundation for Higher Education (2006) *The Leadership and Development Challenges of Globalisation and Internationalisation*, London: Leadership Foundation for Higher Education, Online. Available HTTP: http://www.lfhe.ac.uk/publications/leadership summit2006.pdf (accessed 20 June 2011).

Grant, E. (2008) 'Ënhid! Let's go! Destinations and directions for learning and teaching in higher education', paper given at the Higher Education Academy Annual Conference. Online. Available HTTP: http://www.heacademy.ac.uk/resources/detail/events/annualconference/2008/Ann_conf_2008_Elizabeth_Grant (accessed 3 August 2011).

—— (2010) '21st century learning: implications for academic development', paper given at International Conference, Academic Staff College, Aligarh Muslim University, February 2010.

Greenbank, P. (2009) 'Re-evaluating the role of social capital in the career decision-making behaviour of working class students', *Research in Post-Compulsory Education*, 14, 2: 157–70.

Hansen, T.B. and Stepputat, F. (eds) (2005) *Sovereign Bodies: Citizens, Migrants, and States in the Postcolonial World*, Princeton University Press; cited in E. Obadare and W. Adebanwi (2009) 'Transnational resource flow and the paradoxes of belonging: redirecting the debate on transnationalism, remittances, state and citizenship in Africa', *Review of African Political Economy*, 36, 122: 499–517.

Higher Education Academy (2012) Online at http://www.heacademy.ac.uk/internationaliation (accessed 17 March August 2012).

Kennedy, K.J. (2006). 'Towards a conceptual framework for understanding active and passive citizenship', unpublished report, cited in J. Nelson and D. Kerr (2006) *Active Citizenship in INCA Countries: Definitions, Policies, Practices and Outcomes*, International Curriculum Archive. Online. Available HTTP: http://www.inca.org.uk/pdf/Active_ Citizenship_Report.pdf (accessed 17 March 2012).

Knight, J. (2003a) 'Updated internationalization definition', *International Higher Education*, 33, 6: 2–3.

—— (2003b) *GATS, Trade and Higher Education: Perspective 2003: Where Are We?* Observatory of Borderless Higher Education. Online. Available HTTP: http:// www.obhe.ac.uk/documents/view_details?id=698 (accessed 20 June 2011).

—— (2004) Internationalization remodelled: definition, approaches and rationales, *International Higher Education*, 8, 1: 5–31.

Knight, J. and de Wit, H. (eds) (1999) *Quality and Internationalisation in Higher Education*, Paris: Organisation for Economic Co-operation and Development (OECD), 241–59.

Leadership Foundation for Higher Education (2006) *The Leadership and Development Challenges of Globalisation and Internationalisation*, London: Leadership Foundation for Higher Education. Online. Available HTTP: http://www.lfhe.ac.uk/publications/ leadershipsummit2006.pdf (accessed 20 June 2011).

Liodakis, G. (2003) 'The new stage of capitalist development and the prospects of globalisation', paper prepared for conference on Economics for the Future, Cambridge, UK, 2003. Online. Available HTTP: http://www.econ.cam.ac.uk/cjeconf/delegates/ liodakis.pdf (accessed 3 August 2011).

McDonough, P. (1997) *Choosing Colleges: How Social Class and Schools Structure Opportunity*, Albany, NY: SUNY Press.

Mishra, A. (2010) 'India: innovation universities need foreign help', *University World News*, 18 April 2010, issue no. 120, cited in J. Eastman (2011) *Notes on Higher Education in India: Current Status and Issues*, Association of Universities and Colleges in Canada. Online. Available HTTP: http://www.aucc.ca/policy/documents/higher-education-in-india-status-issues-julia-eastman-e.pdf (accessed 2 August 2011).

Mitchell, K. (2003) 'Educating the national citizen in neoliberal times: from the multicultural self to the strategic cosmopolitan', *Transactions of the Institute of British Geographers, New Series*, 28, 4: 387–403.

Mohamedbhai, G. (2008) *The Effects of Massification on Higher Education in Africa: Report on Behalf of the Working Group for Higher Education*, African Association of Universities. Online. Available HTTP: http://www2.aau.org/wghe/scm/meetings/mai08/adea/ study_massification.pdf (accessed 3 August 2011).

NCIHE (1997) *Higher Education in the Learning Society: Report of the National Committee*, London: HMSO.

Nelson, J. and Kerr, D. (2006) *Active Citizenship in INCA Countries: Definitions, Policies, Practices and Outcomes*, International Curriculum Archive. Online. Available HTTP http://www.inca.org.uk/pdf/Active_Citizenship_Report.pdf (accessed 20 May 2012).

Nilsson, B. (2000) 'Internationalising the curriculum', in P. Crowther, M. Joris, M. Otten, B. Nilsson, H. Teekens and B. Wachter (2000) *Internationalisation at Home: A Position Paper*, Amsterdam: European Association for International Education in cooperation with the Academic Cooperation Association, IAK, IÉSEG, Nuffic, Katholieke Hogeschool Limburg and Malmö University. Online. Available HTTP: http://www.nuffic.nl/pdf/ netwerk/IAH-Booklet.pdf (accessed 17 March 2012).

Obadare, E. and Adebanwi, W. (2009) 'Transnational resource flow and the paradoxes of belonging: redirecting the debate on transnationalism, remittances, state and citizenship in Africa', *Review of African Political Economy*, 36, 122: 499–517.

Robinson, W. and Harris, J. (2000) 'Towards a global ruling class? Globalization and the transnational capitalist class', *Science and Society*, 64, 1: 11–54.

Roman, L.G. (2003) 'Education and the contested meanings of "global citizenship"', *Journal of Educational Change*, 4, 3: 269–93.

Salisbury, M., Umbach, P., Paulsen, M.B. and Pascarella, E. (2009) 'Going global: understanding the choice process of the intent to study abroad', *Research in Higher Education*, 50, 2: 119–43.

Sinha, J., Sinha, T., Verma, J. and Sinha, R.B.N. (2001) 'Collectivism coexisting with individualism: an Indian scenario', *Asian Journal of Social Psychology*, 4, 2: 133–45.

Sklair, L. (2001) *Transnational Capitalist Class*, Oxford: Blackwell.

Smith, M.K. (1996, 2000) 'Curriculum theory and practice', *The Encyclopaedia of Informal Education*. Online. Available HTTP: http://www.infed.org/biblio/b-curric.htm (accessed 20 May 2012).

St John, E.P. and Asker, E.H. (2001) 'The role of finances in student choice: a review of theory and research', in M.B. Paulsen and J.C. Smart (eds) *The Finance of Higher Education: Theory, Research, Policy, and Practice*, New York: Agathon Press.

UK Higher Education Europe Unit (2006) *Policy Briefing: International Trade and UK Higher Education*, London: Association of Commonwealth Universities. Online. Available HTTP: http://www.europeunit.ac.uk/sites/europe_unit2/resources/Europe%20Unit_Trade%20report_final.pdf (accessed 20 June 2011).

World Bank (2003) *Higher Education Development for Ethiopia: Pursuing the Vision*, New York: World Bank Sector Study.

World Trade Organization (1994) *General Agreement of Trade in Services* (Uruguay Round) Annex 1b, Part 1, Article 1. Online. Available HTTP: http://www.wto.org/english/docs_e/legal_e/26-gats.pdf (accessed 17 March 2012).

Part II

Teaching and learning

Chapter 7

Classroom encounters

International students' perceptions of tutors in the creative arts

Silvia Sovic

In recent decades much has been written about the internationalization of universities in the English-speaking world, and this research has focused mainly on international students and their inability to adapt adequately to the processes of teaching and learning in those universities. Globalization, and the accelerated pace of interconnectivity with the help of rapid technological innovations, has thus transformed higher education and its cultural complexity as never before. As Rizvi and Lingard put it, 'the cultural Other is no longer remote, exotic, or mystical and beyond our reach. The Other is all around us. The ensuing cultural diversity has clearly enriched us – hybridity has almost become the cultural norm' (Rizvi and Lingard 2000: 419). However, much less attention has been paid to how these students are being taught. The student body may be increasingly global but the teaching staff often appears to cater mainly for local needs.

These observations apply especially to UK universities in the last decade. The recent commercialization of higher education is particularly associated with internationalization and the pressure to recruit international students who pay higher fees. Yet these international students are then perceived in an inconsistent light, and it is questionable whether higher education has been adequately prepared for such a drastic change of the student body and its teaching practices. 'For many, international students are simultaneously a source of contempt (for their inadequate English language skills), resentment (that we have to accept them at all) and paradoxically, anxiety ("will they like us [and tell their friends to come and study here so that I still have a job])?"' (Devos 2003: 163). Scott has recently pointed out that 'universities that struggle to recruit students at home have targeted less discerning international students to fill their places. Others have attempted to overcome chronic threats to their sustainability, perhaps because they are too small or too specialised, by engaging in what can only be described as foreign adventures, fraught with financial and reputational risks' (Scott 2011). Papastephanou pointed out that 'globalization often becomes an ideological device that states and governments employ as an excuse for imposing certain policies that would otherwise fail to gain public acceptance or support' (Papastephanou 2005: 534). It can be argued that this is true especially of recruitment practices (Morgan 2011). As a consequence of the marketization of higher education the teaching staff has had to become more entrepreneurial, which in practice is often thought of as entailing increased workloads, bigger classes and less funding (Devos 2003, Ryan 2010).

In this situation, artificial identities have been constructed not only for international students but also for academic staff. In the context of public debate over declining academic standards in Australia, Devos stated that the identity of academics was becoming characterized as that of victim 'through his or her role as guardian of academic standards. The discourse of othering is actively at work here with "the other" – the international student – rendered inferior to the "not-other" – the Australian Academic' (Devos 2003: 165). By contrast, the identity of international students has been highlighted and discussed in the mainstream educational literature to a much greater extent. Much-used terms such as 'the Asian, East or south-east Asian, Indian or Chinese learner' – and indeed the term 'international student' itself – can epitomize the widespread tendency to reduce and essentialize all the deficiencies of what is presented as a large, stable, homogenous group. Notably, when the learning characteristics of Asian or Chinese students are discussed, many scholars employ a 'large culture approach' – the term coined by Holliday to denote the process by which scholars seek to represent 'the essential difference between ethnic, national and international entities'. As he remarks, 'the large culture paradigm begins with a prescriptive desire to seek out and detail differences which are considered the norm' (Holliday 1999: 240). The inadequate learning experiences of these students are then interpreted as deriving from their passivity, obedience, collectivism, a tendency to memorize and lack of critical and analytical thinking. Unlike home students, who are perceived as deep learners, many Asian or Chinese students are typified as surface or rote learners who favour a teacher-centred approach and are apparently not capable of learning independently (e.g. Watkins and Biggs 2001). This in turn is often explained in the context of 'Asian values' and the Confucian cultural tradition. Many negative assumptions about teaching and learning are associated with these easy notions, including most recently the belief that Asians have a much greater tendency to plagiarize.[1]

Clark and Grieve rightly pointed out that these stereotypical perceptions have been 'asserted rather than demonstrated. Much of the evidence produced for the way Chinese students behave in classroom settings has been drawn from reports and perceptions by Western instructors, thus filtered through their own values, expectations and standards' (Clark and Grieve 2006: 63; and see also page 100). Ryan and Louie went further and challenged the Confucian–western dichotomy in scholarly research; among other assumptions of international students' deficiency they questioned the 'virtues of Western education' such as concepts of 'critical thinking, independent learning, lifelong and lifewide learning', arguing that these terms are used indiscriminately and with little attempt to provide definition, especially when it comes to international students with Asian backgrounds (Ryan and Louie 2007: 413; and see Ryan 2010: 44). Coate equally warns how tutors' caricature perceptions of their students can have detrimental effects in the classrooms: 'I should not assume every time an Asian-looking student walks into a classroom that I somehow "know" what their particular approach to learning might be . . . We do not "know" who the international students are more than we "know" who the home students are' (Coate 2009: 278). Among the growing number of scholars who have opposed the misconceived portrait of students from South-East Asia are Chalmers and Volet, who pointed out that these negative images of students 'have sometimes been used as an excuse for not addressing the fundamental issue of student learning at university. When the "problem" is attributed to the students, teachers can avoid examining their own attitudes and practices' (Chalmers and Volet 1997: 96). Gu and Schweisfurth claim that 'central to learners' survival and success appears to be learner-quality related influences, essentially learner motivation, agency and determination to thrive. These qualities are individualized and vary greatly even within a monocultural group.' They stress that 'a support system is required in institutions to help learners overcome the stress and frustration caused by initial cultural shock . . . Such support needs to be both socially and academically targeted' (Gu and Schweisfurth 2006: 87). The present study tries to demonstrate how diverse international students are, and will suggest that engagement with them, as individuals rather than in groups, is an indispensable prerequisite for the improvement of the learning experiences of all students in the classroom.

The International Students' Experience Project

The evidence presented here comes from the International Students' Experience Project, an investigation of creative arts students at the University of the Arts, London, conducted at its Creative Learning in Practice Centre for Excellence in Teaching and Learning (CLIP CETL) during the academic year 2007–8. Some 141 first-year international students from Japan, South Korea, Hong Kong, Taiwan, India and the USA were interviewed in their own language. American students were included so that we could assess how much difference language makes in hampering successful transition. Twenty-one home students were also interviewed. While not strictly a control group, the experiences of these students shed light on a number of issues highlighted by international students. To our knowledge this is the largest study of its kind in the UK.

Students who agreed to participate first filled out a questionnaire, which included details of their age, qualifications, programme of study and information about their level of linguistic competence. They then had an in-depth, semi-structured interview with a postgraduate of the same provenance as the student. Quantitative and qualitative information could thus be combined for the purposes of analysis, though it should be stressed that the core of the data was qualitative – the translations and transcriptions of the interviews. The methodology and details of the project have been described elsewhere (Sovic 2008a), as have results on themes such as coping with stress (Sovic 2008b), social interaction (Sovic 2009) and group work (Sovic and Blythman 2009). The focus here will be on students' perceptions of the tutors they encountered in classroom settings. It will reflect on students' experiences of interacting with their tutors, and will explore:

- what the students who were interviewed thought makes a good tutor;
- students' expectations of their tutors;
- how students perceive tutors' engagement with them.

In relation to these topics, it should perhaps be stressed that the significance of the project lay above all in the fact that the interviews were conducted in the native language of the students. In exercises of this kind, the weaker the students' linguistic abilities, the less their voices tend to be heard; either they do not participate at all, or they contribute much less (on paper), or are less open about their views. This was thus above all an exercise in 'bringing in' the 'other' students who were usually 'otherized', and ensuring that their views were fully represented. It was an attempt to fill a significant cross-cultural gap. As Marginson and Mollis remark, 'to the extent that comparative education is focused on difference as well as sameness and on local specific as well as global standards, we can require more curiosity about what non-Anglo-American voices are saying and greater sensitivity to the rights of the other' (Marginson and Mollis 2001: 615).

What makes a good tutor?

A number of students commented on their tutors. Here are a few examples of what students perceived as characteristics of a good tutor:

> A good tutor gives me a clear vision, tells me what is a problem, and what I should improve for the next time.
>
> (Japanese student)

> He/she is very enthusiastic about teaching, and he/she is strict to the students who don't work hard. The tutor remembers all the names and faces of the students.
>
> (Japanese student)

> They put a lot of emphasis on *the student's idea*. In the project, they do give guidelines, but they allow a lot of flexibility for the students to do whatever they want.
>
> (South Korean student)

Respect for teachers who were passionate about their work was very common, as was appreciation of those who care about their students.[2]

Among the advantages of being taught by practitioners were career benefits:

Many of our teachers are artists. They would often share their own experiences with us. For example, they tell us that what they had been through in order to become an artist, which is extremely invaluable to me because they have given me a better idea about my career.

(Taiwanese student)

Some, however, made the point that being a good artist is not the same as being a good teacher:

What I have realised is that some of them could be excellent artists who produce remarkable pieces of work, yet they are just not very good at teaching. There is something that may be very easy to them, both as artists and as teachers, but that could be very difficult to us, as students, as apprentices.

(Taiwanese student)

To sum up, the students in this project valued passion, enthusiasm and effort, but were disappointed and critical where these qualities were noticeably absent.

The student–teacher relationship

Many students were unclear about the relationship that they were expected to have with their tutors. The use of first names threw them in particular.

I was really amazed to hear that students call their tutors by their first name . . . in Taiwan, our tutors give a more authoritative impression than tutors here. Tutors here seem to be relatively friendly, but would still see a clear line separated between tutors and students. I must add that this line appears to be much clearer in Taiwan.

(Taiwanese student)

There are a lot of formalities with teachers here. Just because we address them by their names, it doesn't mean that we have the freedom, that we have any compatibility. Just because we call them by their names, we have this kind of a chilled out relationship, it doesn't mean it works like that.

(Indian student)

The implications of different degrees and conventions of formality appear to be extremely difficult for freshly arrived international students to negotiate.[3] Those who already had first degrees from their home country were especially articulate on this point. Our international students also found it difficult to understand the system of communication. They could easily be disappointed if their tutors – who in this university are almost all part time – were not immediately available to help them despite the friendliness that they had exhibited.

During break times when I want to ask questions, my instructors tell me not to really bother them at that time but to come during their office hours. I find it difficult because any questions that I want addressed and have answered have to come at the instructor's convenience. Of course, this is not to say that they don't try to help students at all.

(South Korean student)

American students were also confused over this issue:

When they're at school, they're great, they're extremely accessible. When they're not at school, they're all working artists, so it's impossible to get a hold of them. They don't give you their email or their phone number, or anything, but when they're at school, they're really easy to talk to. They really respect you and your ideas, which I found really different from talking to teachers in the States. In the States, first of all, they give you their email, and they're like 'call me whenever; contact me if you need any help', but also talking to them is always like, they're a little condescending in a way; not in a bad way, but in a 'I'm your teacher, this is what I think you should do'; here, they just more throw ideas back and forth, and they're more fellow artists.

(American student)

Many also discover that a less authoritarian figure may also be a less interventionist figure:

Taiwanese tutors are more subjective. The way that you do your work could be possibly directed by what the tutor thinks this is right or not. Here, you are free to do what you like to do. But, Taiwanese tutors tend to teach you and show you more stuff, and are more likely to push you to do more work. In comparison with Taiwanese tutors, tutors here don't push you much and seem to be relatively passive. If you don't approach them to ask them some questions or for support, they don't seem to think that they have responsibilities to tell you more than what they taught in the classroom.

(Taiwanese student)

Caution is needed when we compare narratives of 'their' and 'our' education systems. As Holliday reminds us, 'a Chinese student once told me that some of her compatriots admitted feeding their British tutors with exoticized accounts of "Chinese culture" because it seemed to be what was expected . . . I know from experience of being a foreigner in other people's countries, that this sort of exaggeration of Self to suit people's perception of Other can help one to gain acceptance' (Holliday 2005: 21). Although the mainstream educational literature singles out mainly Asian students as not adapting readily to this difference in approaches to teaching, many American students expressed a similar opinion:

In the States, I wouldn't stress this much about my work, because the teacher would be stressing for me, saying 'you have to get this done', and I'm like 'okay, okay!,' but here I have no one saying that to me, so I have to say it to myself. That's stressful!

(American student)

It is not clear to what degree this is a problem specific to the creative arts. However, it is certainly seen as having a positive side:

This is much better because in India you have a lot of spoon-feeding and here you are expected to do things on your own. So, that's good.

(Indian student)

However, some international students clearly had unrealistic expectations.

Like, I just met my tutor. I was talking to her and she said that she has faced this situation a lot that a lot of international students come here and they want us to parent them. And to a certain extent I disagree with that, why can't they parent us? They are women, they are normal human beings, they go through same problems like others do. Tutors have more knowledge than you, they are more experienced than you. If they have more experience in something then why can't they share it with us? Why can't they sit with us and discuss our personal problems?

(Indian student)

Students were very explicit about what they wanted from teachers. The majority of them wanted more support and guidance, especially at the beginning.

An easy thing is a well-organized guideline or outline. A concept of a project is clearly shown at beginning. A project brief tells us what we should do, in detail, like outline, and everything necessary for research . . . I need just simple and clear guidelines. The course gives me both. It is easy to follow.

(Japanese student)

This wish for guidance is despite the fact that students recognized that their studies were supposed to be much more independent than what they were used to. The transition to independent learning needs to be supported.

The underlying advantage of enjoying so much freedom is that we can decide what we need to learn in order that we can produce a project. The disadvantage is that I still need some support and guidance from my teachers.

(Taiwanese student)

This student felt that they had succeeded in developing these skills, but only under great pressure:

unlike the Japanese education system, the students are expected to study on our own here, so at first, I had no idea how to do the work. I had to figure out everything by myself, and it took me until just before the deadline to understand everything. But the volume of work is huge, so it was very difficult at the beginning. Of course, the tutor helps me if I ask, but there will be nothing if I don't do anything on my own. It's like self-teaching. I was confused by this system. It's really free for students and tutors as well, so if you are not capable of deciding your own timetable, you would end up being totally at a loss.

(Japanese student)

Those who overcame this hurdle had no doubt that it was worth it. Many stated that they preferred the freedom that independent study brought with it:

At first, I feel like this was a disadvantage, but in retrospect, I like the freedom. I'm not sure about other people, but for me, I like the freedom to study and move in the direction that I want to pursue. So I think in the end, my experience is better than what I expected it to be.

(South Korean student)

Once again, Americans also noted a difference.

The schooling here is a little different . . . than what I'm used to in the States, it's a little more free flowing, self-motivating and in the States it's more programmed and everyone's kind of laid out. Here you kind of do what you need to and get to explore more on your own terms.

(American student)

Such comments again put the supposed homogeneity of the supposedly 'western', or at least Anglophone, university systems under question.

Tutors' engagement with international students

Our respondents had a variety of opinions on how effectively tutors engaged with international students. Many criticized the tutors' unwillingness to engage with differences in their cultural backgrounds.

Some of our tutors, if they are very open-minded, would accept our ideas. However, some of them may find our ideas are really odd since they don't really understand our cultural background and therefore may not accept what we have done. It depends on individual tutors. I believe that I don't have to accept every comment they make.[4]

(Taiwanese student)

Several of the students we interviewed were disappointed that tutors did not show more interest in their previous experiences and transmission of knowledge. Some already had degrees from their own country, but because of their inadequate language skills some tutors did not get beyond that barrier to appreciate their experience and abilities.

> The course itself is not very difficult for me. As said, I have got relevant BA and MA degrees in Taiwan. I have got some background knowledge that I gained from my degrees in Taiwan. What I struggle academically the most is English language.
>
> (Taiwanese student)

Language issues can so easily disguise the more fundamental point that these students are raising, not least because they allow tutors to disengage with such students by simply ascribing all the problems to linguistic deficiency. Yet the point is central, and is only sporadically discussed in the literature, for example by Ryan, who emphasizes that 'teachers working with students from unfamiliar cultural (or social) backgrounds need to learn how to make connections between students' previous experiences and expectations of learning and help students to make links across different cultural and social practices and expectations' (Ryan 2010: 51), and by Jokikokko, who argues that one of the most fundamental intercultural competences required for a teacher is 'the ability to take students' various cultures, languages, backgrounds and abilities into account in teaching and learning' (Jokikokko 2009: 145).

Clearly some students are generally alienated:

> once, the teacher told me off saying that it's because I don't speak English well. And afterwards, I couldn't speak to that teacher, and I always tried to avoid [the teacher]. It was the teacher of . . ., but this incident made me scared of [the teacher]. I don't feel anything easy in this course. When I couldn't ask the teacher any more, I tried to ask my friends, but there's a limit, so I usually consult the books to finish my works.
>
> (Japanese student)

Whether or not language is the trigger, negative experiences with their tutors appear to have a long-lasting impact on students. In such situations many students find support from their friends. Social networks come to replace the tutor, and become crucial for students in terms of support – more than the formal support mechanisms offered by the university, which (apart from language support) are generally not used much by international students (Sovic 2009).

When tutors do make an effort with international students this is greatly appreciated:

> S/he has great patience. At the end of the term s/he gave us a questionnaire concerning teaching and learning to fill in, and would offer extra support

especially to international students. For instance, s/he told us that if we have problems with writing in English, we could possibly write in our own language. We could make an appointment with him/her, and discuss how to convey our ideas in English.

(Taiwanese student)

However, not all were as positive as this last student. Among international students there was a widespread sense of discrimination, indeed even polarization in how different groups were treated by tutors.

Whatever western students say, no matter whether they attend courses, or whether they submit their works or not, our teachers seem to accept them all. In contrast to western students, international students are treated by our teachers in a completely different manner.

(Taiwanese student)

I feel some different treatment to international students from a teacher. You know, her attitude is different, depends on nationality, between international students and British . . . I think she may get irritated to talk to us, because of our poor English. Her treatment toward students is different, like, how to talk to students, for example, she doesn't come around us while we are making some works in a class, for checking what we are doing. For British students, she often approaches them and looks at their works and speaks to them, whereas for Asian students, just walk through us without any words. She neither explains to the international students nor comments on our works in a class. At first, she seemingly tried to speak to us, but gradually . . . she became avoiding Asians.

(Japanese student)

Language is obviously a key factor here, and a difficult one because international students recognize that their needs are not the only ones. Nonetheless it appears from many responses that international students feel that tutors do not make enough concessions, for example in pace, use of idiom, references to local cultural assumptions etc. which are taken for granted by home students.

Yes, language is a big problem for me. Some of international students went to our teachers and asked if they could possibly slow down their pace of teaching and that of speaking. But, they responded to us, saying that there are some native UK students in the classroom. International students should consider that UK students have got their needs. We have to comprise one another. Probably, they think that our English should be as good as native speakers in order to take this course.

(Taiwanese student)

Reliance on tacit knowledge common to the tutor and home students is about much more than language, however; it extends into the core of the syllabus. International students wish for more explanation and help when it comes to difficult conceptual and theoretical knowledge, which may be easier for home students to assimilate because to a large extent it emanates from their own culture.

> For example if the professors would go over in more detail the theory and hard concepts. For international students, I think the readings can get quite tough and the sheer amount of reading can be a bit overwhelming. But if you had the professors teach more thoroughly during lecture, it would help a lot.
>
> (South Korean student)

However well meaning or dedicated tutors can be, sometimes more can be achieved by greater understanding of the complexities of the learning process for international students. Consider this example:

> In our first term, one of teachers divided us into some small groups for group discussion. We had around five groups. The course director tried to split Asian students into these five groups. I was the only one Asian in my group and the rest are UK students. I was very stressed, particularly during group discussion. These home students would speak very fast, which I couldn't really catch them well. Although I was very stress, I did learn a lot from it. In our second term, we have to do something called 'Business Plan', which is regarded as a serious and important module. These UK students in my class made a request that they would really like to choose their team-mates whom they are happy to work with. So, the mixed-cultural idea in our first doesn't exist any more. My current team-mates are not those who I worked together with in my first term. They are all Asian. One of ex-team-mates asked me if I would like to join their team, which was very tempting and I hesitated a bit. I would be more likely to enjoy more self-autonomy if I joined the Asian student group. However, if I joined UK students, I would learn more, but my ideas would be dominated by them. This is because UK students speak very good English and may not like to listen to me too much. What they think would dominate the ways in which our project is going to work. My ideas seemed to be undermined.
>
> (Taiwanese student)

In difficult situations, and especially in group work, international students would always expect the teacher to take the initiative (Sovic and Blythman 2009).

> Group work is difficult because of the strong character of each student . . . for group work we have to compromise and work together for a goal . . . now my group has six students, but each student's work clashes with the

others. In this kind of situation, I want the teacher to build cooperative relations among the students in the group.

(Japanese student)

Some students from Asian backgrounds commented that tutors did not understand the difficulty of non-native speakers in discussions, and the reasons why they did not participate.

There are some UK students if they don't accept your points, they would show to you that they don't know to listen to you . . . there is a very diverse nature of our student body within this foundation course. I can see there is a phenomenon that these Asian students in my course are relatively quiet. Unlike UK students, these Asian students think more, but talk less. Our teachers can't understand why these Asian students are so quiet.

(Taiwanese student)

Feedback

In oral feedback in particular, international students often felt that they were given less attention than would be the case for home students.

The time to meet the teachers is quite short. I think it's one-way communication. They listen, but I can't have any feedback. I don't think it's a kind of communication. They think we just can't adapt to their style.

(Hong Kong student)

Some teachers are not kind to Asian students with poor English ability. For example, a teacher gives a group feedback for Asians: 4 or 5 students altogether, but an individual tutorial for European . . . This is unfair.

(Japanese student)

Some also felt that the feedback they received could be generic or even peremptory.

For example, the suggestion from tutors is sometimes abstract/vague when I ask. This is due to the nature of Art subjects but I'm even studying this subject in foreign language. This sometimes makes me hard to understand the meaning of these comments/suggestions.

(Japanese student)

Instead of encouraging me to do that, my tutor just told me to change it, and to tell you the truth, I felt it wasn't a good way of teaching. Since then, I don't go to tutors for suggestions. Instead, I read books or ask other students that have more knowledge. I wish the tutors would give me advices that are more constructive, like 'how about this way' and stuff. But the teachers' ways with the students are all different, so I can't generalize too much either.

(Japanese student)

In general, the students interviewed had more constructive thoughts on what good feedback consisted of and could achieve. This student saw the quality of feedback as directly related to small class sizes.

Yes, we are constantly getting tutor feedback in our lessons and then, because we just did our plays on Monday, for all of the teachers, so we just had our big feedback meetings yesterday. That's usually once per term that you're getting your big feedback, but they are constantly telling you. It's very helpful. Because the school is so small, the teacher to student ratio is really good, everyone knows who you are, and it's very helpful.

(American student)

This student felt less fortunate.

The tutors are very busy as they have to deal with a lot of students, so I can't have a deep discussion with them. Of course, it is a good opportunity to learn something though. But it is a bit frustrating because whenever I want to discuss more about a specific matter, they always say that they're too busy to take time for me.

(Japanese student)

Although clearly 'size matters', the personal characteristics and initiatives of teachers could also overcome such problems.

I felt that the teachers give more careful explanations than I have hoped. There are 40 students in the class and it's divided into 2 groups, and the teacher listens to every one of the 20 students. It's only 3 or 4 minutes for each student, but this individual tutoring helps a lot. The UK and international students are mixed together in one group, but I feel that there are a lot more international students.

(Japanese student)

The student in this quote makes the important point that for international students, written feedback is especially valuable to them given their language problems.

The feedback describes by each section and gives me written detail of the comments. When I get the paper-based feedback, it is useful. However, in course, there are only one lecture and some technicians toward 50 students.

My lecturer is always extremely busy. This lecturer is really nice and all my classmates like him or her.

(Japanese student)

Conclusion

Throughout our interviews it was an eye-opener to see how engaged and perceptive the students were on the issues of teaching and learning (as on so much else). The richness and depth of the data itself gives the lie to the notion that Asian students are incapable of critical thinking. So what does this mass of respondents reveal about their teachers and the roles they play?

It is clear that stereotyped, ethnocentric views about different learning traditions and cultures are highly detrimental. The standard, 'large culture' approach, even where well-intentioned, is a totally inadequate framework for understanding students from different parts of the world. Holliday argues that 'generalized conclusions about the educational ability of a whole group of people defined by culture or ethnicity is still discriminatory, no matter how many examples of professional experience it is based on, because it denies *individuality*' (Holliday 2005: 30). It can also be counter-productive for quite specific reasons, as it is likely to lead to disengagement on the part of the students themselves. This may be because students find it easier to accept the identity that is foisted upon them than to challenge it, or for the more negative reasons described here by Clark and Grieve:

> in a learning environment which is perceived by the learner as a client/ provider relationship . . . not being given what is seen as "good instruction" might well lead to frustration and resentment, and withdrawal of interactive cooperation rather than engagement in it. This constitutes a very different interpretation of the behaviour of apparently passive Asian learners.
>
> (Clark and Grieve 2006: 65)

Grimshaw is even more explicit:

> just because the students operate in a receptive mode, this does not imply that they are less engaged. Conversely, just because students in anglophone Western classrooms are seen to be verbally participatory, this does not necessarily guarantee that learning is taking place.
>
> (Grimshaw 2007: 302)

The recent fixation with apparently different pedagogic traditions has perhaps run its course.

> There is no reason to assume that any pedagogic culture has a simply explained provenance. Categories like 'the far east learner', 'national teaching scripts',

the 'Socratic and Confucian' tradition or more broadly, 'western or non-western pedagogies' yield to this simplicity and to cultural relativist readings of the world.

(Cousin 2011: 592)

Many scholars have concluded over the last decade that it would be wiser to think outside such categories and treat all students as students first and foremost. In a fast-moving, globalized world, cosmopolitan learning is surely the way forward – not just for those who choose migration as a route to study but for 'home' students as well. Cosmopolitan learning 'underscores the importance of understanding others both in *their* terms as well as *ours*, as a way of comprehending how both our representations are socially constructed' (Rizvi 2009: 266). Teachers have an absolutely pivotal role in this. Whatever the reasons for misunderstanding, disaffection or failure of engagement, the students in our study clearly, and rightly, *expected* tutors to play an active role in enabling learning, and were disappointed if they did not see this in action. Teachers perform best in this respect when, rather than seeing international students as a problem and a challenge, they take their presence as an opportunity to engage: Jokikokko claims that, for tutors, 'the importance of other people' is one of the most important components of an intercultural learning environment, notably as 'attitudes and behaviours of teachers have an effect on students' attitudes' (Jokikokko 2009: 161), and further observes that 'teachers mediate certain values and attitudes in their teaching either consciously or unconsciously' (ibid.: 149). Such engagement by teachers can also extend to taking the lead in helping home students to overcome their limited view of their international peers.[5]

Notes

1   See Ryan 2010, the most recent and comprehensive discussion of the whole debate on 'the Chinese learner'.

2   Trust and caring have been singled out as important indications of good teaching practices in research on intercultural learning. Jokikokko points out that 'good teaching starts with the construction of trusting relationships and works continually to build on the foundation of trust ... Although a teacher's fundamental tasks are defined in norms and regulations, and the curriculum specifies the content of the teaching, teachers need to act and make decisions that are based on their ethical deliberations every day' (Jokikokko 2009: 158).

3   The problem is not confined to 'Asian' students; Continental European academic cultures have the same formality. This is an aspect of 'tacit knowledge' that is barely addressed in the literature on international students.

4   Compare the study of Jokikokko which found tutors aiming 'at creating a learning environment that is safe and open for different ideas and opinions' (Jokikokko 2009: 158).

5   For an admirable example of practical suggestions of how such teaching can work, see Carroll 2011.

References

Carroll, J. (2011) 'What would inclusive teaching and learning be like?', in M. Foster (ed.) *Working with Cultural Diversity in Higher Education*, SEDA (Staff and Educational Development Association) Special 28.

Chalmers, D. and Volet, S. (1997) 'Common misconceptions about students from South-East Asia studying in Australia', *Higher Education Research and Development*, 16, 1: 87–98.

Clark, R. and Grieve, S.N. (2006) 'On the discursive construction of "The Chinese Learner"', *Language, Culture and Curriculum*, 19, 1: 54–73.

Coate, K. (2009) 'Exploring the unknown: Levinas and international students in English higher education', *Journal of Educational Policy*, 24, 3: 271–82.

Cousin, G. (2011) 'Rethinking the concept of "Western"', *Higher Education Research and Development*, 30, 5: 585–94.

Devos, A. (2003) 'Academic standards, internationalisation, and the discourse of "The International Student"', *Higher Education Research and Development*, 22, 2: 155–66.

Grimshaw, T. (2007) 'Problematizing the construct of "the Chinese Learner": insights from ethnographic research', *Educational Studies*, 33, 3: 299–311.

Gu, Q. and Schweisfurth, M. (2006) 'Who adapts? Beyond cultural models of "the Chinese Learner"', *Language, Culture and Curriculum*, 19, 1: 74–89.

Holliday, A. (1999) 'Small cultures', *Applied Linguistics*, 20, 2: 237–64.

—— (2005) *The Struggle to Teach English as an International Language*, Oxford: Oxford University Press.

Jokikokko, K. (2009) 'The role of Significant Others in the intercultural learning of teachers', *Journal of Research in International Education*, 8, 2: 142–63.

Marginson, S. and Mollis, M. (2001) '"The door opens and the tiger leaps": theories and reflexivities of comparative education for a global millennium', *Comparative Education Review*, 45, 4: 581–615.

Morgan, J. (2011) 'In it for the money? UK needs to rescue overseas reputation', *Times Higher Education*, 14 July: 10.

Papastephanou, M. (2005) 'Globalisation, globalism and cosmopolitanism as an educational ideal', *Educational Philosophy and Theory*, 37, 4: 534–51.

Rizvi, F. (2009) 'Towards cosmopolitan learning', *Discourse: Studies in the Cultural Politics of Education*, 30, 3: 253–68.

—— and Lingard, B. (2000) 'Globalization and education: complexities and contingencies', *Educational Theory*, 50, 4: 419–26.

Ryan, J. (2010) '"The Chinese Learner": misconceptions and realities', in J. Ryan and G. Slethaug (eds) *International Education and the Chinese Learner*, Hong Kong: University Press.

Ryan, J. and Louie, K. (2007) 'False dichotomy? "Western" and "Confucian" concepts of scholarship and learning', *Educational Philosophy and Theory*, 39, 4: 404–17.

Scott, P. (2011) 'Internationalisation may be a "Good Thing", but it has an ugly side', *Education Guardian Higher*, 7 June: 6.

Sovic, S. (2008a) *Lost in Transition? The International Students' Experience Project*, London: CLIP CETL. Online. Available HTTP: http://www.arts.ac.uk/librarylearningand teaching/clipcetl/projects/internationalstudentsexperience (accessed 13 September 2011).

—— (2008b) 'Coping with stress: the perspective of international students', *Art, Design and Communication in Higher Education*, 6, 3: 145–58, and in N. Austerlitz and

A. Shreeve (eds) *Unspoken Interactions: Emotions and Social Interactions in the Context of Art and Design Education*, London: CLTAD.
—— (2009) 'Hi-bye friends and the herd instinct: international and home students in the creative arts', *International Journal of Higher Education and Educational Planning*, 58: 747–61.
Sovic, S. and Blythman, M. (2009) 'Group work and international students in the creative arts', *Dialogues in Art and Design*, ADM-HEA/GLAD: 109–15.
Watkins, D. A. and Biggs, J. B. (eds) (2001) *Teaching the Chinese Learner: Psychological and Pedagogical Perspectives*, Hong Kong: CERC.

Chapter 8

The critical meets the cultural

International students' responses to critical, dialogic postgraduate education in a western university

Margaret Kettle and Allan Luke

Introduction

International education is Australia's third largest 'export' industry, generating 18 billion dollars in 2009 (AEI 2010a) which, according to former Education Minister and now Prime Minister Julia Gillard, makes a significant contribution to Australia.[1] Since the 1980s when the Australian government moved from education as 'aid' to education as 'trade', higher education has been actively marketed and 'sold'. Key selling points have been English as the medium of instruction, the provision of degrees in internationally mobile fields such as management/commerce and information technology (IT), and the opportunity to migrate (Marginson 2006). Australia allows international students to settle in the belief that this makes the country more attractive as a study destination and contributes to its knowledge economy (OECD 2008).

For students and sending nations alike, an international education is a means of broadening horizons and giving students greater understanding of different languages, cultures and knowledge systems (ibid.). International education with its global flows of students to overseas universities is rich with stories of academic and institutional adjustment, language anxieties, cultural challenge, exchange and alienation, agency and personal transformation. These stories sit alongside other accounts – documented in the files of student unions, university managers and, in some instances, legal experts and press reports – of cultural misunderstanding and miscommunication, discrimination and unfair practices, failure, fraud and academic misconduct. If we are to go by the comments of Australian academic colleagues working with international students, currently constituting over a fifth of all students in Australian universities (ABS 2010), it is a mixed picture and experience for all. The position taken in this chapter is that the accounts of these students and their authored tales of the Australian academic experience provide an opportunity to better understand the students' dynamic and strategic programmes of action during their study programmes. The stories lay the ground for challenging the reductive and deficit views held by some university staff and students.

This chapter introduces two students from China and Thailand respectively and presents their stories of undertaking a Master of Education (MEd) course at an

Australian university. The course was one that typifies many humanities-based postgraduate courses: it comprised a relatively small student cohort and was conducted in a seminar style with high levels of interaction between the lecturer and students. Typically the reading of course content was conducted out of class and classroom sessions were used to probe key concepts, often through lecturer-led class discussions. At times, additional content was delivered didactically by the lecturer.

The students' accounts presented here show their 'readings' of the course: its valued ways of knowing, doing and being, and the implications for their views of the world, actions and interactions, and identities. They tell the story of border-crossing and transition as they implement change, or not, to accommodate the new academic situation. The questions for us are the epistemological and experiential shifts identified by the students and the cross-cultural relevance and value ascribed to these shifts by the students.

Our decision to work with students from two Asian countries is not arbitrary. Rather it is linked to the significance of the Asian region for Australian education. In 2009, a total of 203,324 international students were enrolled at Australian universities, 83 per cent of whom were from Asian countries (AEI 2010b). Lead source countries were China and India, followed by Malaysia, Singapore and Indonesia. During the 2000s the lead countries have varied but the percentage of Asian enrolments has changed little. The chapter focuses on the experiences of postgraduate students, which is a response to the increasing attractiveness of this level of study. In 2009 Australian universities recorded a 10 per cent increase in international postgraduate enrolments on the previous year, with 80 per cent of the total opting for coursework masters courses. The majority of students were from China, India, Thailand and Nepal (AEI 2008). The postgraduate students in this chapter are from two major source countries, China and Thailand. We recognize that their narratives are not generalizable but consider them valuable nonetheless, as representations of the complex cultural dynamics and exchanges at work in postgraduate study.

The chapter begins with our standpoints, as a means of explaining our researcher positions and experience in international education. It then introduces the students and their accounts of the MEd course. It concludes with a discussion of the relevance of western critical, dialogic postgraduate education as judged by the two students.

Standpoint

We have been involved in second language teaching and learning at the school, adult and university level for three decades. During the mid-2000s, Margaret Kettle (2007) designed a doctoral research project investigating a group of international students' educational, cultural, social and linguistic resources and experiences while studying a Master of Education course titled *Issues in Educational Theory*[2] at an Australian university. Allan Luke was the dean of the faculty running the course and had been directly involved in the recruitment and development of the programme, with some teaching and supervision. We both had institutional investments in how these students engaged with Australian postgraduate teaching and learning, as well as with their overall experience of living in Australia. The larger study included both field and participant observer notes and critical discourse analysis. Here the focus is on excerpts from two narrative accounts. Both of us envisioned the project as providing new empirical insights into a topic that has been riven with entrenched theoretical positions and controversy.

Key debates in the area of Australian international education have centred on students' learning approaches, English and the role of teaching. Kettle's (2007) study opted for a comprehensive, ethnographically oriented investigation of the student learning experience informed by transdisciplinary theories of discourse formation, identity construction, pedagogy and classroom interactions, learning strategies, second language acquisition and language use. The students were the authorial authorities on international education: what constitutes valued practices in a western university course; what learning approaches are deemed appropriate; how are they acquired and enacted; what are the facilitating factors that aid uptake and transition to new practices; how do new knowledge and practices relate to existing ones; what are their value and relevance?

The study found that the students were strategically engaged in recognizing key course practices and deploying cognitive, social, linguistic and personal resources to enact them. The students were agents of their own change. They identified facilitative factors as the lecturer's explicit teaching of academic reading and writing, and her scaffolding of knowledge construction and class participation. The notion of voice was relevant, both in terms of the students' capacity to represent themselves and their ideas, and the lecturer's distribution and guardianship of speaking rights. The study aligned with our views on the importance of research that provides exemplars of transformative practice. The two student accounts provided in this chapter exemplify the complexity and nuance of the lived experience made visible in the research but often missing in the discussions and literature on international education.

An example of the debate about the international student experience was on display at the 2009 Australian International Education Conference (AIEC). Academics in research forums challenged the predominance of trade-related words such as 'industry' and 'market' to describe international education. They argued instead for terms that emphasize student learning and engagement. Indeed, questions were raised about the use of the term 'international student' itself and its power to differentiate and divide student groups. Meanwhile at the same conference in a plenary speech, the then Education Minister (and now Prime Minister) Julia Gillard praised 'Australia's innovativeness, quality and global reputation for world-class education, training and research' (Gillard 2009). Our questions in this chapter go beyond the rhetoric and assumptions about 'quality' in Australian international education. Rather we ask the students for their representations, with a particular interest in the relevance and value of the Australian experience for them as globally conscious and nationally committed citizens.

Margaret Kettle is an applied linguist working in the fields of sociolinguistics and second language teaching and learning:

> My first instructive experience of second language learning was as an undergraduate student in an ESL programme for migrant Italian women. The programme was ostensibly to teach English to the women who had migrated to Australia in the 1950s. It soon became clear that the women had little interest in English and the classes were largely opportunities to meet and talk, and to teach me Italian. Later, informed by Second Language Acquisition theory, I recognized the agency of the women and their ongoing allegiance to the values and practices of their first culture community. Living in Australia but predominantly in an Italian-speaking community, their English language needs were minimal and easily met by their second language repertoire that was functional if not highly fluent. The experience was an introduction to the complexities of citizenship, acculturation, agency, and motivation in second language learning.
>
> My own experience of second language learning is German. I lived in Germany and attended university language courses in Munich where being an international student meant a close-knit group of colleagues from overseas but little or no contact with local German students. Work involved teaching English for specific purposes (ESP) courses in German companies and publishing articles in German magazines. Later in Australia and Thailand, I taught at universities focusing on ESP theory and practice, always with an increasing understanding of the complexities and constraints of context. When I embarked upon my doctoral study, my own experience no doubt informed the critical orientation of the project. Agency, strategic action and investment, alienation and transformation – these were aspects of the students' experiences that resonated with my own. This is not to suggest that I expected their accounts to mirror mine. However, I was empathetic to the magnitude of their undertaking and keen to capture the full extent of their engagement with the academic, personal, social, cultural and linguistic demands of their course.

Allan Luke is an educational researcher who has worked in the field of language and literacy education for over three decades in Canada, Australia and Singapore.

> I began my career teaching migrant children in British Columbia primary schools in the early 1970s and secondary school ESL programs in the late 1970s, working principally with Vietnamese and East Asian migrant adolescents. Subsequently, I developed programmes and taught in Thailand

and Singapore, and have worked as a policy consultant in those countries, as well as in Hong Kong, Ontario, New Zealand and Kiribati.

Growing up Chinese-American, my work as teacher, educational researcher, university manager and government bureaucrat has been informed by a commitment to social justice, and specifically to redressing the histories of exclusion, marginalization and, indeed, racial and linguistic discrimination experienced by cultural and ethnic minorities, and students from lower socioeconomic backgrounds. Though my writings and teaching would nominally be classified as critical sociology and curriculum theory, I am interested in any and all educational interventions that have some demonstrable ameliorative effects on social injustice in education.

Because of my own cultural and linguistic background as a North American trained and raised academic – a Western intellectual by any description – of visible Chinese ethnicity, the complexities of working in Asia and with East Asian students were not always straightforward. I have written extensively on the optics of seeing both as cultural insider and outsider, of experiencing racialization and linguistic power and marginalization on several fronts, often simultaneously.

(Luke 2009a, 2009b; Luke and Luke 2001)

While we share a strong commitment to the success of these students, the ethical and political question of 'what is to be done' educationally is less than straightforward. Both of us have taught second language and migrant students as part of our own educational histories, but we view this as part of a larger commitment to educational access, opportunity and equity – not a focus on linguistic and second language teaching/learning efficacy per se. We share normative aspirations of intercultural communication, cosmopolitan identity, linguistic equality and equitable access to educationally acquired cultural capital. The international student literature has led us in many directions and emerges in three discernible themes. Initially, the Australian literature moved from policy interventions stressing English language competency that constituted a *de facto* 'deficit' approach to East Asian students. This entailed continuing strong sanctions around language assessment benchmarks for admission (e.g. Auditor-General 2002), 'bridging' and transition coursework to upgrade skills, and an acrimonious public and media discourse around 'soft marking', inflated credentials and lowered standards which continues to capture the public imagination (e.g. Livingstone 2004a, 2004b). In effect, this marked out a classic diagnosis/remediation model for non-English-speaking students venturing into the Australian tertiary model. This, in turn, was superseded by a decade-long literature that 'culturalized' the problem: explaining issues of cultural transitions, differential cultural 'learning styles' and patterns of intercultural communication (e.g. Chalmers and Volet 1997; Renshaw and Volet 1995). This literature, in turn, has been supplanted and augmented by critical studies that have stressed issues of differential 'power', drawing on models of feminist and critical pedagogy and post-colonial theory (e.g.

Bullen and Kenway 2003; Currie *et al.* 2002; Ninnes 1999). In this way, the approaches to explicating the experience of overseas students in Australian universities have, however unintentionally, mirrored the general movement in migrant ESL education from psychological to cultural to sociological explanation.

Yet there are empirical issues in the unproblematic application of these models to account for the Asian, second language student in university postgraduate study. These students are different from Asian migrant second language learners in white/English-dominated cultures: phenomenologically and experientially, culturally and sociodemographically. The cohorts are heterogeneous; some students come from privileged class backgrounds and institutional positions at the centre of their own countries' educational and bureaucratic systems: some are from ethnic/linguistic/religious affiliations that confer power, others not. They come voluntarily, with different professional, cultural and personal motivations: some self-funded at great family sacrifice, some the beneficiaries of western 'aid' programmes, yet others funded by their governments and institutions. Some come as cultural tourists (Robertson *et al.* 1994), principally for the experience of living with their families elsewhere (Kennett 2003).

With the increasing infusion of internationalization into Australian higher education, questions arise about western education and its 'reading' by overseas students. By studying in Australia the students may not be necessarily casting their lot with long-term mobility and the power of Anglo/European education systems, institutions and societies. Even for domestic students, the andragogical and curriculum 'zones' of Australian postgraduate education, the discourses, practices and aims of postgraduate study are radically different from those of schooling. In the case of our faculty, they were strongly informed by critical educational theory and scholarship, dialogic exchange and an academic culture that generated critical, comparative analyses of educational phenomena. This was the focus of the Issues in Educational Theory course that the students here participated in.

Hence, while we remained committed to the students' educational engagement and achievement, we wanted to avoid unselfconsciously replicating a 'comparative victimology' (Luke 2009b), that is, the assumption that their 'difference' conferred deficit, 'disadvantage' or, for that matter, a romantic nobility that is conferred to cultural minorities of colour fronting up to white- and English-dominated institutions and political economies. As the students' stories show, the archetypal sociological tensions of structure and agency, and cultural questions of 'insider' and 'outsider', were continually in play in ways that defied tidy, binary summation. These, further, were complicated by the 'critical' dialogic experiences of their Australian postgraduate education.

Background

The stories presented here are those of Anna from China and Sonny from Thailand. At the time of the study, Sonny was in the first semester of the Master of Education programme, and Anna in her second. Both Sonny and Anna were funded by an Australian government AusAid scholarship, although Sonny was part of the final Thai cohort receiving Australian support due to a Royal Thai Government request to cease being an aid recipient (AusAid 2005).

Anna was a 29-year-old civil servant in a provincial government education department. Mandarin Chinese was her first language and English her second. Her undergraduate degree was a Bachelor of Arts English completed in China. Prior to her husband's arrival in Australia three months after the start of the masters programme, Anna shared a house with two other Chinese women in a suburb adjacent to the university. They found the food difficult to get used to; one woman disliked it so much she ate only potatoes. The lack of obvious security in the house was disconcerting to the women. One night when there was screaming outside the house, one of the women called the police. The officers identified the problem as possums but returned later to reassure the women, a gesture that surprised and impressed Anna. By the end of her second semester, Anna was working in two part-time jobs: one waitressing in a Tibetan restaurant and the other cleaning and waitressing in a sushi bar. She regarded managing work and study as a challenge and was interested in learning how to balance the two.

Sonny was a 33-year-old English communication teacher at a sports institute in northern Thailand. His family were rice farmers in the north-east of Thailand, near the Laotian border. Thai was his first language and English his second. He majored in English in his Bachelor of Education degree in Thailand. During his first semester in Australia, Sonny shared a house with seven students from China, Vietnam, Taiwan, Singapore and Australia. The lingua franca of the house was English and he reported that everyone got on well. He joined four clubs on campus, mainly to meet people and see free movies: the Australian Space Association (an interest), the Romance Languages club (the free movies), the Thai student association and the Taiwanese student club (with a housemate). During his second semester he took a part-time job cooking in a Thai restaurant. He regarded his sojourn in Australia as possibly his only opportunity to travel overseas. For him it allowed him to learn about education but also to experience the people and culture of another country.

Anna and Sonny were enrolled in the Issues in Educational Theory course as a compulsory component of the MEd programme. The course had an enrolment of 21 students: 10 international and 11 domestic. The lecturer was a senior academic who had a reputation for excellence as a teacher. She conducted the class sessions as a mixture of lectures and discussions, and was adamant that international students should be supported to be active members of the class community. She recognized a difference between world knowledge and second language resources and addressed this in her teaching by explicitly scaffolding second language users' contributions to discussions. Her aims and pedagogic approach were based on Freirian principles of dialogic communication and critical consciousness. Students, particularly international students like Anna and Sonny, understood the lecturer's intentions and responded to her support. Despite her help, both found the experience of presenting ideas in the public forum of the class, especially in front of English first-language users, linguistically and socially daunting.

The difficulties of dialogic exchange in a second language, especially in the presence of first-language speakers, are well documented in the literature (e.g. Horwitz 2001; Miller 2003). The demands involve marshalling the requisite linguistic, pragmatic and social resources to present ideas comprehensibly and to respond to questions and comments from the group, while ensuring one's 'face' and legitimacy within the group. The inherent threats to face and self-representation are significant and have been found to contribute significantly to second-language users' reticence and anxiety (e.g. Tsui 1996). For Anna and Sonny, participation in class discussions and the dialectical demands of managing activity, language and identity (Kettle 2011) were challenges to be negotiated in the Issues course. Their representations of these and other salient practices in the course are presented below in assembled excerpts from interviews conducted at the beginning of the course and after it had finished. The students' voices are retained – their language features and views are presented as recorded and transcribed from the interviews. Spoken features such as fillers, false starts and repetitions have been removed.

Study in an overseas university

Anna

I first applied for this programme because I thought there is something lacking in myself. I need to promote my theoretical knowledge and I applied for this programme. I got approval from my unit and then I came here. What shocked me most about Australian teaching methods and content was the teaching, also the learning methods. The teaching methods are much more flexible and the content is quite flexible as well. There's no set text. We are advised to read some books; the teachers give us some reading lists. That's the most difference between here and my home country. Back in China we are actually reading some set books and we are constantly pressed to learn the books. I mean page by page heart. At the very beginning in Australia, I think it's a bit hard for me because I think I was lost but gradually I got used to that kind of method.

In China the teacher taught us and told us you need to learn something and this is the course, the main content. You need to memorize it. But here in Australia you have to grasp them yourself. You need to pick up the main points and if you want to do your assignments, you need to read a broad literature. I think back at home we learn to be a good student but here you are learning to be a thinker. You need to learn to be more critical. You need to question more. Reality is very complex and if we only learn to remember something or to believe what someone is saying, it is only one way of life. But the life is so complex and there's not only one true thing for this world. So you need to be more critical and more flexible – more agile to change.

In China they actually realise that students need to be more creative, more creative thinkers. Last week I was just surfing the net, I read some news that the Department of Education advocates that we have to make some reforms in the education – in the teaching methods to foster a kind of critical thinking at the elementary school. The local government has some authority to actually add some curriculum which has local characteristics and for teachers to have a broader range of teaching.

Of course I think the main function of education is to educate people to be a good citizen or to be a good person morally. Maybe that's because of the Asian educational system. I think it originated thousands of years ago and people have adapted to this kind of learning. I am thinking about this. When I read the literature now, I think 'why does the author have this opinion and what's my response to this?' Actually the lecturer's helping us to develop this kind of habit – asking questions and questioning the author.

One of the lecturer's unique methods is that she's teaching you techniques of reading and writing. This kind of method can help some beginners because, for example this semester, most people are in their first semester. I think that's good especially for Asian or for international students. They are not used to this kind of writing style. She's helping us gradually to adapt to this kind of writing. I think the lecturer loves her students. She really cares about her international students and whenever she has a question, she asks every nationality.

Sometimes I feel little bit uncomfortable because of the question she's asking. Maybe I'm not quite familiar with how to answer but it feels good. It's a big challenge for me. The most important things I learned in the Issues course are being comfortable to think in a more critical way and what you call voice. It's a kind of difficult situation where you put yourself in an embarrassing situation. While you think that you don't have anything to contribute, it's very important to say something. In first semester, I just try to make up any sentences to say something. I think I'm saying nonsense all the time. But it's not my character to be quiet. If you ask one of my best friends, they will think that's not me to be quiet. I really want to be myself. I mean to be my true self. But here it's totally different because of English and also because of the old stuff in my mind. We never think of these kinds of theoretical issues before. In first semester I think maybe 50 per cent about my English when I'm speaking. In second semester, I participated often in class discussions. When you really think about things, you will not care about your English. You should talk.

I think the critical approach works well. I mean it stretches you; it stretches your brain to help you think deeper. It really feels painful. I see the Issues course like a kind of ambition. It helps you to be more critical because when

I participate in the discussion in class, I begin to think. Actually the content of the course sometimes relates to the Australian context, to the west, developed countries. Normally the lecturer asks international students about their countries. She invites them to think, to relate this kind of issue to our own context. But overall the content mainly focuses on developed countries – globalization in the developed countries.

At the very beginning when I arrived here, I had a language crisis whenever I wanted to approach someone. I wasn't confident and I wasn't comfortable to talk with native speakers. It's a bit hard but now I get used to it. At the beginning whenever I wanted to use the language, I was incredibly nervous but now I'm not. Since I have been in Australia, language is one thing that has changed. I realise that my listening has improved a lot. When I speak to an Australian I think I adopt their accent sometimes; at the end of the sentence I tend to use the up-tone.

I think I change a lot. I begin to think in a slightly Australian way. I feel much more comfortable to live here. When I first arrived at the university I think I was a stranger and now I'm part of it. When a foreign person comes to a new place, you feel you have to familiarise yourself and you are strange – not in people's minds but in your own. I didn't like it at the very beginning. I just feel a little bit timid to go out and I'm afraid I will get lost. Now I just get on the bus and if I take the wrong bus, I get off and catch another bus back. That kind of thing is quite comfortable now.

I'm beginning to observe myself and to think what my future will be, what kind of person I want to be and that kind of thing. In China I never have time to think about these issues. Since I'm here on scholarship, I have to go back to China in July. To be frank I don't want to work in the government anymore. I'm thinking maybe I should change jobs but it's a bit hard. I just want to identify that when I go back to China. My advice to someone coming from China to study in Australia would be to be more optimistic, to be more open-minded, to be more adaptable, to be open to all things. I'm changing to be a more flexible person and more optimistic. I have become increasingly confident in myself and comfortable in myself. If you take care how you position yourself, if you position yourself in a more inferior situation or position, you tend to feel pessimistic, in the dark side. If you put yourself to the brighter side of the road, everything will be fine. When I talk with my friends back in China, I think I've changed. That's the old stuff. Before I was like an old clock – there's no grease, no oil. I might have stopped working but now I've got oil and keep on.

What is Anna's account telling us?

Anna's representations of English and language use on arrival are marked by negative attributes. However, as her time references shift to the present, there is greater inclusion of positive attribution, in relation to English language use, enactment of course practices and participation in Australian life beyond the classroom. There is a shift from negative experience to positive experience linked to increased familiarity and incremental enactment of the practices she recognizes as integral to the course: 'At the very beginning, I think it's a bit hard for me because I think I was lost but gradually I got used to that kind of method.' There is a decrease in the acuteness of the relationship between English and the 'self': 'In first semester, I just try to make up any sentences to say something. I think I'm saying nonsense all the time. But it's not my character to be quiet . . . I really want to be myself. I mean to be my true self.' Across the duration of the two semesters, her account details a shift from a concern with English to an engagement with concepts and ideas. English was initially 'overdetermined' (Fairclough 2001) in its impact on her levels of engagement, that is, in its mediation of her ways of knowing, acting/interacting and being in the course. However, as her competence and confidence in English grew, concern about the language recedes and the course disciplinary content becomes her priority. She refers to the 'old stuff in my mind' and the new theoretical perspectives presented in the Issues course. For her, there is a rich relationship between English as her second language, new theoretical perspectives, class participation and 'voice', self-representation and critical thinking. She contrasts her Chinese and Australian educational experiences as the former valuing the good student and the latter valuing the thinker. For her the relevance and value of critical thinking derive from the recognition that there is no one truth and that possibilities always exist for dealing with changing realities. Simply remembering and reproducing established views are not enough for dealing with the complexities of life. Questions and 'agility for change' are necessary. Anna describes her own developing practice of critiquing authors' positions in her reading of course literature. In play in her interrogations are her pre-existing, culturally, socially and educationally contextualized knowledges, new disciplinary understandings from the Issues course and the facilitative modelling by the lecturer. It can be argued that she is in the process of reworking and reformulating her knowledges, practices and identities. She recognizes initiatives in China to promote critical thinking in elementary schools, with the emphasis on critical as being creative. Her metaphors for critical thinking in the Issues course include stretching the brain, pain and deeper thinking. She is eloquent in her view that critical thinking promotes flexibility and the existence of alternative possibilities.

Anna's account indicates a project of self-transformation; a crafting of the self: 'I'm beginning to observe myself and to think what my future will be, what kind of person I want to be. I think I've changed. That's the old stuff. Before I was like an old clock – there's no grease, no oil. I might have stopped working but now I've got oil and keep on.' She used metaphor constantly to articulate the abstract and unformalized conceptualizations of her experience (Kettle 2007). For her, the space and distance of overseas study appear to have afforded revitalization and possibilities of a new future.

Sonny

The Master of Education programme is related to my previous field. I don't imagine that after I finish this Issues in Educational Theory course, I can be a principal of schools. I can't imagine that because it's very competitive. I know how I can apply this knowledge to my field, how to apply to my class and my lessons, to my experience. I love teaching. I love my students. It's my pleasure to see them interact with me in class.

The teaching methods between Thailand and Australia are very different. In Thailand, the room, the classes are very, very big but here in Australia, it's just only 10, 20 students, not more than 20. And actually the style of teaching in Thailand is not to stimulate students to thinking by themselves, rather the lecturer tells everything. So, I think it's different. The students in Thailand can't provide their ideas, can't correct. The teaching systems are not the same because it's the nature of Thai students – they are just passive students. We are accustomed to this in Thailand. When I came here and I studied, I found something different, very different. I'm very surprised that students try to respond to lecturers' questions. For me, I try to do that but sometimes I have problems. I really worry about how to formulate my ideas and how to respond to questions.

Like my own experience, when I began to learn English in Thailand, the teacher taught me at the beginning, grammar. It was also very, very difficult for me when I want to speak – how to speak correctly according to grammars. I was ashamed when I speak something wrong so it made me sad for my students, when they are not confident to speak English. I think the cultures between Thailand and Australia are different. In Thailand, everyone must obey or listen to the Buddha. Whatever the Buddha say must be right. But here, no matter who you are, you don't believe something that someone said. You can express your idea and show your idea. This is a surprise because this situation rarely happens in Thailand. Students just sit and listen. They don't interact with teachers but here when the lecturer says something and some students don't agree, they can immediately argue. I think here it is because everybody is equal and so everybody is exposed to how to expose their ideas to each other; how to interact, how to argue with each other's idea. It is the issue about culture. In Thailand, it is something that we can't do and it makes the roles different.

I think when I first got here, it was very difficult to get myself involved in class activity. In Thailand, there's no problem if a student just sits and listens but here I just feel like I was very ashamed for myself. I don't have any participation in class just like I am nobody. I can't express my ideas in class. It is very hard and very uncomfortable for me. I've tried very much to cope with this problem but for a first time, I don't even know what other students are expressing because of the language. I'm not familiar with their styles or their expressions but now I think I'm better. I know more what they are expressing. It is still a problem for me, that is, how to express my ideas. I think when I have more confidence, everything will be better. I think confidence will help me to have more action, more reaction in class.

I tried to tell myself that I should show my idea because nobody knows about me and because nobody knows about the situation in Thailand. I want to let them know but the first thing I try to understand myself is how to express my idea, how to interrupt in class, how to deal with problems, how to make me confident. There is no need to worry about grammar. I think sometimes, it takes time for me to formulate my ideas because I try to concentrate and get closer to other students' ideas. I have to think about my own language and it's not like I understand what the other students are saying immediately. It's very hard.

I think the lecturer conducts the classes very good because I found that she tries to motivate students to participate in lessons. She names a student to say something. And I think it's very, very good because it stimulates the ideas for students. If I don't understand, she makes me try to understand and makes me try to say something that will show my idea. It doesn't matter if it is right or wrong. It is more important to have the idea. So it's very good. I like it when the lecturer uses my name but sometimes I don't have any idea to say.

Another problem that I think about when I express my idea is when somebody interrupts me and asks me about something. This is a problem because I am concentrating on my own idea. Someone is interrupting me and asking me about another point. It takes time for me to think about that. I worry that I don't understand some points because of my English and if I say something, that it is irrelevant, it's nonsense. But our lessons helped me because I've got a friendly environment; I don't have to feel that I can't have a friend.

Writing an assignment is a very, very difficult step. It's difficult to begin. So when I write I'm not sure it is the right way. It's very useful to be critical, to be analysed. It helps in learning, just like in Thai culture you don't believe anything without it being stated carefully. But being critical in Thailand is not quite similar because it's not going deeper. The study here goes deeper than my country. Here issues are being more criticized, more critical, more analytical.

Something has changed since I have been in Australia because I stay here alone. In Thailand I am more with the people that understand the same culture and here I have to change my idea. I'm staying here alone, so how can I improve myself? How can I stay here happily – without stress, without homesick, or without a problem with lessons? I have had to be strong. I had to overcome problems. But whatever will be will be but I always think that everything is not like a smooth road so everything has problems. The question is how we can pass this point in order to achieve our goals.

My advice to someone coming to study in Australia is that you have to be ready for the changes because it's not like Thailand. You have to study by yourself; you have to read a lot; you have a lot of assignments. First of all, English is very important. Everybody says that there's no problem because we can study English here. But I don't think it is enough because study, understanding the context, understanding the content is very important from the beginning. So they must have excellent English, especially in speaking. Here, you stay alone. You do everything on your own. I don't mean that they find problem here and they surrender. It's just like anybody who goes to another country. They don't know about many things and they have to cope with difficulties. So for somebody that didn't have the chance to go abroad before, when they came here I think the experience will teach them how to live. But the thing that I would like to say is that they have to prepare their knowledge. And I would like to say to them, be confident in yourself, say whatever you want to say, do whatever you want to do, especially in class.

At the beginning of the first semester, I was strange here. I knew no one. I didn't know much about the educational system here, how to study a Master's degree and Australia was a foreign country with a different language and different culture. So from the first semester I learned and I got familiar with things. I thought I came here to learn, to study so I don't have to be afraid of anything. I should adapt myself into the new environment. At first, I think it's hard. It's very hard because I don't know how to but right now I think I have nothing to lose. I have to try. Nobody is like kill me if I do something wrong.

A change for me during my time in Australia is that I see everything broader. I have focused not only on my studies but also on the life in Australia. I want to know how the life is in this country and how the educational system goes on. These are two things that I focus on because I'm not sure that I have time to go abroad in the future so this chance is the only chance in my life. I can't see different things in my own country. I try to understand. I don't judge that my country is better than here or here is better than mine. But there is something different to understand.

What is Sonny's account telling us?

Sonny's story is marked by references to the features of spoken English that he associates with classroom interaction. The references are specific and include expressing ideas, responding to questions from the lecturer and colleagues, interrupting in class and speaking 'correctly according to grammars'. Prominent in his list and referred to repeatedly is the need to express his ideas. Sonny's foregrounding and detailed specification of the features of dialogic interaction point to his recognition of their importance in the course. But while he indicates an interest in acquiring them, and indeed an embryonic competence in enacting them, his primary focus is his English level. He is concerned that he lacks the capacity to interact as needed. Not surprisingly the aspect of the lecturer's teaching that he finds most helpful is her use of students' names to draw them into class discussions: 'she makes me try to say something that will show my idea'. For Sonny, the priority is not whether the idea is right or wrong, rather 'it is more important to have the idea'. His summation of the relationship between language and ideas is that learning English on arrival is too late for students enrolled in university programmes. Rather, his advice is to ensure that their proficiency is 'excellent' on arrival so that they can focus on 'understanding the content . . . from the beginning'.

Sonny posits culture as the reason for Thai and Australian students' different approaches to class interaction. To account for his difficulties, he refers to Buddhist hierarchical principles in Thailand and the requirements to sit and listen to teachers. He contrasts this with what he sees as Australian values of equality, which allow students to interact and argue with each other's ideas, and indeed with the lecturer's as well. He regards critique and analysis as useful and helpful to learning. He compares the emphasis on critical thinking in the Issues course with Thai culture where 'you don't believe anything without it being stated carefully'. Differences are conceptualized in terms of depth: 'the study here goes deeper than my country. Here issues are being more criticized, more critical, more analytical.'

Sonny's account is filled with binaries and contrasts: Thailand and Australia; passive and interactive; before and now. Much of his story is concerned with acquainting himself with the unfamiliar priorities and practices of the Issues course. Most acute and almost anguished are his representations of class interaction and the impact on 'self'. His lexical choices are dense with negative attributes – 'nobody', 'hard', 'problem'. But there are also indications of transformation and change: 'When I first got here it was very difficult . . . but now I think I'm better . . .'. Striking in Sonny's descriptions of difficulty and struggle are his references to self-reliance, coping, acceptance and strength. Evident are a sense of purpose and strategies for improvement. Notwithstanding his willingness of purpose in relation to the Issues course, Thailand remains to the fore for Sonny, as a reference point for academic issues and as a source of national identity that he feels compelled to share with colleagues.

Negotiating culture and western critical, dialogic education

Striking similarities exist in Anna's and Sonny's accounts, despite their backgrounds. Both express initial unfamiliarity with Issues practices and a lack of confidence in their capacity to negotiate the academic and social demands of the course. For both, their English language levels are at the root of their concerns, although for Anna in her second semester of study, the dialectical relation between language and content has shifted to greater engagement with content and less with English. A threshold of acceptable and appropriate practice appears to have been reached. While she expresses a 'coming to know', Sonny recognizes what is required in the course but indicates only partial enactment. Both students identify the critical imperative operating in the course, and recognize moves towards critical approaches to teaching and learning in their respective countries. Interestingly both use the metaphor of depth and thinking deeper to differentiate the approach to critical thinking in the Issues course from those being applied in their home contexts.

In line with metaphors about academic literacy and apprenticeship (e.g. Gee 2002), Anna presents herself as being apprenticed into critical course practices through the modelling and explicit teaching of the lecturer. Notwithstanding her commitment to the course, Anna discerns a focus on developed countries in the course content and orientation, despite the lecturer's invitation to international students 'to think, relate this kind of issue to your own context'. For Sonny, the lecturer's strength lies in her acknowledgment of the interactive demands of class discussions and her facilitation of participation. Through her cued elicitation (Mercer 1995) of responses by calling students' names, she affords speaking rights to students such as Sonny and invests their ideas with legitimacy. The way we are 'heard' by others is crucial to self-representation (Miller 2003) and impacts on our ability to 'impose reception' (Bourdieu 1991) and be listened to as a legitimate member of a community. For Sonny, the lecturer made efforts to provide a supportive environment of 'receptive others' in which he could express his ideas and gain legitimacy within the class (Kettle 2005).

But this is not a 'language' issue per se. Across both Anna's and Sonny's accounts there is a sense of the disruptiveness of the critical approach of the course. Both would have come from institutional experiences with the interactional competences affiliated with 'East Asian pedagogy' (Mok 2006): where critique of ideas, other students' views and those of the teacher/lecturer are not common practices. Sonny attributes this to Buddhist teacher/student relationships, while Anna refers to it simply as being 'constantly pressed to learn the books. I mean page by page heart'. In the Issues course they were placed in a situation where reciprocal speaking rights were exchanged and expected, with direct invitation and ethical responsibility to respond (Young 1992). This created not just a linguistic challenge of appropriate and effective response – which visibly expanded in grammatical and conceptual complexity, verbal fluency and pace as the course went on – it also created a socio-cultural and intellectual challenge: asking them to engage in normative educational practice as a model for 'what might be' in their own educational contexts. Sonny comments on the destabilizing effect of the experience and its challenge to his beliefs and personal systems. Anna comments that it has had an influence on her attitudes towards work and that she might leave the government system upon return. It appears that both have been exposed to the possibility of positions beyond the known and the orthodox. In Anna's case, critical questioning has meant an understanding that life and reality are complex and cannot be defined by just one 'true' explanation; for Sonny, the chance to travel has led to a broadening of views. There is a sense that they have become acquainted with the idea of alternatives, and that spaces and possibilities are always available. The potential of this idea lies in its logic that orthodoxies that were once considered immutable are now open to scrutiny and change.

Sonny and Anna indicate a commitment to the practices of the Issues course, albeit with differing degrees of recognition and enactment (Fairclough 2003). Their efforts might be seen as investments (Norton Peirce 1995) that have reaped personal and professional rewards. The social and intellectual space of the course and life generally in Australia seem to have offered them new possibilities – increased English proficiency, expanded knowledge and skills, changed worldviews, job alternatives, travel opportunities, and personal challenges and confidences – although not without sacrifice and struggle. Their talk indicates they are 'managing' themselves, their resources, academic demands and the significant 'others' in the course. They reveal a certain understanding of their own agency. They are crafting situated identities for their personal trajectories and the new context. As it was, both students were successful – eventually – in the Issues course. Anna passed with a High Distinction. Sonny failed his second assignment but rather than follow the lecturer's advice and resubmit, he chose to fail the course and repeat it the following year so that he could 'learn more'. His agency paid off and he passed on the second attempt.

Is this a case of 'empowerment' via engagement with a critical education in an unfamiliar cultural and institutional context? Might it entail a restructuring of these students' investments and agency via the linguistic and cultural exchanges of this particular dialogic approach to pedagogy? Many of the paradoxes and contradictions of the experience of this particular approach to critical education are on the table here. The pattern entails a movement out of one's routinized cultural and linguistic practices into the domain of a cultural Other. The readjustment of everyday life, of patterns of work, leisure, consumption and, indeed, family and collegial relations sets a broad cultural 'zone' within which the pedagogic, textual exchanges of the classroom take place.

Within that, the new patterns of exchange, and the approach to critique and analysis constitute a major, new interactional learning zone for both Anna and Sonny. It would be naively determinist to assume that this was either a case of the colonization of these students by a Euro/centric western critical pedagogy or a matter of epiphanic 'empowerment'. And one of the interesting gaps in the literature on critical pedagogies is the absence of longitudinal studies (Luke and Chang 2007). The naive assumption of critical approaches to education, including those in TESOL (cf. Norton and Toohey 2004), is that there is a hypodermic effect of dialogic exchange: somehow that 'critical consciousness', once acquired via dialogue, necessarily has 'transformative' effects on student consciousness (Freire 1972) and leads to fundamental changes in epistemology, and political and cultural standpoint.

These students' lives and their prior pedagogical knowledge and experience were indeed destabilized by the experience, but neither left subscribing to a 'west is best' educational ideology (Luke 2001). On the one hand, the curriculum and approach used by this faculty and lecturer were indeed transformative, systematically moving students from the known to the new in ways that were sensitive to the textual and linguistic hurdles they faced. But what they do with this new experience, exchange and capital remains an unfinished story. If there is a lesson here, it is that pedagogical exchange and learning are always situated, spatially, geographically and temporally located in enabling and disenabling material and cultural locations. Further, transnational movement between institutional and pedagogical spaces is a complex empirical and phenomenological matter: travel, in all of its various forms, entails the recontextualization and realization anew of practice, knowledge and identity that may take idiosyncratic, unpredictable forms and outcomes. Whether, how and in what ways Anna's and Sonny's experiences of cultural Otherness, their introduction to a new, different set of pedagogical exchanges, and their augmented textual and discourse resources will 'make a difference' in their life choices and career trajectories in Thailand and China remains an unfinished story.

Notes

1   For the full text of 'Internationalisation – its contribution to Australia' see http://
    www.deewr.gov.au/Ministers/Gillard/Media/Speeches/Pages/Article_090527_
    093411.aspx (accessed 22 September 2009).
2   The names of the course and the students have been changed.

References

ABS (Australian Bureau of Statistics) (2010) *Year Book Australia 2009–10: Overseas Student Enrolments with Higher Education Providers*. Online. Available HTTP: http://www.abs.gov.au/AUSSTATS/abs@.nsf/Lookup/1301.0Chapter12082009%E2%80%9310 (accessed 3 November 2010).

AEI (Australian Education International) (2008) *International Higher Education Students by Level of Course*. Online. Available HTTP: http://aei.gov.au/AEI/Publications AndResearch/Snapshots/38SS08_pdf.pdf (accessed 29 November 2009).

—— (2010a) *Export Income to Australia from Education Services in 2009*. Online. Available HTTP: http://aei.gov.au/AEI/PublicationsAndResearch/Snapshots/2010052810_pdf.pdf (accessed 3 November 2010).

—— (2010b) *International Student Enrolments in Higher Education in 2009*. Online. Available HTTP: http://aei.gov.au/AEI/PublicationsAndResearch/Snapshots/201004 16HE_pdf.pdf (accessed 3 November 2010).

Auditor-General (2002) *International Students in Victorian Universities*. Online. Available HTTP: http://www.audit.vic.gov.au/reports_par/agp7601.htm (accessed 2 May 2003).

AusAid (2005) *Thailand*. Online. Available HTTP: http://www.ausaid.gov.au/country/country.cfm?CountryId=32 (accessed 10 May 2005).

Bourdieu, P. (1991) *Language and Symbolic Power*, trans. G. Raymond and M. Adamson, Cambridge MA: Polity Press.

Bullen, E. and Kenway, J. (2003) 'Real or imagined women? Staff representations of international women postgraduate students', *Discourse: Studies in the Cultural Politics of Education*, 24, 1: 35–50.

Chalmers, D. and Volet, S. (1997) 'Common misconceptions about students from South-East Asia studying in Australia', *Higher Education Research and Development*, 16, 1: 87–98.

Currie, J., Thiele, B. and Harris, P. (2002) *Gendered Universities in Globalized Economies: Power, Careers and Sacrifices*, Lanham, MD; Oxford: Lexington Books.

Fairclough, N. (2001) *Language and Power*, 2nd edn, Essex: Pearson Education Limited.

—— (2003) *Analysing Discourse: Textual Analysis for Social Research*, London: Routledge.

Freire, P. (1972). *Pedagogy of the Oppressed*, trans. M. Bergman Ramos, Harmondsworth: Penguin.

Gee, G.P. (2002) 'Literacies, identities, and discourses', in M. Schleppegrell and M.C. Colombi (eds) *Developing Advanced Literacy in First and Second Languages*, Mahwah, NJ: Lawrence Erlbaum.

Gillard, J. (2009) 'Address to the Australian International Education Conference, Sydney', 15 October 2009. Online. Available HTTP: http://www.deewr.gov.au/Ministers/Gillard/Media/Speeches/Pages/Article_091015_120915.aspx (accessed 29 November 2009).

Horwitz, E. K. (2001) 'Language anxiety and achievement', *Annual Review of Applied Linguistics*, 21: 112–26.

Kennett, B. (2003) 'Resourcing identities: biographies of Australians learning Japanese', unpublished manuscript, University of Queensland, Australia.

Kettle, M. (2005) 'Agency as discursive practice: From "nobody" to "somebody" as an international student in Australia', *Asia Pacific Journal of Education*, 25, 1: 45–60.

—— (2007) Agency, discourse and academic practice: reconceptualising international students in an Australian university', unpublished manuscript, University of Queensland, Australia.

—— (2011) 'Academic practice as explanatory framework: reconceptualising international student academic engagement and university teaching', *Discourse: Studies in the Cultural Politics of Education*, 32, 1: 1–14.

Livingstone, T. (2004a) 'Foreign students fail on their own terms', *The Courier-Mail*, 19 February: 9.

—— (2004b) 'Universities face tests on cash and credibility', *The Courier-Mail*, 14 Februrary: 12.

Luke, A. (2009a) 'Another ethnic autobiography? Childhood and the cultural economy of looking', in R. Hammer and D. Kellner (eds) *A Critical Cultural Studies Reader*, New York: Peter Lang.

—— (2009b) 'Race and language as capital in school: a sociological template for language education reform', in R. Kubota and A. Lin (eds) *Race, Culture and Identities in Second Language Education*, London: Routledge.

Luke, A. and Chang, B. (2007) 'Foreword', in K. Kumashiro and B. Ngo (eds) *Six Lenses on Anti-Oppressive Education*, New York: Peter Lang.

Luke, A. and Luke, C. (2001) 'A situated perspective on cultural globalisation', in N. Burbules and C. Torres (eds) *Globalisation and Education*, New York: Routledge.

Luke, C. (2001) *Globalization and Women in Academia: North/West-South/East*, Mahwah, NJ: Lawrence Erlbaum.

Marginson, S. (2006) 'Dynamics of national and global competition in higher education', *Higher Education*, 52: 1–39.

Mercer, N. (1995) *The Guided Construction of Knowledge: Talk amongst Teachers and Learners*, Clevedon, England: Multilingual Matters.

Miller, J. (2003) *Audible Difference: ESL and Social Identity in Schools*, Clevedon, England: Multilingual Matters.

Mok, I. (2006) 'Shedding light on the East Asian learner paradox', *Asia Pacific Journal of Education*, 26: 131–42.

Ninnes, P. (1999) 'Acculturation of international students in higher education: Australia', *Education and Society*, 17, 1: 73–101.

Norton, B. and Toohey, K. (eds) (2004) *Critical Pedagogies and Language Learning*, Cambridge: Cambridge University Press.

Norton Peirce, B. (1995) 'Social identity, investment and language learning', *TESOL Quarterly*, 29, 1: 9–31.

OECD (Organisation for Economic Co-operation and Development) (2008) *Education at a Glance 2008: OECD Indicators*. Online. Available HTTP: http://www.oecd.org/dataoecd/23/46/41284038.pdf (accessed 10 September 2009).

Renshaw, P.D. and Volet, S.E. (1995) 'South-East Asian students at Australian universities: a reappraisal of their tutorial participation and approaches to study', *Australian Higher Educational Researcher*, 22, 2: 85–106.

Robertson, G., Mash, M., Tickner, L., Bird, J., Curtis, B. and Putnam, T. (eds) (1994) *Travellers' Tales*, New York: Routledge.

Tsui, A.B.M. (1996) 'Reticence and anxiety in second language learning', in K. Bailey and D. Nunan (eds) *Voices from the Language Classroom*, Cambridge: Cambridge University Press.

Young, R. (1992) *Critical Theory and Classroom Talk*, Clevedon, England: Multilingual Matters.

Chapter 9

Transformative learning and international students negotiating higher education

Ly Tran

The international sojourners who have the courage and determination to move beyond their cultural comfort zone and work through intercultural experiences often possess the potential to be effectively engaged in transformative learning. Brown (2009) states that moving between different life worlds can represent the catalyst for self-discovery and self-reconstruction. Overseas learning indeed entails transformative power. The nature of the sojourn experience in a new intercultural and academic environment involves complex and multidimensional operations. Changes and adaptation to changes underpin the sojourn experience. The specific ways in which individual international students make changes, and their process of adapting to an unfamiliar learning and social environment, are the manifestation of how they exercise personal agency. This process often requires much self-determination, investment and strategy. Such a transformative process involves international students viewing their world from a different perspective (Taylor 1994), and in some cases enables them to develop multiple frames to make sense of the world around them.

This chapter aims to explore the theory of transformative learning as a possible explanation for the changes international students make in their journey to negotiate higher education. The chapter is derived from a doctoral study that involved international Chinese and Vietnamese students' adaptation to Australian higher education academic practices (Tran 2007). Within this chapter, transformative learning is viewed as a changing process in which international students construct reality through revisiting their existing assumptions and moving towards life-changing developments in their personal and professional perspectives (Cranton 2002; Mezirow 2000). It will be argued in this chapter that international students' process of negotiating higher education is a dynamic interplay between challenges and transformative power. Cross-border intercultural experiences are intimately linked to opportunities for self-transformation, and the challenging experiences that international students go through indeed foster the conditions for professional development and life-enhancing changes to take place. Given the current lack of theoretical and empirical research on the transformative power of international students, there is a critical need for more research on the transformative characteristics of international students and how best to capitalize on their potential. In this chapter, I draw on excerpts from two rounds of interviews with individual international students to illustrate the specific ways in which international students have the capacity to transform their own learning and develop life-enhancing skills. The discussion shows that they experience evolution in professional outlook, attitudes and personal qualities through the process of critical self-reflection and adaptation to disciplinary demands in higher education.

The chapter also highlights the contradictions regarding the discursive practices within the current context of international education export. English-medium institutions seek to project themselves as sites where 'transformations' take place. But, in reality, the onus of adaptation and intercultural transformation appears to be mainly placed on international students themselves rather than on academics. In addition, whilst theories about international education and the international-ization of the curriculum view transformative learning as being central (Bond 2003; Leask 2005), the majority of the literature on international students' learning experiences tends to position this student cohort from a problem-based vantage as opposed to transformative learning. In the media, international students are often constructed as 'commercial products' and their images are linked to 'transformations' and 'contributions' to the institutions and host countries but predominantly in the economic sense. In particular, there is little discussion related to how to support the emergence of new, challenging and valuable discourse through validating the transformative potential and diverse dimensions of knowledge that international students bring to academia.

Transformative learning as projected on university web pages for international students

To maintain confidentiality, the universities referred to in this section are not named. University websites have indeed emerged as the dominant sources of information for international students on which to select and base their choice of study destination (Nguyen 2007). Through their websites, universities draw on vocabularies that embrace transformative meanings to construct their institutional identity and promote their image to prospective students. Interestingly universities, regardless of their differing status, utilize similar wordings such as 'enrich', 'empower', 'develop' and 'change' to position themselves as a transformation site for international students. For example, the following statement is from the web page specified for international students at a university in Victoria, Australia: 'this environment ensures all our international students are given the tools that will enrich and empower them both academically and personally'. It appears that this university is linguistically manifested as nurturing a transformative environment for international students to flourish and enrich themselves. Transformative learning is thus promised within this university context. Also drawing on transformation-related language but in an alternative dimension, another university from England tries to connect with international students through positioning itself as being a world-leading university in which its international student members are capable of contributing to transforming the university and to building its prestige: 'our growing cohort of international students informs and enriches our activities, contributing to our ranking as one of the world's leading universities'. This university is ranked in the top five universities of the world. Clearly the promotional dimension of these universities is shown through the linguistic choices used in their website. It can be seen that host educational providers tend to connect with international students through the discourse of transformative learning through their websites. In other words, through their web pages for international students that work as a recruiting tool and promote the institutions' status, universities tend to position themselves as supporting and nurturing a transformative learning environment and other-position international students as having the potential to transform their learning.

The official website of the Australian Government, which is used to provide prospective international students with information about studying in Australia, conveys the message: 'the benefits of living and learning in Australia are both personal and academic. Your years in Australia will give you the best platform to succeed in your career, and prepare you for the challenges of the work place. It won't just be your mind that develops – your time in the classroom will change you as a person' (Study in Australia 2011). The key message communicated here is that study in Australia will provide international students with the opportunity to go through both personal and academic transformations. The messages from these universities and the Government website work to construct an identity for both the universities and international students in connection with transformative learning. This discourse places international students in a position to imagine they are the ones who have the potential to transform, and if they take up the invitation to join the university they will become part of a community that nurtures transformative processes.

Literature on the experiences of international students in host countries

Ironically the majority of research literature on international students tends to view their learning experiences in the host countries from a problem-oriented vantage as opposed to transformative learning. These studies seem largely to focus on the challenges that international students may encounter in relocating in an unfamiliar environment and in particular their study problems in the host institution (Samuelowicz 1987; Elsey 1990; Ballard and Clanchy 1995; Robertson *et al.* 2000; Lacina 2002). This line of research also explores the coping strategies of international students and how to support them to overcome challenges. As Coate (2009) mentions, while this stream of literature has useful implications for the teaching of international students, it seems to imply that these difficulties are unique to international students, and the overall discourse seems to be orientated toward discussing the deficit aspects of cross-border learning. Kettle (2005) seems to be among the very few authors who explore the process of a Thai international student in negotiating his disciplinary routes in Australian higher education. This paper documents the transformative power of an international student and re-conceptualizes international students as mobile people who could act as 'active agents' in gaining access to their academic world. Apart from Kettle's work, there is insufficient research examining the issue of how to support international students to maximize their potential and to create a learning environment that nurtures students' transformative learning in their academic subjects. In particular, the personal transformation and academic growth as a result of cross-border experiences and integration into a new academic culture appear to be largely overlooked in scholarly work on international students. There is also apparently a lack of research and practices examining the ethical commitment to realizing what is promised to offer students in relation to the conditions to transform skills and perspectives in the real classroom context.

The small proportion of literature that looks at the transformative power of international sojourns and migrants tends to draw on theories of culture shock and focus on the aspect of intercultural growth rather than transformation in relation to international students' learning practices in their discipline (Taylor 1994; Ward *et al.* 2001; Cushner and Karim 2004; Brown 2009; Milstein 2005). Furthermore, most of these studies investigate the intercultural experiences of migrants or students in exchange programmes rather than in their degree study in the host countries. Shearer (1994, cited in Fenimore 1997) identifies five dimensions of an intercultural identity: 1) acceptance of original and new cultural elements; 2) increased scope, depth and perspective in perception; 3) increased self-knowledge, self-trust and self-directedness; 4) increased inner resilience that facilitates further development; 5) increased creative resourcefulness to deal with new challenges. In fact Kim and Ruben (1988) propose a framework exploring intercultural transformation from two vantages, which they refer to as an adaptation-as-problem perspective and an adaptation-as-growth perspective. These two dimensions imply that the process of adaptation can involve challenges and at the same time foster the condition for growth. The study reported in this chapter draws on examples from international students' journeys to adapt to higher education academic writing practices in order to illustrate how this process can create space for transformative learning, and how international students are capable of being engaged in transforming themselves and their own learning.

The literature on international sojourns seems to highlight the idea that intercultural experience has transformative potential (Taylor 1994; Ward *et al.* 2001; Cushner and Karim 2004; Brown 2009). The potential to enhance cross-cultural understandings through international sojourns is often cited as an aspect of this transformative power (Bochner 1996; Ward *et al.* 2001; Brown, 2009). Bochner, for example, mentions that international sojourns may facilitate individuals' development of more ethno-relative views of the world around them. According to Taylor (1994), during the sojourn process the migrant sojourners often adapt to and shift their perspectives in order to accommodate the new experience and integrate into the host environment. This author attempts to link the transformative power of sojourners to their process of becoming interculturally competent. In particular the author highlights that competent sojourners are not passively conditioned by the new environment but rather are capable of negotiating 'purpose and meaning' in intercultural communication. There may be a number of factors that affect this integration process as sojourners differ in their own motivations, personalities, preferences and expectations. Brown (2009: 505) suggests that sojourners' personal transformation can be linked to 'a journey of self-discovery as removal from the comfort of the familiar forces them to test and stretch their resourcefulness and to revise their self-understanding'. However, it should be noted that Green (2009) argues for a less idealistic treatment of the automatic connection between studying abroad with cross-cultural under-standing. This author calls for more detailed research on the affective factors for transformation or cross-cultural learning to take place.

In short, the majority of the past studies of international students' academic experiences tend to position them from a deficit model. The body of literature that does explore international students' transformative potential often focuses on their process of developing intercultural competence and acquiring intercultural knowledge and skills such as tolerance and cultural relativity (Ward *et al.* 2001; Brown 2009) rather than on their capacity to transform in relation to their academic practices in the host countries. A personal change in outlook and self-understanding is also highlighted in the literature (Taylor 1994; Brown 2009). These areas are the main focus of research on international sojourners partly because these studies are grounded in a tourism-related theoretical framework. However, the changes that are conceptualized within international students' disciplinary study seem to be little-captured.

Transformative learning and international education

Transformative learning refers to a changing process in which learners make meaning and construct reality through revisiting their existing assumptions and moving towards life-changing developments in philosophy and outlook. Cranton (2002), Mezirow (2000) and Taylor (1994) discuss useful perspectives related to transformative learning that can be applied in the context of international students' changes in personal and professional attitudes and outlooks. Mezirow links transformative learning to a process by which individuals:

> transform our taken-for-granted frames of reference (meaning perspectives, habits of mind, mindsets) to make them more inclusive, discriminating, open, emotionally capable of change, and reflective so that they may generate beliefs and opinions that will prove more true or justified to guide action.
>
> (Mezirow 2000: 7–8)

Mezirow highlights the relationship between transformative learning and how the lenses through which individuals can view and interpret the world around them can be reconstructed. In a similar vein, Cranton (2002: 64) relates transformative learning to individuals' ability to critically examine their own existing views, be willing to appreciate alternatives and shift the ways they make sense of the world. These three studies view individuals' critical reflection on their own perspectives and experiences as instrumental in their transformative learning process.

Transformative learning is viewed to be fundamental in research on international education and internationalizing the curriculum. In a study on international students on a Malaysia-based campus of an Australian university, Pyvis and Chapman (2007) found that the aspiration to transform their own perspective and enrich their international experience is the primary motive for international students to undertake an international education. These authors termed this type of investment in international education as 'self-transformative' investment. This finding is echoed by Kingston and Forland (2008), who argue that one of international students' primary purposes in choosing to study overseas is to transform themselves rather than conforming to a fixed set of academic conventions of the host institutions.

Research also conceptualizes the internationalization of the curriculum as being related to transformative learning. Indeed both Morey (2000) and Bond (2003) highlight transformative capacity in their definition of the internationalization of the curriculum. Morey (2000: 28) argues that internationalizing the curriculum should be seen as a process that involves different levels of transformation rather than a 'static outcome'. In the model of an internationalized curriculum proposed by this author, a 'transformed stage' is the highest level of development in which both international and domestic diversity play key roles in the internationalized curriculum. Bond (2003) identifies three approaches to internationalizing the curriculum: the 'add-on' approach, the 'infusion' approach and the 'transforma-tion' approach. The add-on approach represents the process of simply adding international or intercultural dimensions to the existing curricula. Infusion refers to a curriculum that provides students with the opportunity to be exposed to international and multicultural perspectives. This approach is more systematic than the add-on and more commonly used. The transformation approach, which is seen as the most advanced approach in internationalizing the curriculum, aims to encourage international and domestic students into new ways of thinking and making sense of the world, critically examine existing assumptions within the traditional curriculum and construct their reality through the lenses of diverse groups. A study conducted by Leask (2005) also shows that staff and students construct the internationalization of the curriculum as being related to the opportunity to be transformed by intercultural interactions.

Theories about international education and the internationalization of the curriculum inherently view transformative learning as a core component. In the relatively limited number of studies on international students' purposes in undertaking an international education, many international students are found to be motivated in pursuing an international education with the aspiration to transform their perspectives (Pyvis and Chapman 2007; Tran and Nyland 2010). Within the most advanced frameworks of internationalizing the curriculum, international students are similarly positioned to be involved in a process of critical examination and transcendence of the 'taken for granted' assumptions while transforming their personal and professional attitudes. Clearly there is an immense gap between the positioning of international students in relation to international education and the internationalization of the curriculum, and the literature on international students' experiences, which largely looks at international students from a deficit viewpoint. Such a mismatch of the theory related to the inter-nationalization of the curriculum and the literature on international students also shows that institutions and current academic practices do not focus on capitalizing on international students' potential to transform their perspectives and translate their presence and the 'capital' that they bring to academia into valuable resources for transformative learning for both international and domestic students.

In the public domain, international students are often described in relation to the education export industry. In Australia, for example, the picture of international students is often depicted in relation to a $18 billion industry. International students are often compared to commercial products such as coal or iron ore. The media also draws on terms such as 'transformation' or 'transform' in talking about international students but in another sense: for example, an article entitled 'Foreign students transform city' (Rout 2007) focuses exclusively on how international students transform Melbourne in terms of the cash flow to the city. Others refer to how the $18 billion dollars from education export help to transform Australia in economic terms. Therefore despite educational institutions' efforts in positioning themselves as transformation sites and other-positioning of international students as possessing the transformative power in relation to academic and cultural aspects, international students are ironically constructed in the local media as 'cash cows' whose transformative power is linked to their contribution to the host country's economy.

The study

The study reported in this chapter analyses how eight Chinese and Vietnamese international students exercise personal agency and mediate their academic writing to adapt to disciplinary practices in Education and Commerce at an Australian university. Chinese and Vietnamese international students of education and economics were selected for this study for a number of reasons. China is one of the leading sources of international students for Australian higher education. At the university where this study was conducted, international students from China comprise the largest proportion of international students. In addition, at this university, there has been an emerging postgraduate student growth from Vietnam. Economics is the biggest faculty and it has the largest enrolment of international students at the university where this study was conducted. Education is one of the disciplines of the university that has recently seen a rising trend in the international student cohort. The students in this study were required to meet the cut-off IELTS score of 7.0 and 6.5 in order to gain entry to their one-and-a-half year masters course in education and economics respectively (Tran 2007).

The data were a combination of two rounds of interviews with the students and their own assignments. The methods for data collection include the *talk around text* with students (Lillis 2001), the positioning interviews six months later and their written texts. With the consent of the students, their first written assignments at the Australian university were collected. These texts would then be used for the students to reflect on their specific experiences of writing them. The first essays written by the Vietnamese and Chinese students have been chosen to be the focus of the study because these are probably the most challenging for international students to write. International students' first texts for their masters course are often where the clash between disciplinary requirements and their former interpretations of writing occurs. Hence, the first written work is often the place where students have to negotiate their initial interpretations of academic writing and the disciplinary requirements. Each student participant was invited to a one-hour interview in which she/he was asked to talk about the selected text. The talk aimed to engage students in an exploration of their practices of writing these specific texts and how they exercised personal agency to mediate their writing and adapt to their disciplinary requirements. The *talk around text* (Lillis 2001) was conducted from four to eight weeks after the students had completed these texts. The positioning interviews with the Vietnamese and Chinese international students were conducted six months after the *talk around text*. The positioning interviews allow space for the students to reposition their views and reflect on any changes with regard to their interpretations and expectations of academic writing they may go through as they progress through their course. Semi-structured interviews with open-ended questions were adopted. The interviews were then transcribed. All respondents presented in this study have been given pseudonyms.

The issues of personal agency and personal transformation of Vietnamese and Chinese international students in their participation in disciplinary writing practices are important concerns in this study, as academic writing is a central dimension of meaning making in higher education. New (1994) argues that people, as agents, can act intentionally and have potential choice to make changes to the world in which they live. International students' process of making meaning at the tertiary level can also be referred to as a process of negotiation. This in part originates in their effort to meet course requirements and lecturers' expectations, which to some degree represent the disciplinary systems of knowledge and beliefs. This process is also related to the values and beliefs shaped by students' cultural and personal preferences. In this chapter, the analysis of the data will draw on the theory of transformative learning as a framework to interpret and analyse international students' aspiration and capacity to be engaged in transformative learning. The following key dimensions of transformative learning identified by Mezirow (1991) and Taylor (1994) are used to shed light on the analysis of international students' process of negotiating meaning and transforming their personal and professional perspectives: engaging in critical reflection, linking to prior experiences and developing intercultural competency. In addition, Brown's (2009) assumption about the connection between the confrontation of challenges and the development self-efficiency is also drawn on to interpret international students' personal growth.

Transforming perspectives through critical reflection

Mezirow (1991) and Taylor (1994) identify reflection as an important dimension of perspective transformation. In his discussion of the learning process of intercultural competency, Taylor (1994: 170) links reflective orientation to a cognitive process whereby 'participants made a conscious connection between their cultural disequilibrium, possible behavioural learning strategies and necessary change towards competency'. All the participants in this study engaged in reflection throughout their process of negotiating their ways of constructing knowledge in higher education. An example of reflective orientation was described by Wang, a Chinese international student, in her talk around how she constructed meaning for her first assignment for her masters course at the Australian University. She recalled a milestone that has helped to shape her view on the use of personal experience and personal pronouns:

> When I read Jill's [the lecturer] doctoral thesis, it's just like I read a novel . . . It's very interesting about personal experience. It's amazing at that time and after I read her thesis, I talked to Jill about her thesis and I said 'I can never expect you wrote your Ph.D. thesis like that' because it's her personal account – my experience in China and how I dealt with different kinds of situations. At that time, I feel that it's like a process, first you use 'I' and at that time you don't know anything about academic writing and then you adapt to the Western style of writing, you avoid using 'I' and after that when you are mature enough in the field, you start using 'I' again because you know how to use 'I' appropriately in your writing . . . Now I think I am not competent enough to use 'I'. Maybe 5 years later when I, for example, develop myself as a beginning scholar, after I finish the thesis, I can label myself as a beginning scholar. And then 5 years later when I do a lot of research in the area, I gain more confidence with the understanding of the knowledge and of the theory, have my own understanding, when you understand something or you think you really understand something, I think you are brave enough to say 'I think' or 'According to my experience'.
>
> (Wang)

The quote above illustrated that Wang's initial belief about the use of 'I' and personal experience of academic writing, which she developed when entering her disciplinary discourse, appeared to be challenged as she read her lecturer's thesis and had a conversation with her lecturer. Wang's word usage, 'It's very interesting', 'It's just like I read a novel', 'It's amazing . . .', 'I can never expect . . .', indicated how powerful the role of her lecturer's thesis and her lecturer's way of writing was in reshaping her attitude. She repositioned her interpretation of the use of the personal pronoun and personal experience in academic writing in light of what she learnt from her lecturer's writing. The international student here positioned herself as an active constructor of knowledge in discourse and also a reflexive constructor of the self. From Wang's perspective, her previous use of 'I' and personal experience in writing sprang from her ignorance of academic writing practice and her identity as a novice in the field of language teaching. As for Wang, her latter use of personal terms like 'I' or 'my' to express her views and her experience, which she believed to be more appropriate than her former use, was associated with her deeper awareness of academic writing conventions, her growing confidence, her understanding of professional knowledge and her maturity as a 'beginning scholar'. Wang's attempt to express her personal agency through using personal experience and personal pronouns was like a journey of constructing meanings, through which she experienced shifts in her perceptions as she deepened her understanding. Her account illustrates that transformative learning emerged from her capacity to critically reflect on her exposure to different ways of meaning making which provides her with the condition for the discovery, negotiation and reconstruction of the self (Giddens 1991). In other words, the international student's capacity to engage herself in reflective orientation (Taylor 1994) actually leads to a change in meaning perspective.

The international students in this study tended to be flexible in adapting to what they interpreted as the academic requirements of their own discipline. They continuously reshaped their interpretation of ways of constructing knowledge in their discipline through self-reflection and reflection on others' views. For example, Ying, a Chinese student of commerce, articulated her approach to mediate meaning and understanding in her disciplinary practices in Australian higher education:

> You need to think from other perspectives but not always from your own side to see the things. You must try different angles and sometimes you argue with yourself because you need to tell if your opinion is sustainable or has a standing . . . I have to evaluate other people's work, that's my critical thinking . . . You need to argue with yourself. When I write, of course I did argue with myself.
>
> (Ying)

Ying demonstrated a strong sense of self-reflection and critical thinking in her process of negotiating understanding in higher education. She referred to her efforts in raising and answering questions as the ways she argued with herself: 'Is this valid?', 'Is this appealing to myself at least?', 'Do I trust this statement?' The ways Ying mediated and constructed knowledge were linked to posing questions concerning the validity and reliability of others' work and re-examining her own perspective. Ying self-positioned as a student who projected an outlook that was not locked in her own circle but instead interacted with alternative perspectives. In particular, the sense of self was shown to be integrative, developmental and evolving. Ying's illustration emulates Cranton's (2002) view of transformative learning which is related to individuals' ability to critically examine their own existing views, be willing to appreciate alternatives and shift the ways they make sense of the world.

Engaging in transformative learning through linking to one's own prior experiences

Cranton (2002) and Taylor (1994) view individuals' critical reflection on their own perspectives and experiences as being instrumental in their transformative learning process. In this study all the students indicated that they actually drew on their previous personal or professional experiences, either explicitly or implicitly, in their process of constructing knowledge in Australian higher education. However, they did not always demonstrate such a validation of prior experiences on the surface of their text due to the understanding that such experiences were not expected in academic writing by their lecturers. Making the links between the theories learnt from the course and their personal experiences could lead to the development of disciplinary knowledge and the change in perspective. This is illustrated by Lin and Bình when they revealed how they drew on their personal experiences in their process of developing knowledge in their discipline during the second interview:

> Yeah. While I was reading those experts and those authors . . . I will justify my own criteria whether it suits my situation, my particular context or not.
>
> (Lin)

> Sometimes the evidence from the book is not appropriate in your own context, so you need something from your own to compare with their opinion, you can say that 'it's nice in other context but in my case, my learners are blah blah . . . so it's not appropriate'.
>
> (Bình)

Both Lin and Bình viewed their personal experience and knowledge about the specific context in their home countries as valuable resources to reflect on and be critical of the experts' opinion. Most learners indeed have a personal history, life and professional experience that they can carry with them during their journey to live and study in another country for an extended period of time. When international students move across national borders and engage in a new learning environment, memories of their life history and past experiences can become vivid and can provide them with a springboard for reflection and building upon. Lillis (2001) refers to this as the voice of experience that international students embrace in their intercultural learning context.

Both international students in the above excerpts positioned themselves as learners who are able to identify the gaps between published research they were exposed to in their study in Australia and what was actually happening in their Vietnamese and Chinese contexts. This finding echoes Taylor's (1994) comment on the relationship between transformative learning and the development of intercultural competency, and that the participant is not a 'passive recipient' of knowledge in the host learning environment but instead appears to be capable of actively negotiating their understanding of knowledge. The students' capacity to integrate and justify the validation of the knowledge they learn, based on their understanding of their own contexts and their personal experiences, matches the description by Mezirow (1991: 167) of a transformed perspective as a 'more inclusive, discriminating and integrative perspective'. However, while Mezirow's model of transformative learning does not highlight the impact of students' prior experiences on their transformative learning, this study indicates that international students actually draw on their prior experiences in their process of knowledge construction and perspective transformation in the new learning context.

Despite international students having the potential to transform their professional outlook and develop new approaches to learning, most often the unfamiliar and diverse ways of learning and constructing knowledge that they bring with them into the new learning context are considered unfit, problematic or even inferior to the conventions and the academic practices taken for granted in the host institutions (Cochran-Smith 2003). In addition, their different experiences as a result of their prior schooling, working and socialization in their home countries are often viewed as being limited or negative (Carrington 2007). If those unfamiliar experiences and transformative potential are not recognized in the educational transaction in the new context, this is a waste of pedagogical resource and cultural vistas that can be utilized to open up positive, new and challenging learning opportunities for international students, local students and teaching staff themselves.

Seeing the confrontation of hardship as the opportunity to learn and transform themselves

The international students in this study indicated that an initial source of challenge and stress could provide the foundation for personal growth and the enrichment of knowledge. For example, Wang, a Chinese student, revealed:

> Now I know everything because I went through the process and I gain a lot. I think the big success for me is that now I am confident . . . Yes, even I have to struggle and I consider the process of struggle as the way to learn things and I don't want to stick to my own ways.

> (Wang)

Wang indicated that the challenging process of meaning making in her discipline led to a consequent rise in her self-belief and confidence as well as in the development of new knowledge. This echoes Brown's (2009: 510) statement that 'self-efficacy was therefore the product of the confrontation with hardship'. The process of struggle and negotiation, the development of internal strength and the accumulation of knowledge are positively associated with one another during the international student's negotiation of higher education. The student indeed felt empowered after going through this process of negotiation.

In a similar vein, Vy, a Vietnamese student, and Ying, a Chinese student, elaborated on how their initial feelings of being challenged and pressured could be translated into a new capacity to learn and transform their ways of constructing knowledge for their course:

> In general, I love this assignment because even though I found it challenging, finally I found that I learnt something from there, the language I learnt it, new words, new kinds of expressions.
>
> (Vy)

> The whole process you work on writing the assignment, including research, finding the materials and writing is quite interesting, even though you feel pressured, sometimes depressed . . . I think that's real experience, we learn something . . . I want to make it interesting and I need to use words with imagination. This is really my understanding of things.
>
> (Ying)

The words 'struggle', 'challenging', 'hard' and 'pressured' were used by the students in association with the word 'learn' in order to refer to the growth in both personal and academic terms that they experienced as a result of the confrontation with the challenges in constructing and negotiating meaning in their discipline.

The development of new learning skills and knowledge as a result of the tough process of participating in disciplinary writing practices indeed has the potential to influence international students' further study and future life. This is also highlighted by Lin, a Chinese student:

> But here I mean though it's genius, it's quite hard, quite tough at first . . . quite a complicated learning process . . . I think what I learnt which is more important and will contribute to my further learning and my future life, not just to learn to write in English is how to do a writing, an academic writing, I mean the writing process is actually involves a lot, not just writing . . . I think, for many other things for making a presentation, for many other things, you need that kind of ability, to integrate different parts, to give order to them and to come up with the product. That's what's helpful.
>
> (Lin)

Lin attempted to make sense of her own experience through which she developed new academic skills and capacities that have long-term implications for her professional growth as well as personal life. The challenging and complex nature of the process of relocating to a new learning environment and adapting to new academic demands represents the springboard for transformative learning to take place. Importantly, the examples from international students' personal journeys of negotiating higher education show that they viewed the hardship that they went through as being positive and rewarding. This is because such hardship helps to enrich their lives, increase their resourcefulness and prepare them to deal with new challenges. This has been presented by Shearer (1994, cited in Fenimore 1997) as one of the important qualities of an 'intercultural identity' that international sojourners possess.

Conclusion

This chapter has explored the discourse of 'transformative learning' in relation to international students within the university context by looking at different vantages: the literature on international students' learning experiences, the theoretical frameworks of international education and transformative learning, university websites, the media and data from a study on international students' negotiation of disciplinary writing in higher education. The analysis reveals the contradictions of the discursive practices related to transformative learning and international students within the current context of international education. As shown in the above discussion, the international students in this study self-position as embracing an aspiration to transform themselves and actually underwent significant moves in their participation in Australian higher education. The process of negotiating higher education represents a dynamic interplay between challenges and transformative power; the removal from comfort zones and the need to overcome challenges and navigate a plurality of academic demands and values actually creates spaces for international students to undergo fundamental personal and academic changes. It is the challenging and complex nature of the process of negotiating higher education that enables international students to negotiate shifting borders, discover their internal strength and experience movements in their perspectives. This process also provides the springboard for the emergence of the newly constructed self. This study shows that international students are capable of reflecting on their own experiences, appreciating the need for change and plotting new strategies to transform themselves personally and academically. Critical self-reflection is identified as being central to international students' process of mediating higher education.

Within the current discursive practices, universities through their web pages are strategically drawing on the metaphor of 'transformative learning' as an attraction to international students. In this sense, international students are other-positioned by the university as having the potential to transform in the host learning environment, and the university self-positions as creating the environment in which international students can be effectively engaged in transformative learning. The theory of international education also constructs the internationalization of the curriculum as being related to the opportunity for both international and domestic students to be transformed. Ironically, in the public domain international students are often constructed as 'cash cows', 'users of educational services' or 'commercial products'. Furthermore, in the literature international students are mainly viewed from a problem-focused vantage. In other words, an adaptation-as-problem approach (Kim and Ruben 1988) is the dominant framework shaping the majority of studies on the academic experiences of international students. Also, within the current institutional context, most often the English and learning support unit focuses predominantly on remedying the difficulties international students face, while there is an absence of efforts placed on developing specific practices and exploring approaches to validating international students' potential and their existing but perhaps 'hidden' strengths in negotiating higher education. This discourse is contrary to the ways universities attempt to project themselves as sites embracing transformations and other-position international students as being capable of influencing academic practices and transforming their learning.

Based on the findings of this study, I would argue for the need to move beyond the discourse that problematizes international students' learning, to recognizing and reconstructing international students as having the potential to transform their learning as well as their lives. I do not view their study journey as a smooth sail, but instead acknowledge that the challenges that have been captured in the majority of the literature concerning international students studying in English-medium institutions are part of a cross-border journey and relocation in another country. However, I believe that the process through which international students' transformative potential is identified and validated deserves more empirical research and should be added to the current practices where it is mainly their challenges that are highlighted and dealt with. More research is needed to explore their aspirations in relation to transformative learning, and in particular the different layers and dimensions of international students' transformative capacity. This study also highlights the significance of the past experiences that international students draw on as a springboard for their transformative learning in the host institutions. Therefore it is critical for academics to learn about their international students' past experiences and learning traditions, and draw on these aspects as valuable resources for facilitating international students' transformative learning. This is associated with academics' attempts to adapt and change pedagogies and curricula in teaching international students. In order to capitalize on international students' transformative power, it is also imperative to identify what represents opportunities for transformative learning in working with international students in specific courses, how to create these opportunities and how to promote them effectively. This aspect should be highlighted in any conceptual framework as well as any toolkit that provides instructions about internationalizing the curriculum. This is a significant step towards ensuring that what is promised on university websites in relation to the teaching and learning of international students, and what has been theorized as central to international education, can be translated into the development of curriculum and pedagogic practices. Those practices that recognize and capitalize on international students as agents capable of mediating their own academic practices will help address international students' intrinsic motives that are bound to transformative learning, and empower them to negotiate and draw creatively on institutional practices.

References

Ballard, B. and Clanchy, J. (1995) 'Generic skills in the context of higher education', *Higher Education Research and Development*, 14, 2: 155–66.

Bochner, S. (1986) 'Coping with unfamiliar cultures: adjustment or cultural learning', *Australian Journal of Psychology*, 38, 3: 347–58.

Bond, S. (2003) *Untapped Resources: Internationalization of the Curriculum and Classroom Experience: A Selected Literature Review* (CBIE Research Millennium Series No. 7), Ottawa, ON: Canadian Bureau for International Education.

Brown, L. (2009) 'The transformative power of the international sojourn: an ethnographic study of the international student experience', *Annals of Tourism Research*, 36, 3: 502–21.

Carrington, S. (2007) 'Developing an inclusive school culture', in M. Keefe and S. Carrington (eds) *Schools and Diversity*, 2nd edn, French's Forest: Pearson Education Australia.

Coate, K. (2009) 'Exploring the unknown: Levinas and international students in English higher education', *Journal of Education Policy*, 24, 3: 271–82.

Cochran-Smith, M. (2003) 'The multiple meaning of multicultural teacher education: a conceptual framework', *Teacher Education Quarterly*, 30, 2: 7–26.

Cranton, P. (2002) 'Teaching for transformation', *New Directions for Adult and Continuing Education*, 93: 63–71.

Cushner, K. and Karim, A. (2004) 'Study abroad at the university level', in D. Landis, J. Bennett and M. Bennett (eds) *Handbook of Intercultural Training*, Thousand Oaks, CA: Sage Publications.

Elsey, B. (1990) 'Teaching and learning', in M. Kinnell (ed.) *The Learning Experiences of Overseas Students*, Suffolk: The Society for Research into Higher Education and Open University Press.

Fenimore, M.A. (1997) 'The grammar of self in second and other language learning', *International Journal of Language, Culture and Society*, 1: 1–11.

Giddens, A. (1991) *Modernity and Self-identity: Self and Society in the Late Modern Age*, Cambridge: Polity Press, in association with Oxford: Blackwell.

Green, W. (2009) 'Beyond the myths: an exploratory study of the experiences of mobile Australian students', paper presented at a seminar on researching international students' perceptions of their learning experiences, The University of the Arts, London, June 2009.

Kettle, M. (2005) 'Agency as discursive practice: from "nobody" to "somebody" as an international student in Australia', *Asia Pacific Journal of Education*, 25, 1: 45–60.

Kim, Y.Y., and Ruben, B.D. (1988) 'Intercultural transformation: a systems theory', in Y.Y. Kim and W.B. Gudykunst (eds) *Theories in Intercultural Communication*, Newbury Park, CA: Sage.

Kingston, E. and Forland, H. (2008) 'Bridging the gap in the expectations between international students and academic staff', *Journal of Studies in International Education*, 12, 2: 204–21.

Lacina, J.G. (2002) 'Preparing international students for a successful social experience in higher education', *New Directions for Higher Education*, 17, 1: 21–7.

Leask, B. (2005) 'Internationalisation of the curriculum and intercultural engagement – a variety of perspectives and possibilities', refereed paper presented at the Australian International Education Gold Coast, Queensland. Online. Available HTTP: http://www.idp.com/aiec2005/program/article17.asp (accessed 28 September 2010).

Lillis, T. (2001) *Student Writing: Access, Regulation and Desire*, New York: Routledge.

Mezirow, J. (1991) *Transformative Dimensions of Adult Learning*, San Francisco: Jossey-Bass.

—— (2000) 'Learning to think like an adult: core concepts of transformation theory', in J. Mezirow and Associates (eds) *Learning as Transformation: Critical Perspectives on a Theory in Progress*, San Francisco: Jossey-Bass.

Milstein, T. (2005) 'Transformation abroad: sojourning and the perceived enhancement of self-efficiency', *International Journal of Intercultural Relations*, 29: 217–38.

Morey, A.I. (2000) 'Changing higher education curricula for a global and multicultural world', *Higher Education in Europe*, 25, 1: 26–39.

New, C. (1994) 'Structure, agency and social transformation', *Journal for the Theory of Social Behavior*, 24, 3: 197–205.

Nguyen, C. (2007) 'A Victorian university's online identity (re)constructions: Indian international students' perspectives', paper presented at the EDUCAUSE Australasia 2007 conference, Melbourne, Australia.

Pyvis, D. and Chapman, A. (2007) 'Why university students choose an international education: a case study of Malaysia', *International Journal of Educational Development*, 27, 2: 235–46.

Robertson, M., Line, M., Jones, S. and Thomas, S. (2000) 'International students, learning environments and perceptions: a case study using the Delphi technique', *Higher Education Research and Development*, 19, 1: 89–102.

Rout, M. (2007) 'Foreign students transform city', *The Age*, 22 August 2007. Online. Available HTTP: http://www.theaustralian.news.com.au/story/0,25197,22285275-12332,00.html (accessed 28 September 2010).

Samuelowicz, K. (1987) 'Learning problems of overseas students: two sides of a story', *Higher Education Research and Development*, 16, 2: 121–32.

Study in Australia (2011) Online. Available HTTP: http://studyinaustralia.gov.au/Sia/en/Home.htm (accessed 28 September 2010).

Taylor, E. (1994) 'Intercultural competency: a transformative learning process', *Adult Education Quarterly*, 44, 3: 154–74.

Tran, L.T. (2007) 'Journey of adaptation of Chinese and Vietnamese international students to academic writing practices in higher education', unpublished Ph.D. thesis, University of Melbourne.

Tran, L.T. and Nyland, C. (2010) 'International vocational education and training: the migration and learning mix', paper presented at the 13th AVETRA conference, Gold Coast, Queensland, Australia.

Ward, C., Bochner, S. and Furnham, A. (2001) *The Psychology of Culture Shock*, Hove: Routledge.

Chapter 10

Bringing forth the graduate as a global citizen

An exploratory study of masters-level business students in Australia

Michelle C. Barker, Raymond T. Hibbins and Peter Woods

This research aims to assist researchers and practitioners to integrate internationalization principles into the formal and informal curricula of higher education so that university graduates possess the knowledge, skills and attributes of a 'global citizen'. Internationalization has been defined in the literature as 'the process of integrating an international, intercultural or global dimension into the purpose, functions or delivery of post secondary education' (Knight 2003: 1). Although definitional approaches vary widely among scholars (Francis 1993; Knight and de Wit 1995), there is general academic consensus that successful internationalization involves the integration of three interrelated aspects: 'international' (relationships between and among nations), 'intercultural' (interaction between cultures within countries, communities and institutions; the 'at home' aspect of the process) and 'global' (worldwide scope). Within this framework, internationalization involves a culmination of strategies to embed an international, multicultural and/or multilingual dimension into curricula and pedagogy, extracurricular activities, research, community and organizational policies and management systems. When designed and delivered successfully, a fully internationalized curriculum enriches the emotional, attitudinal, cognitive and behavioural elements of learning. Moreover, it builds the human and social capital that an inclusive educational institution – and the global community more broadly – requires for long-term social cohesion, economic prosperity, political stability and environmental sustainability.

The global graduate and internationalization of the curriculum

In light of the strong representation of international students in both undergraduate and postgraduate university courses throughout Australia, the higher education context provides students and staff with a unique opportunity to develop a cross-cultural awareness, appreciation and understanding of the diverse people and environments comprising the world. At present, the full potential of this learning environment is not being realized in many tertiary institutions. In particular, there is limited research in the higher education literature that examines the 'student voice' in relation to what it means to be a 'global citizen' – that is,

> a person with the ability to work, play and live somewhere other than the land of their birth . . . this person exhibits agency (is proactive and engaged in civic life) and primacy (has the capacity to make change happen). At the emotional and philosophical level, the global citizen considers herself to be transnational: committed to the human issues no matter in what nation state they occur.
>
> (Bryant 2006: 2)

According to current literature, individuals who are classified as global citizens demonstrate the *knowledge*, *skills* and *attitudes/values* needed to thrive in a world characterized by global mobility and social, cultural, economic, political and environmental interconnectivity (see Figure 10.1). First, it is widely recognized that global citizens possess *knowledge*, *awareness* and *understanding* of areas such as: a) equity, social justice, human rights and related social, economic and political issues; b) globalization and interdependence, and the implications for sustainable development; c) intercultural and transnational issues relevant to professional practice; and d) one's own culture and its perspectives, and other peoples' cultures and their perspectives. Second, global citizens demonstrate the unique ability to: a) think globally and consider controversial international issues from a variety of perspectives (e.g. social, cultural, economic, political, religious); b) critically analyse and challenge conventional thinking, injustice and inequalities; and c) interact, cooperate and empathize with people from different social, cultural, religious and linguistic backgrounds, both locally and globally. Finally, global citizens also demonstrate attitudes, beliefs and values such as: a) an appreciation of, and value and respect for, global, multicultural and multilingual diversity; b) a commitment to engage in informed debate about topical issues of equity, social justice, human rights and related social, economic and political issues; c) a desire to participate in, and contribute to, creating an equitable and sustainable community; d) an appreciation of the complex, interacting factors that contribute to diversity of language, culture and multicultural relationships; and e) sensitivity to, and awareness of, complex human–environment relationships, and a willingness to act in a manner consistent with the new needs and demands facing society.

In sum, global citizenship reflects the capacity of individuals to adapt to different people, cultures and environments throughout the world and the ability to manage this interconnectedness harmoniously and productively. It is achieved through an interactive process whereby students and staff from different socio-cultural backgrounds exchange knowledge, skills, attitudes and experiences so as to enhance their understanding and appreciation of, and capacity to operate successfully within, a range of local, national and international communities.

However, the concept of global citizenship is contested by some researchers, who suggest that we should aim to produce students who have developed a

Key characteristics of a 'global citizen'

Knowledge and understanding	Skills and abilities	Attitudes and values
– Knowledge of equity, social justice, human rights and related social, economic and political issues – Knowledge of globalization and interdependence, and the short- and long-term implications for sustainable development – Understanding of how the world operates (socially, culturally, economically, technologically, politically and environmentally) – Recognition of the impact of local, national and international actions and decisions for local, national and international communities and environments – Understanding of how knowledge may be constructed differently across cultures in different disciplines – Recognition of intercultural and transnational issues relevant to professional practice – Awareness of own culture and its perspectives, and other cultures and their perspectives – Recognition of one's membership of, and responsibilities within, both a local and a global society	– Ability to think 'globally' to consider issues from a variety of different perspectives (e.g. social, cultural, economic, political, religious, etc.) – Critical analysis of (and the ability to challenge) conventional thinking, injustice and inequality – Ability to interact and empathize with people from different social, cultural, religious and linguistic backgrounds, both locally and globally – Effective leadership, cooperation and teamwork skills – Ability to engage in problem-solving, shared perspective-taking and negotiation to resolve conflicts	– Appreciation of, and value and respect for, global, multicultural and multilingual diversity – Commitment to engage in informed debate about issues of equity, social justice, human rights and related social, economic and political issues – Committed to justice, equality, environmental sustainability and civic obligations – Commitment to participate in, and contribute toward, creating an equitable and sustainable community at a range of levels (from the local to the global) – Appreciation of the complex interacting factors that contribute to diversity of language, culture and multicultural relationships – Sensitivity to, and awareness of, complex human–environment interactions and a willingness to act in a manner consistent with the changing needs and demands facing society – Sense of identity, self-esteem and belief that people can make a difference to the world

Figure 10.1 Summary of some of the key characteristics that define an individual who is categorized as a 'global citizen'.

Source: Based on an integration of conceptual definitions from Brownlie (2001), Bryant (2006), Edwards *et al.* (2003), Hower (2003), Oxfam (2006) and Tarrant and Sessions (2008).

global mindset (Earley *et al.* 2007) or 'cultural intelligence'. Cultural intelligence is defined as a person's capability to adapt effectively to new cultural contexts, and it has both process and content features (Earley and Peterson 2004). The three facets in the structure of the concept are the cognitive and meta-cognitive facet, the motivational facet and the behavioural facet, as outlined in Figure 10.2. The first facet relates to Earley and Erez's theory (1997) on explaining cultural influences on work behaviour by focusing on an individual's self-identity as an active interpreter of a society's norms and values. The self is understood to be a person's mental representation of their own personality and identity formed through experience and thought (Earley 2002). Knowing oneself, coupled with the cognitive flexibility to be able to reshape and adapt one's cognitive self-concept, is an important part of effectively relating across cultures. Within the cognitive facet, a person also needs strong reasoning skills to be able to engage in inductive reasoning to help sort out and make sense of many social and environmental clues when in a multicultural environment (Earley 2002). Metacognition, or 'thinking about thinking', is important as it enables someone in a culturally unfamiliar environment to reflect on what they are thinking and then put together 'patterns into a coherent picture even if one does not know what this coherent picture will look like' (Earley 2002: 277). Given the recent research on US college students by Arum and Roksa (2011) where they found critical thinking and complex reasoning to be skills developed in either an exceedingly small proportion of the students or empirically non-existent, it will be interesting to see the extent to which students in this present study will have developed these higher cognitive and meta-cognitive skills so essential to cultural intelligence.

A relatively unique aspect of cross-cultural adaptation presented by the cultural intelligence framework is the inclusion of a motivational facet (Earley and Peterson 2004). Self-efficacy is an important component of the motivational facet, as successful intercultural interactions depend on the individual's belief in their own

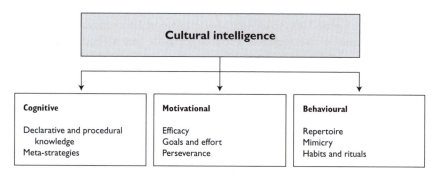

Figure 10.2 Facets of cultural intelligence.
Source: Earley 2002: 274.

ability to navigate social discourse in an unfamiliar setting. Coupled with this is the perseverance to re-engage despite obstacles and setbacks. The individual's goals in the new cultural environment will also play a role in the amount of effort they will be willing to expend in succeeding in cross-cultural interactions.

The model of cultural intelligence argues that knowing what to do and being motivated to persist in getting it right in a culturally unfamiliar environment must be complemented by the possession of a repertoire of situation appropriate behaviours. This repertoire should include some aptitude for learning languages, as Earley (2002) argues that a person with a low aptitude for acquiring languages will have low cultural intelligence. The ability to mimic can also help a person to copy appropriate behaviours and then learn the circumstances to which the behaviour can be applied. Thus, the model would appear to add weight to those who argue for an emphasis on the requirement for university undergraduates to learn a foreign language (Altbach and Knight 2007). This practice is still common in universities in non-English and some English-speaking countries (Nunan 2003).

However, in regard to international students, developing these attributes in addition to adapting to an unfamiliar cultural climate can be particularly challenging. Throughout their adaptation to a new cultural climate, international students may experience unrealistic parental pressures, time management problems, loneliness, problems in adjusting to different learning styles and assessment regimes, and language-specific demands of assignments. According to Ong (2009) they could also be experiencing depression, discrimination in the workplace, difficulties establishing friendships, inter-group conflict, intra-group conflict and relationship problems. In addition, international students may be finding that the pedagogy and curriculum are highly at odds with their prior learning experiences and the educational traditions of their own culture (Wallace and Dunn 2008). These international students may be experiencing culture shock or cognitive dissonance, thus making the learning experience problematic.

Accordingly, it is necessary to examine current international students' definitions of global citizens to determine what aspects of internationalization need to be addressed in curriculum by trained facilitators that may assist future international students. Specifically, the present study applied contemporary research on global citizenship (see Figure 10.1) to identify how international students defined a global citizen in terms of the required knowledge, skills and attitudes. Students' definitions of a global citizen will also be discussed in light of the cultural intelligence framework (see Figure 10.2).

Method

Participants

The sample comprised 62 postgraduate students (26 females, 35 males and 1 unspecified) who were enrolled in a postgraduate business course entitled International Human Resource Management (IHRM) at a large Australian university. The course provided students with the opportunity to explore international dimensions of the core aspects of IHRM, such as linkage with international business strategy and structure, recruitment, compensation and reward management, training and development, performance management and industrial relations. The course aimed to provide students with a working knowledge of some contemporary approaches to international HRM using highly interactive teaching methods. Thus, active student participation and contribution during classes and group work activities were vital for effective learning. Throughout the 13-week course, students were required to complete three assessment tasks: 1) an oral presentation (30 per cent) in which students formed small groups (≈ 5 members) and chose a HRM function or issue – such as performance management, staff retention, recruitment, expatriate repatriation – and analysed how the function or issue is addressed in two different cultures or countries; 2) a written critical essay (30 per cent) in which students engaged in research, critical analysis and discussion about the nature of particular issues in IHRM; and 3) a final exam (40 per cent) which assessed students' understanding, application and critical analysis of the theory, practice and case studies relevant to IHRM that were discussed during the lectures and tutorials. Thus, the course aimed to develop the cross-cultural knowledge and skills of students, and provide a 'cross-cultural experience' as students worked together in multicultural groups.

The vast majority of the course participants (93.5 per cent) were enrolled on a full-time basis and had been studying at university for either one to two semesters (39.3 per cent) or three to four semesters (36.1 per cent). The sample comprised both domestic students (8.1 per cent) and international students (91.9 per cent), with slightly more than half (54.8 per cent) of all international students residing in Australia for one to three years (54.8 per cent). Forty-four students (74.1 per cent) were 21 to 26 years of age, seven students (11.5 per cent) were 27 to 30 years of age, and ten students (16.4 per cent) were 30 to 45 years of age. The total sample comprised students with highly diverse countries of origin, including India (37.1 per cent), China (12.9 per cent), Australia (8.1 per cent), Vietnam (6.5 per cent) and Colombia (4.8 per cent), among many others. The ethnic identity of participants was equally as diverse, with the majority of students identifying themselves as either Indian (29 per cent), Chinese (6.1 per cent), Anglo-Australian (8.1 per cent), Vietnamese (4.8 per cent), Latin-American (4.8 per cent), African (3.2 per cent) or Hindu (3.2 per cent). Accordingly, 29 per cent of students spoke at least one language other than English, including Chinese (8.1 per cent), Gujarati Hindi (3.2 per cent), Gujarati Hindi/Marathi (3.2 per cent), Hindi (4.8 per cent), Japanese (3.2 per cent) and Punjabi Hindi (3.2 per cent). Most participants rated their oral and written English ability as being strong (52.5 per cent and 46.7 per cent, respectively) or moderate (42.6 per cent and 54.7 per cent, respectively). Finally, participants demonstrated varying levels of prior work experience, with 29.5 per cent of participants having no previous experience, 24.6 per cent of participants having less than one year of experience and 31.1 per cent of participants having two to five years of experience. Of the

32.3 per cent of participants who had some form of prior work experience, specific occupations were largely centred on the professional areas of finance and accounting (4.8 per cent), management (9.6 per cent), human resources (8.0 per cent), information technology (6.4 per cent), customer service (6.4 per cent) and marketing (3.2 per cent)

Procedure

We collected qualitative data from participants by conducting nine small focus-group sessions using the nominal group technique, lasting for approximately 90 minutes in duration. Each session was coordinated by a well-trained group facilitator and involved approximately eight to ten participants in nine groups. The general procedure for the data collection process proceeded as follows. First, upon arrival at the classroom the focus-group facilitator welcomed participants and provided a brief summary of the background, rationale and overall objectives of the research. Participants were explicitly informed that they were free to: a) withdraw from the group session at any time without explanation or prejudice; and b) withdraw any unprocessed data previously supplied. The focus-group facilitator also reiterated that confidentiality and anonymity of participants' verbal and written responses would be safeguarded, and that no identifying or personally sensitive information would be collected. For ease of data collection and analysis, participants were then asked to provide informed written consent for the sessions to be audio-taped. After agreeing to participate, participants were asked to provide basic demographic information (i.e. age, gender and ethnic background).

Next, the focus-group facilitator prompted participants to engage in a collaborative discussion about what it means to be a graduate who is a 'global citizen'. This discussion made specific reference to the following question: 'This University aims to produce graduates who are "global citizens". How would you describe someone who is a "global citizen"?' A nominal group technique (see Delbecq et al. 1975) was utilized to facilitate effective, efficient and equitable group decision-making. This technique involves four rounds where participants write individual answers to questions, which are listed on a board, followed by the group combining and refining common answers. Finally, participants deliver three 'votes' on the best answer to each question, with three points for the best answer, and so on. Votes are delivered simultaneously, with participants placing coloured stickers next to their chosen responses on the board. This technique requires responses from all participants, and helps to reduce domination of the discussion by any one participant. At the conclusion of the session, participants were verbally debriefed and thanked for their participation.

Nominal group technique

As mentioned above, we utilized the nominal group technique (ibid.), as it produces information related to the issue under investigation that can be prioritized within the group discussion to develop group answers (Potter et al.

2004). It is an effective technique for increasing a group's capacity to generate ideas and can be an effective and efficient decision-making technique (Ng 2000). The main advantage of the nominal group technique is that it allows for each member of the group to have equal participation or voice in sharing ideas. Potter *et al.* (2004) explain that researcher bias is minimized by using the nominal group technique due to the highly structured nature of the process and the direct involvement of participants in both data collection and analysis. The technique enabled us to produce a useful range of responses to our question on student views of the meaning of the term 'global citizen' and we report these in the next section.

Results

In all, nine groups of participants responded to the discussion question, 'This University aims to produce graduates who are "global citizens". How would you describe someone who is a "global citizen?"' Guided by the nominal group procedure, each group provided their top three descriptions of a 'global citizen' to the research team (see Table 10.1).

Content analysis (Weber 1990) was employed to assign descriptions into three categories by two independent coders, based upon the components of global citizenship: knowledge, attitude and skills. Audio-taped segments of the activity were also used to aid analysis. An overview of the types of responses assigned to each category is discussed in the following sections.

Knowledge

Seven out of nine groups provided at least one description that related to the knowledge component of global citizenship. Overall, descriptions covered a number of facets of the knowledge component of global citizenship but were general in nature. For example, groups frequently described a global citizen as someone who had 'knowledge', 'awareness' or an 'understanding' of people from different cultures.

Attitude

Seven out of nine groups also provided at least one description that related to the attitude component of global citizenship. Similar to the descriptions contained in the knowledge category, descriptions of attitudes of global citizens were general in nature. Descriptions of attitudes included either being accepting or respectful of other cultures.

Skills

Out of all three components of global citizenship, the skills component was the most frequently mentioned type of response amongst the nine groups. Each

Table 10.1 Group descriptions of someone who is a global citizen

Group	Response
Group 1	1 Ability to work in a multicultural environment/team
	2 A person who shares his/her knowledge with people from other countries
	3 Someone who is able to adapt to whatever global environment they are in
Group 2	1 Being aware of other people's and one's own culture, respecting and adapting not through stereotypes but through understanding and exposure
	2 Being able to accept cultures and adopt their best practices
	3 Cooperate
Group 3	1 Being able to master two languages and has experience as an expatriate
	2 Culturally understanding and sensitive, willing to learn about other cultures
	3 Good communication skills and can work in any environment
Group 4	1 Respect and tolerate and use an appropriate communication style
	2 Awareness and acceptance of cultural diversity
	3 Integrate and understand other cultures and be a 'people person'
Group 5	1 Someone who can adopt any culture and work in a multicultural team
	2 One who has knowledge and skills of different cultures and one who is flexible and adaptable
	3 Someone who respects others' cultures, opinions and beliefs regardless of their race, ethnicity and religion
Group 6	1 Respect
	2 Definitional concerns with the label 'global citizen'
	3 Knowledge of many cultures
Group 7	1 Openness/awareness
	2 Fluidity/global acceptance
	3 Flexibility
Group 8	1 Be accepting – national and international
	2 Someone who can integrate well in other cultures
	3 'Global mind'– influenced by mass communication
Group 9	1 An individual who can adapt to new environments, i.e. is flexible
	2 Thinks 'globally' (e.g. understands the world beyond their local region) and acts 'locally'
	3 Can contribute by work and practice locally, nationally and internationally for the development of humanity and communities to make the world a better place

group mentioned at least one description that related to the skills component of global citizenship and four groups provided descriptions relating to this component more than once. The skill descriptions of global citizens were also more detailed across groups than the former two categories.

Descriptions relating to effective communication skills were the most frequently cited. This included general descriptions such as 'good communication skills', 'a people person' and an 'appropriate communication style', as well as descriptions relating specifically to cross-cultural communication such as 'a person who shares his/her knowledge with people from other countries' and the ability to 'master two languages'.

Two other types of skill were also cited as skills of a global citizen. First, participants recognized that a global citizen should be able to 'adapt to new environments' and be 'flexible'. Second, participants also recognized that the abilities to 'work in a multicultural team' and 'cooperate' with others were also important skills of a global citizen in a professional setting.

Conclusion

For the present study, students were able to provide more extensive descriptions of the skills required to be a global citizen than the knowledge and attitudes. In particular, students were able to identify that effective communication with people from cultural backgrounds different from their own was an important skill. Students also recognized that effective communication needs to be tailored to professional contexts that involve working with others in a team, especially with people from different cultural backgrounds. However, students did not identify skills of a more cognitive nature, such as the ability to think analytically about other peoples' perspectives, a feature of the previously described cultural intelligence model. This lack of development of higher-order cognitive and meta-cognitive skills is consistent with the findings in the US study of college students by Arum and Roksa (2011). According to the cultural intelligence framework (Earley 2002), a person also needs strong reasoning skills to be able to engage in inductive reasoning to help sort out and make sense of many social and environmental clues when in a multicultural environment.

Students' descriptions of the knowledge and attitudes of global citizens suggest that future curriculum needs to focus on these aspects of global citizenship in particular. Descriptions of knowledge and attitudes were less frequent and detailed than skill descriptions, suggesting that the knowledge and attitudes of global citizenship may be too abstract for students. In regard to the knowledge component of global citizenship, students were able to identify that global citizens should be able to understand and be aware of other cultures. However, there are many different facets to take into account when understanding other cultures and their impact on a global mindset. This involves being aware of and understanding not only the differences between one's own culture and other cultures, but also how these differences in perspectives interact and affect a number of different global issues (see Figure 10.1). This would include an understanding of the influence of ethnocentrism on members of particular cultures, including one's own, and the role stereotyping plays in cultural interactions.

For the attitudes component of global citizenship, students recognized that global citizens need to be accepting and respectful about cultures different from their own. Future curriculum may need to further aid students to recognize that attitudes of global citizenship involve many factors that stem from the acceptance and respect of other cultures. For example, it is also necessary for global citizens to be committed to, and open to, engaging in informed debates, about a variety of global issues, and believe that it is possible to change the world for the better (see Figure 10.1). Appreciation of the values underpinning particular national/ cultural positions on particular issues like climate change, the role of entrepreneurship in business, collectivity versus individualism, appropriate gendered behaviour in business enterprises and deference to age in business organizations would be essential here.

There is the opportunity in multicultural educational institutions to engage in strategies that emphasize experiential learning that will facilitate students to develop the knowledge, skills and attitudes of being global citizens. Experiential learning of these components of global citizenship may aid students in understanding these components from a less abstract nature. These three components (shown in Figure 10.1), when introduced to students, could potentially result in cognitive dissonance because they are being decoded by individuals from different cultures with inherited frameworks with differing perceptions and values. Such dissonance, if handled by skilled facilitators and enablers in the classroom, could provide opportunities for building emergent understandings and new frameworks from personal experience (Wang 2008). This latter outcome recognizes the power of human agency by privileging reflective dialogue, and seeks to enhance intercultural sensitivity, mutual understanding and reciprocal relationships during the interactive process between partners in intercultural construction. This may be facilitated where students are made aware, through appropriate learning experiences and reflection, of how their own culture affects their perceptions and judgements.

In addition, future research could address whether personal or socio-cultural difficulties experienced by international students (Ong 2009) influence their abilities to define global citizenship. It may be that there are particular barriers and constraints to interactions in educational institutions that affect international students' ability to interact with and adapt to environments culturally different from those to which they are accustomed. In turn, these variables may affect the reasoning skills required to understand the reality of displaying global citizenship qualities in daily and professional practice. Hence, further intervention for these students, or tailored programmes addressing these barriers, may be necessary.

In conclusion, it was clear to students from the present study that communication skills are central to the development of global citizens, but there are also further skills, knowledge and attitudes that are important as well. Of utmost importance for future academic staff will be the handling of value analysis, with particular emphasis on the use of strategies and experiential learning that will facilitate an ability to work effectively and productively in diverse workplaces that may reside in complex and sometimes unpredictable contexts.

Acknowledgement

The authors acknowledge with thanks the assistance of Melissa Legg in the analyses and review of this chapter.

References

Altbach, P.G. and Knight, J. (2007) 'The internationalization of higher education: motivations and realities', *Journal of Studies in International Education*, 11: 290–305.

Arum, R. and Roksa, J. (2011) *Academically Adrift: Limited Learning on College Campuses*, Chicago: University of Chicago Press.

Brownlie, A. (2001) *Citizenship Education: The Global Dimension*, London: DEA.

Bryant, D. (2006) *The Everyone, Everywhere: Global Dimensions of Citizenship*. Online. Available HTTP: http://www.compact.org/resources/future-of-campus-engagement/the-everyone-everywhere-global-dimensions-of-citizenship/4259/ (accessed 17 April 2009).

Delbecq, A.L., Van de Ven, A.H. and Gustafson, D.H. (1975) *Group Techniques for Program Planners*, Glenview, IL: Scott Foresman and Company.

Earley, P.C. (2002) 'Redefining interactions across cultures and organizations: moving forward with cultural intelligence', in B.M. Staw and R.M. Kramer (eds) *Research in Organizational Behavior* (Volume 24), Oxford: Elsevier Science.

Earley, P.C. and Erez, M. (1997) *The Transplanted Executive*, Oxford: Oxford University Press.

Earley, P.C. and Peterson, R.S. (2004) 'The elusive cultural chameleon: cultural intelligence as a new approach to intercultural training for the global manager', *Academy of Management Learning and Education*, 31: 100–15.

Earley, P.C., Murnieks, C. and Mosakowski, E. (2007) 'Cultural intelligence and the global mindset', in T. Devinney, T. Pedersen and L. Tihanyi (eds) *The Global Mindset: Advances in International Management* (Volume 19), Bradford: Emerald Group Publishing Limited.

Edwards, R., Gosling, G., Petrovic-Lazarovic, S. and O'Neill, P. (2003) 'Internationalisation of business education: meaning and implementation', *Higher Education Research and Development*, 22, 3: 183–192.

Francis, A. (1993) *Facing the Future: The Internationalization of Post-Secondary Institutions in British Columbia*, Vancouver, BC: British Columbia Centre for International Education.

Hower, M. (2003) 'The making of a global citizen', in B. Holland and J. Meeropol (eds) *A More Perfect Vision: The Future of Campus Engagement*, Providence, RI: Campus Compact. Online. Available HTTP: http://www.compact.org/category/resources/future-of-campus-engagement/ (accessed 11 June 2012).

Knight, J. (2003) 'Updated internationalisation definition', *International Higher Education*, 33: 2–3.

Knight, J. and de Wit, H. (1995) 'Strategies for internationalisation of higher education: historical and conceptual perspectives', in H. de Wit (ed.) *Strategies for Internationalisation of Higher Education*, Amsterdam: EAIE.

Ng, P. (2000) 'Applying nominal group method to needs identification in Hong Kong mental health services', *Administration and Policy in Mental Health*, 27: 247–52.

Nunan, D. (2003) 'The impact of English as a global language on educational policies and practices in the Asia-Pacific region', *TESOL Quarterly*, 37: 589–613.

Ong, D. (2009) *The International Student's Handbook: Living and Studying in Australia*, Sydney: UNSW Press.

Oxfam (2006) *Education for Global Citizens: A Guide for Schools*, Oxford: Oxfam.

Potter, M., Gordon, S. and Hamer, P. (2004) 'The nominal group technique: a useful consensus methodology in physiotherapy research', *New Zealand Journal of Physiotherapy*, 32: 126–30.

Tarrant, M. and Sessions, L. (2008) 'Promoting global citizenship: educational travel and study abroad programs in the South Pacific', paper presented at the ISANA International Education Association 19th International Conference, Skycity Convention Centre, Auckland, New Zealand.

Wallace, M. and Dunn, L. (2008) 'Experiences of transnational learning: perspectives from some undergraduates in the People's Republic of China and Singapore', in L. Dunn and M. Wallace (eds) *Teaching in Transnational Higher Education: Enhancing Learning for Offshore International Students*, New York: Routledge.

Wang, T. (2008) 'Intercultural dialogue and understanding: implications for teachers', in L. Dunn and M. Wallace (eds) *Teaching in Transnational Higher Education: Enhancing Learning for Offshore International Students*, New York: Routledge.

Weber, R.P. (1990) *Basic Content Analysis*, Newbury Park, CA: Sage.

Chapter 11

Entrepreneurial identities of international students at UK business schools

Yu-Ching Kuo

Introduction

This chapter aims to propose a new way of considering international students as entrepreneurs and as autonomous agents of their lives in the context of entrepreneurial discourses. The entrepreneurial identity construction of international students is produced and reproduced through negotiations of entrepreneurialism and its interrelated and competing discourses, such as international students as victims, problems, beneficiaries, learners and customers. In this chapter, I explore international students' entrepreneurial identity by considering them as autonomous agents who demand long-term perspectives and plans for their own lives to face future challenges and opportunities. I then examine how the negotiating space for gaining ownership of their learning is generated in the context of entrepreneurial discourses.

Approaching the study

My ontological and epistemological positions were oriented towards social constructivism, which influenced my selection of literature and shaped the methodological features and analytical scope. This study draws out the theoretical perspectives of interactionists, focusing on identity theorists. More specifically, three theoretical foundation features are identified and contextualized: international students have multifaceted selves consisting of multiple identities; identity construction is a process of stimulus and responses; and international students are both recipients of and contributors to entrepreneurial discourses.

This study focuses on business schools in the United Kingdom, which have relatively more international students than other disciplines, according to the data released by the Higher Education Statistic Agency (HESA) in the UK (Kuo 2010). Drawing on ethnographic approaches, the empirical aspect of the study consisted of a qualitative analysis. Semi-structured, in-depth interviews were conducted with more than 50 international students and 22 university staff at different levels across universities (vice/deputy chancellors, deans of school, heads of international offices and academic staff) in four UK universities' business schools: two were pre-1992 universities (here called Greenford and Whiteford) and two were post-1992 universities (Bluefield and Redfield).

For the reason of ethical concerns, I refer to interviewees without giving their real names, as they were guaranteed confidentiality. Each institution and interviewee is given a unique code whenever they are mentioned in this chapter. I adapt the voice-centred relational method from Mauthner and Doucet (1998; also see Brown and Gilligan 1992) in which there are four categories of reading involved: reading for the plot and for our responses to the narrative; reading for the voice of the 'I'; reading for the relationships; and placing people within cultural contexts and social structures (Mauthner and Doucet 1998). My analytical scope is influenced by both interactionism and post-structural concepts of discourses and ideas. The scope spans the micro–macro continuum, from individual overseas students, to interpersonal relationships between overseas students and university staff at different levels, to the role that the UK higher education institutions (HEIs) play in the construction of entrepreneurial discourses.

Limitations

This study has three major limitations. First, I did not examine the influence of demographic characteristics, for instance, how international students' nationality, religion, ethnicity, age, social class or linguistic background could influence the way in which they negotiate their entrepreneurial identity. Therefore, I recommend that future studies investigate the dimensions and dynamic relationships between demographic characteristics and the way in which international students construct their entrepreneurial identity.

The second limitation is that my empirical research focused on business schools. Therefore, I cannot answer the question of whether the experiences of international students in business studies might be different from students in other disciplines without conducting further empirical studies. To address this limitation, I recommend that future studies include university staff and international students from different ranges of academic disciplines.

Third, the issue of a relatively small sample may be challenging. As mentioned previously, I conducted this study at two post-1992 and two pre-1992 universities, both focusing primarily on teaching postgraduate business courses. Undergraduate and postgraduate study courses (M.Phil., Ph.D.) were excluded. However, I am aware that a future study may need to consider to what extent interactions between different levels of international students and university staff affect the entrepreneurial identity constructions of international students.

International students as victims and as problems

The identity of the international student as an entrepreneur is under-researched. This is partly because, in the discourse of entrepreneurialism, the debates and discussions are latently entwined with the construction of international students as victims (who are unfairly treated in the UK), as problems (tarnishing the higher quality of UK higher education, as a result of which HEIs over-promote and emphasize the synthesis between their learner and customer identities) and as beneficiaries of the marketization of higher education (who enjoy exercising their rights as customers) (Kuo 2010).

The view of international students as victims, problems or beneficiaries is a partial picture depicted by some literature that overshadows many out-performances of international students. For example:

> We have seen no evidence beyond anecdotal, often anonymous, reports that entry standards are being lowered for overseas students. In fact, the highest performing students at Russell Group universities are just as likely to be international students as they are UK students. In 2006/07, according to HESA data, 16% of overseas (non-EU) students at Russell Group institutions obtained a first class honours degree, compared to 15% of UK students. This is a clear indication of the high standard of overseas students that achieve a place at our universities and the commitment they have to their studies.
>
> (Russell Group of Universities 2009: 409)

There are many other facets of international students' lives that are either omitted or misinterpreted in the literature. Leonard and Morley argue that 'some studies use it valuably to explore inter- and intra-personal student experiences', while 'others are in danger of medicalizing and socially decontextualizing stress, isolation etc.' (2003: 5). International students were constructed 'in a victim role – as in need of rescue and "help"' (ibid). Bartram notes that there is a danger in which 'students themselves might also come to accept this rather impoverished view – a view clearly antithetical to supporting the development of the independent and self-directing learner that higher education arguably aims to promote' (2006: 3). Aligned with Leonard and Morley and Bartram, arguably, if university staff consider that these international students are victims or problematic objects, and accordingly in need of rescue, then the former could transmit a pessimistic feeling to the latter through their daily interactions and communication. Not only could these pessimistic feelings harm international students, it can also bring about a revictimization.

Furthermore, the discourse of international students as a 'problem' is politically articulated through recent debates and policy developments with regard to international student visa regulations. This discourse has been publicly debated in two respects. In respect of academic performance, the quality and the English language proficiency of international students has received sufficient public attention in the UK since the summer of 2008. The former chief executive of the Quality Assurance Agency, Peter Williams, expressed his concern with regard to the tendency of some UK HEIs to be over-dependent on international student fees. Williams noted 'the current degree classification system is arbitrary and unreliable', warning of 'universities which have become financially dependent on the higher fees of international students' (Coughlan 2008). Alderman added:

In my view, over the past twenty or so years, there has been a systemic failure to maintain appropriate academic standards in British higher education, with the result that these standards have measurably declined. I place the primary responsibility for this at the door of university chief executives (generally vice-chancellors) . . . In particular, vice-chancellors have permitted and indeed encouraged the decline in academic standards in the desperate search for . . . increased income from 'full cost' fee-paying international students.

(Alderman 2009: 73–4)

In the political respect, 'a link appears to have been drawn between low levels of English (of international students) and high risk immigration profiles' (Schmitt 2010: presentation slide 11). As Theresa May, the UK Home Secretary, puts it:

In higher education alone, international students contributed some £2.2 billion in 2008/09 to their institutions in tuition fees, and if personal off-campus expenditure is included, we estimate the figure approaches £5 billion . . . But it also raises questions about consistency of the quality of international students and the courses they follow. I am concerned that the UK is attracting students who aren't always the brightest and best. The Government wants to ensure that those who enter on a student visa genuinely come here to study, not to work or with a view to settling here.

(UK Border Agency 2010: 3)

These two different debates concerning international students as problems are politically articulated. The discourse of international students as problems, as Sen (2006) may say, includes 'not only descriptive misinterpretation, but also the illusion of a singular identity that others must attribute to the person to be demeaned' (2006: 8). The legitimated international students are likely to be penalized by this political articulation. The danger of this discourse is to cause international students unnecessary stress, while undertaking their academic and socio-cultural challenges in the UK, wasting efforts that the university student teams made to enhance their experiences.

Negotiating the entrepreneurial identity

The idea of international students as entrepreneurs is not new. Mars *et al.* argue that students are not simply targets and victims of the trend of this com-mercialization of education. Students can be 'active entrepreneurial agents promoting a new knowledge regime' (2008: 638). Their study was contextualized in the setting of which state-sponsored students learn knowledge and entre-preneurial strategies from faculty members in academic faculties initiated for commercial ventures. They suggest that the development of students' roles, as learners of entrepreneurship and as entrepreneurs are shaped by professors and student peers within and beyond the classroom as well as by an array of organizations and social structures inside and outside of universities

(Mars *et al.*: 639).

In the same vein as Mars *et al.*'s study, the present contribution suggests that the entrepreneurial identity of international students is different from their customer identity. Some international students in this study had entrepreneurial spirit, which was marked by personal commitment to:

- 'create something new, something different; they change or transmute values' (Drucker 1994: 20);
- understand themselves in terms of 'their success or failure in acquiring the skills and making the choice to actualise oneself' (Rose 1999: 87);
- have belief in their own destiny, welcome changes and are not frightened of the unknown (Heelas 1991: 73);
- be willing to 'take the initiative to make changes in their own lives and take responsibility for themselves' (ibid.); and
- be determined to prepare themselves for 'survival and success in their own economic futures and to develop entrepreneurial skills and an attitude of self-reliance' (Hartshorn 2002: 150).

As I argued in my doctoral study, the concept of the customer relationship is adapted from for-profit organizations by many HEIs to 'look after' international students as customers, because their financial contributions are considered to be significant to their institutions. Some HEIs could 'deliver' what international students want and need by blurring the lines between regarding them as learners and as customers (Kuo 2010).

Some UK HEIs introduce customer care policies to manage student experiences. International students 'could be dehumanised by the current mechanical and bureaucratic systems, which, paradoxically, are designed to enhance their experiences' (ibid.: 212). Along with UK governments' international student visa policy, mechanical and bureaucratic systems of the HEIs reveal signs of dehumanization that might have deprived international students of human character or attributes (op. cit.), on the one hand. On the other hand, it can be argued that the mechanical and bureaucratic systems of the HEIs might jeopardize international students' experience by seeing them as 'infantilised adults' (Nayak and Beckett 2008: 408).

Some international students in this study were aware that their institutions were increasingly enterprising. They felt that some university staff regarded them as customers. Nevertheless, these students preferred not to look at themselves as customers, largely because, in an educational context, they were not authorized to exercise rights like customers in the commercial world. Furthermore, some international students rejected their customer identity and have been persistent in their learner identity, because they have strong intrinsic motivations for their study in the UK. What they looked for was pleasure and satisfaction from their study. These international students tend to believe that their study would increase their employability prospects and enrich their life experiences after they finished.

Customers and entrepreneurs are two different identities. Unlike customer identity, which emphasizes the way international students, as customers, consume knowledge-based products as a market good and a saleable commodity (Newson 1998; also see Buchbinder 1993; Blackwell and Gibson-Sweet 1998), the entrepreneurial identity highlights the fact that they are self-reliant individuals, enthusiastic to pursue their self-defined interests energetically and determined to achieve personal satisfaction. In other words, international students with entrepreneurial identity are more likely to have 'self-governing capabilities' (Rose 1996: 155) and 'aspire to autonomy' (Rose 1998: 151). These international students are autonomous agents of their lives and want to take responsibility for the consequences of their decisions. Yet, the components of self-governing capabilities or autonomy of international students have not yet received much attention when it comes to the issue regarding the *international student experience*. Under the market mechanism, in which international students are regarded as customers, the student experience becomes a measurable concept, suggesting that there is interplay between a high level of student customer satisfaction and good student experiences (Douglas *et al.* 2007; Middlehurst and Woodfield 2007). Neither were self-governing capabilities or student autonomy considered to be criteria for the student experience surveys, nor were these components of international students measurable.

Additionally, in the majority of this study, participants stated the reasons that UK HEIs were attractive to them. These reasons included 'the academic reputation of UK degrees', 'wider range and variety of courses' and 'requiring new knowledge and competencies'. Despite slight differences, these reasons are interconnected. International students either come with scholarships (sponsored either by their governments or by their employers) or come to the UK self-funded with the purpose of making innovative transformations in their lives, such as creating a new career path.

International students tend to believe that their experience of studying in the UK would eventually meet 'a desire for self-realisation and personal enrichment' (Wagner 1999: 130). However, some scholars have linked student mobility and academic or cultural imperialism (e.g. Bourdieu and Wacquant 1999; Alatas 2003). For many research participants, undertaking business-related masters degrees involves 'gaining acceptance as an integral element of entrepreneurial practice and study' (Cope 2005: 373). Some of them were extremely eager to perform as entrepreneurs who 'come to understand themselves in terms of their success or failure in acquiring the skills and making the choice to actualise oneself' (Rose 1999:87). These students, as Rose (2000a) would say, have not 'opened up, in diverse ways, to interventions conducted in the name of subjectivity'. However, they are the motivated subjects who have been 'equipped with an internal dynamic orientation to the world, with needs to be shaped and satisfied' (2000a: sub-section Ethics, para. 4). They also have been the creative subjects who strive 'for autonomy through fulfilment and choice' (ibid.).

For example,

> Definitely, it is good for my career development, because before I'm coming here I went to work for some companies in Japan. I need to get some changes and English and business is one way to develop my career. Actually, I really would like to broaden, widen my knowledge in business, because MBA's really a good cause to know everything about business.
>
> (Fukuda, Japanese, Greenford University)

> I wanted an English speaking country and my options were just limited to the States, Canada, and UK and the UK seemed to be the best option in regards with a choice of culture and traditions and history of the country. And also I thought that it would be valuable for me to get outside of my continent of South America and just explore what the education is like in Europe . . . I wanted to develop my knowledge in management studies and I do realise there are very good schools in my home country, but I wanted to know something different to get outside my circle of the things I already know and want to explore something different, to learn something different.
>
> (Castillo, Mexican, Greenford University)

> The main reason is I want a bright future, because you know the competition in China is very intense. So I just want to brush up my English and improve myself to find a good job . . . The main reason for me to study in the UK I said just now to improve myself, to get a masters degree just for one year and so that I can stay in my town. I think time is limited for everybody, especially for girls. If I had to say, I just want to learn something I am really interested in.
>
> (Wen, Chinese, Greenford University)

Underpinned by human capital theory, Walker argues that students in HE may have viewed their education as 'instrumental and investments' for their future earnings (2010: 219). My interview data confirmed Walker's view, to some extent, revealing an emerging trend that studying abroad is considered to be a good investment in human capital to increase the probability of exploring their 'nascent entrepreneurial activities' (Davidsson and Honig 2003: 6).

From an economic perspective, 'qualifications and knowledge acquired through formal education' and 'skills, competencies and expertise acquired through training on the job' are the main components of human capital (Blundell *et al.* 1999: 2). Blundell *et al.* state that 'the accumulation of human capital is seen as an investment decision' (ibid.: 2). The concept of 'value for money' emerged as a vital element that many international students in my study assessed. More specifically, they were concerned with what they may receive from their institutions in terms of return on investment. Many international students also thought that studying abroad would be an expensive investment; however, they would give up some proportion of income hoping there are 'returns for increased future earnings' (ibid.: 2).

International students were determined to undertake a masters degree in the UK to enhance their entrepreneurial journeys, even if they have to sacrifice things such as family life and financial security.

> Just for the knowledge or the contact when I came here, I think it is quite valuable. I know that it's a big amount of money being funded by my parents, but I told them because I borrow it, when I go back, plus some interest.
>
> (Kai, Chinese, Redfield University)

Their determination in the UK reflects Hisrich and Peters' description of entrepreneurship:

> the process of creating something new with value by devoting the necessary time and effort, assuming the accompanying financial, psychic, and social risks, and receiving the resulting rewards of monetary and personal satisfaction and independence.
>
> (2002: 10)

The non-pecuniary incentives

Many international students were motivated by the increased earnings they may receive after their studies. They paid significant attention to the extrinsic value of their study in the UK, looking at it as a means of searching for better prospects in life or in employment. Some international students, in contrast, are not primarily motivated by 'pecuniary incentives' (Licht and Siegel 2006: 514), searching for intrinsic aspects of their study in the UK, such as vision, stability, lifestyle, leadership, innovation, independence, contribution and challenges (ibid.). For instance, despite knowing that his institution had financial incentives towards international student markets, Dinda highly valued the intrinsic aspects of his education.

> I think the real value for money comes in if you take in much more than just the education. If you came here, stayed in your room, went for your lectures, did the studies, went back to your room and did this continuously, for however many years, you would not get your value for money. I think the real value for money is getting to the culture, apart from education, which is the primary aspect, apart from that, knowing the culture. You become independent . . . Different way of thinking, I've become more open minded, I think that's another big change.
>
> (Dinda, Indian, Greenford University)

Some international student study participants tended to think that there are intrinsic motivations for attending HEIs in the UK. They also said that they would neither regard themselves, nor perform, as customers, because the intrinsic value of receiving education and training from UK universities is essential to them. For instance, Saha, studying at Redford University, considered himself a learner, not a customer.

> What I'm looking is not because I've paid money. I want to do something, it is because I'm looking at a certain relationship is that I want to develop within me, the concept's very clear of what I've applied like I've taken up international finance as a subject. So those concepts have to be developed within me. That is the reason, that relation is what I'm looking from the study . . . So I don't feel as a customer that is true.
>
> (Saha, Indian, Redfield University)

The customer relationship often implies an exchange between tuition fees (from non-EU international students) and educational services (from HEIs). Saha rejected his customer relationship with his institution, even if he paid more than his home student peers for his study in the UK. His denial of the customer identity emerged from his strong, intrinsic motivation in learning 'something', making him say 'I want to do something, it is because I'm looking at a certain relationship is that I want to develop within me'. It was his strong 'inner commitment' (Lickona 1996: 97) that motivated him to take the masters course. His intrinsic commitments could be a result of 'several constructs such as exploration, curiosity, learning goals, intrinsic intellectuality and finally the IM (intrinsic motivation) to learn' (Vallerand et al. 1992: 1005). In the end, he received pleasure and satisfaction from his participation in the UK HEIs.

Negotiating ownership of learning

Negotiation is a vital concept when it comes to the way that international students and university staff engage with one another for the purpose of negotiating ownership of learning. From the perspective of interactionism (Callero 1994; Ritzer and Goodman 2003; Stryker and Burke 2000), they are reflective units that make up a societal entity and should not be confined within a static structure (Meltzer 1972). They are neither silent nor thoughtless vessels waiting to be filled with knowledge. Their capacity for thought is shaped and refined throughout the process of their interactions with university staff. Their minds are not a physical structure, but a continuing process that consists of the larger process of stimulus and responses. The process of negotiating ownership of learning is dynamic.

The issue of negotiating ownership of learning appeared repeatedly in many of my interviews, both with university staff and international students. When this issue was discussed in our interviews, the negotiation and contesting of notions of students as customers, and as learners, was highlighted by university staff. In contrast, for many international students, the right of a student customer made them eligible to participate in negotiating their ownership of learning. Hence, their entrepreneurial characteristics seemed to play a significant role in the ways they interacted and negotiated with university staff.

Coleman, a marketing lecturer who was also responsible for student recruitment and services for Redfield University, regarded the notion of the learner and that of the customer as ambivalent, in comparison with the conventional view, which is to see these two notions as incompatible.

> Every student is a customer, irrespective of whether they're overseas and they've paid more money than the British student . . . We aggressively market to the home students as well, but through a different set of mechanisms. So the student-centred approach is the customer approach, the customer focus . . . So if you like, there is a hybrid between these two. Because you have this student-centred focus, which is about we're going to focus on you and deliver the things that you need, but we are going to identify what it is you need, because we're going to provide the services.
>
> (Coleman, lecturer in marketing, Redfield University)

The concept of 'hybridity' was suggested by Coleman to resolve this 'incompatibility' in the context of entrepreneurial discourse. This implies that there is a hybrid solution to international students' identities as learners and customers. From Coleman's point of view, the integration, or hybridity, of the student-centred approach and the customer approach has generated a space for international students negotiating the ownership of their learning. In this specific negotiating space, the voices of international students were taken into account when it comes to curriculum design. In addition, international students took responsibility for their learning, while using self-paced and/or cooperative learning (Mundhenk 2004).

Coleman did not consider international students as entrepreneurs of their own lives, but as either a learner or customer in this specific negotiating space. The possibility of international students as entrepreneurs of their lives was not illuminated in my interview with Coleman. As stated, these international students in my study were from four UK university business schools. These students were 'learners of entrepreneurship', and their identity as entrepreneurs was 'shaped by professors and student peers' (Mars et al. 2008: 639).

With business studies 'as the subject they aspire to participate in and with the context in which that participation takes place' (O'Neill and Barton 2005: 292), international students engaged with university staff in the space of negotiating their ownership of learning. In this negotiating space, international students seemed to act less as customers and more as entrepreneurs in the way that Drucker may describe them: 'always search for change, respond to it, and exploit it as an opportunity' (1994: 25).

The concept of exploitation, as Davidsson and Honig suggest, 'should not be associated with the negative connotations it might have in other contexts' and 'refers to an opportunity being acted upon rather than merely contemplated' (2003: 6). In this study, I suggest that this concept may need to be investigated as an opportunity for international students to exploit their entrepreneurship by negotiating to gain ownership of their learning. Their entrepreneurial character-istics made them take initiatives to make changes in the way they were taught. They were willing to accept personal responsibility for the ways in which they were involved with these initiatives or changes. The Student Consultative Council at Greenford University, for instance, was considered by many international students as an opportunity to negotiate their ownership of learning. It also functioned as a channel that facilitated communications between the university and its students.

Along with students, academic staff representatives at Greenford University were expected to attend meetings to understand and discuss in what ways their teaching would better fit the needs of their students. For example:

> There is no need having the Students Consultative Council at the end of the semester when we are graduating and getting our degree . . . we will have experience obvious response, well it is an error we will make some changes next semester and things like that. We are not here to pay a huge sum of money not to be involved in the future generation . . . So there should be a robust system that monitors the way lecturers teach a class, immediate changes can be made, and any wrongdoings can be brought to their attention.
>
> (Biya, Cameroonian, Greenford University).

> There is a committee (Student Consultative Council) that deals with this kind of concern . . . So the university is making sure that our voice is heard by setting up these committees . . . so students are pleased with the quality of teaching of one professor we have many channels to have our voice heard. We can raise these issues very easily.
>
> (Castillo, Mexican, Greenford University)

These meetings of the Student Consultative Council Committee were expected to bring outcomes that can improve the quality of teaching and learning. Thereafter, as some international students reported, they seemed to have benefited from the decisions and actions that resulted from these meetings. Some inter-national student interviewees said that they liked being involved with discussions, particularly concerning the curricula, the teaching and learning process and the contents of teaching.

Through their participation in the meetings of the Student Consultative Council Committee, international students at Greenford University explored their entre-preneurial selves. These international students were to 'aspire to autonomy' (Rose

1998: 151). Their participation was driven by the way that they interpreted 'reality and destiny as a matter of individual responsibility' (ibid.). They seemed to be eager to find meaning for their existence by shaping their life through acts of choice (ibid.).

Despite the fact that there is a concern that the negotiating space for the ownership of learning was initiated from the thought of 'market fundamentalism' (Walker 2010: 219), in which people 'often fail to acknowledge the ways that the market can undermine autonomy, by producing conditions for the characterless who lacks an identity' (O'Neill 1998: 78), my study aligned with Buss's observation that 'the value of autonomy is tied to the value of self-integration' (2008: 1). Many international students in this study appeared to be self-governing agents, because they want to be accountable for what they do (ibid). The way that I looked at their participation in the process of negotiating their ownership of learning is a process of empowerment. 'The beauty of empowerment is that it appears to reject the logics of patronising dependency' (Rose 2000b: 334). Their voices seemed to be heard and their opinions were transmitted into the changes of curriculum design and the ways they were taught. The Student Consultative Council Committee at Greenford University seemed to perform not as a way of patronizing, but a way of respecting student choice, and most importantly, empowering students.

From a constructivist viewpoint of learning, international students are to 'encourage the growth of student responsibility, initiative, decision making, and intentional learning; cultivate collaboration among students and teachers' (Grabinger and Dunlap 1995: 5). The creation of a negotiating space for ownership in learning is particularly useful for many international students who come to study, for instance, an MBA or MA in marketing. Many of the students in this study were mature students. They already had many years of working experience prior to taking their postgraduate courses in the UK in the hope that they could 'integrate new knowledge with old knowledge and hereby create rich and complex knowledge structures' (ibid.) More importantly, many expected that their study in the UK would enhance their entrepreneurial journeys.

Conclusions

The identity of international students as entrepreneurs is under-investigated. There is a need to investigate international students in a new way. In this chapter, I have proposed considering international students as entrepreneurs, as autonomous agents of their lives in the political, economic, social, cultural and academic contexts in the UK. Many international students in this study regarded their study in the UK university business school as part of their life journey in search of their entrepreneurial identity.

To explore the idea of international students as entrepreneurs of their own lives in detail, I have emphasized that international students have self-governing capabilities and aspire to be autonomous. The notion of autonomy is significant in the process of the identity construction of international students. Autonomy, as Rose stated, 'is now represented in terms of personal power and the capacity to accept responsibility – not to blame others but to recognise your own collusion in that which prevents you from being yourself' (2000b: 334).

International students are multi-faceted individuals. My international student study participants' responses and attitudes towards their studies in the UK challenged the way in which some literature has described them as victims, problems or beneficiaries. The international students' generally optimistic attitudes and positive experiences and their determination to confront challenges they encounter in the UK have not been exemplified in the literature.

It is 'challenging enough' and 'radical' (Sen 2006: 8) to remove the identities of international students as victims, problems and beneficiaries. It is even more challenging for me to propose an alternative way of investigating them as entrepreneurs of their own lives. By exploring the entrepreneurial identity of international students, I highlight the characteristics of their autonomousness, assertiveness and self-reliance as individuals. Despite financial and emotional sacrifices and tremendous stress, international students are eager to learn, become independent, pursue their self-defined interests and eventually achieve personal satisfaction. They take responsibility for themselves and for what they do. They are protagonists taking charge of their own lives.

References

Alatas, S.F. (2003) 'Academic dependency and the global division of labour in the social sciences', *Current Sociology*, 51, 4: 599–613.

Alderman, G. (2009) 'Memorandum 14', submission to Department for Innovation, Universities and Skills, *Students and University – Memoranda of Evidence*. Online. Available HTTP: http://www.publications.parliament.uk/pa/cm200809/cmselect/cmdius/memo/170/170memo0902.pdf (accessed 26 January 2011).

Bartram, B. (2006) 'Supporting international students in higher education – some reflections on changing motivations and possible effects', paper presented at the British Education Studies Association Conference, University College Chester, Chester, UK, 1 July 2005. Online. Available HTTP: http://www.leeds.ac.uk/educol/documents/155851.htm (accessed 26 January 2011).

Blakewell, C.J. and Gibson-Sweet, M.F. (1998) 'Strategic marketing in a changing environment: the new universities in danger of being struck in the middle', *International Journal of Educational Management*, 13, 4: 187–98.

Blundell, R., Dearden, L., Meghir, C. and Sianesi, B. (1999) 'Human capital investment: the returns from education and training to the individual, the firm, and the economy', *Fiscal Studies*, 20, 1: 1–23.

Bourdieu, P. and Wacquant, L. (1999) 'On the cunning of imperialist reason', *Theory, Culture and Society*, 16, 1: 41–58.

Brown, L.M. and Gilligan, C. (1992) *Meeting at the Crossroads*, Cambridge, MA: Harvard University Press.

Buchbinder, H. (1993) 'The market oriented university and the changing role of knowledge', *Higher Education*, 26: 331–47.

Buss, S. (2008) 'Personal autonomy', in Edward N. Zalta (ed.) *Stanford Encyclopedia of Philosophy*. Online. Available HTTP: http://plato.stanford.edu/archives/fall2008/entries/personal-autonomy/ (accessed 26 January 2011).

Callero, P.L. (1994) 'From role-playing to role-using: understanding role as resource', *Social Psychology Quarterly*, 57, 3: 228–43.

Cope, J. (2005) 'Toward a dynamic learning perspective of entrepreneurship', *Entrepreneurship Theory and Practice*, 29, 4: 373–98.

Coughlan, S. (2008) 'Watchdog: Degree Grades Arbitrary', BBC News, 23 June. Online. Available HTTP: http://news.bbc.co.uk/1/hi/education/7469396.stm.

Davidsson, P. and Honig, B. L. (2003) 'The role of social and human capital among nascent entrepreneurs', originally published in *Journal of Business Venturing*, 18, 3: 301–31. Online. Available HTTP: http://eprints.qut.edu.au/5832/1/5832.pdf (accessed 26 January 2011).

Douglas, J. McClelland, R. and Davies, J. (2007) 'The development of a conceptual model of student satisfaction with their experience in higher education', *Quality Assurance in Education*, 16, 1: 19–35.

Drucker, P.F. (1994) *Innovation and Entrepreneurship: Practice and Principles*, 2nd edn, Oxford: Butterworth-Heinemann.

Grabinger, R.S. and Dunlap, J.C. (1995) 'Rich environments for active learning: a definition', *Association for Learning Technology Journal*, 3, 2: 5–34.

Hartshorn, C. (2002) 'Understanding notions of enterprise in the higher education sector', *Industry and Higher Education*, 16, 3: 149–58.

Heelas, P. (1991) 'Reforming the self: enterprise and the characters of Thatcherism', in R. Keat and N. Abercrombie (eds) *Enterprise Culture*, London: Routledge.

Hisrich, R.D. and Peters, M.P. (2002) *Enterpreneurship*, 5th edn, New York: McGraw-Hill.

Kuo, Y.-C. (2010) 'Learner, customer or ambassador? Identity constructions of overseas students in the discourse of entrepreneurialism', unpublished doctoral thesis, Institute of Education, University of London.

Leonard, D. and Morley, L. (2003) *The Experiences of International Students in UK Higher Education: Preface*. Online. Available HTTP: http://www.ukcosa.org.uk/about/pubs_research.php (accessed 26 January 2011).

Licht, A.N. and Siegel, J.I. (2006) 'The social dimensions of entrepreneurship', in M. Casson and B. Yeung (eds) *The Oxford Handbook of Entrepreneurship*, Oxford: Oxford University Press.

Lickona, T. (1996) 'Eleven principles of effective character education', *Journal of Moral Education*, 25, 1: 93–100.

Mars, M.M., Slaughter, S. and Rhoades, G. (2008) 'The state-sponsored student entrepreneur', *Journal of Higher Education*, 79, 6: 638–70.

Mauthner, N.S. and Doucet, A. (1998) 'Reflections on a voice-centred relational method of data analysis: analysing maternal and domestic voices', in J. Ribbens and R. Edwards (eds) *Feminist Dilemmas in Qualitative Research: Private Lives and Public Texts*, London: Sage.

Meltzer, B.N. (1972) 'Mead's social psychology', in J.G. Manis and B.N. Meltzer (eds) *Symbolic Interaction: A Reader in Social Psychology*, Boston: Allyn and Bacon.

Middlehurst, R. and Woodfield, S. (2007). 'International activity or internationalisation strategy? Insights from an institutional pilot study in the UK', *Tertiary Education and Management*, 13, 3: 263–79.

Mundhenk, L.G. (2004) 'Toward an understanding of what it means to be student centered: a new teacher's journey', *Journal of Management Education*, 28, 4: 447–62.

Nayak, A. and Beckett, A. (2008) 'Infantilized adults or active consumers? Enterprise discourse in the UK retail banking industry', *Organization*, 15, 3: 407–25.

Newson, J. (1998) 'Conclusion: repositioning the local through alternative responses to globalisation', in J. Currie. and J. Newson (eds) *Universities and Globalisation: Critical Perspectives*, London: Sage.

O'Neill, J. (1998) *The Market: Ethics, Knowledge and Politics*, London: Routledge.

O'Neill, T. and Barton, A.C. (2005) 'Uncovering student ownership in science learning: the making of a student created mini-documentary', *School Science and Mathematics*, 105, 6: 292–93.

Ritzer, G. and Goodman, D.J. (2003). *Sociology Theory*, 6th edn, Boston and New York: McGraw-Hill.

Rose, N. (1996) *Inventing our Selves: Psychology, Power and Personhood*, Cambridge: Cambridge University Press.

—— (1998) *Inventing Ourselves*, Cambridge: Cambridge University Press.

—— (1999) *Powers of Freedom: Reframing Political Thought*, Cambridge: Cambridge University Press.

—— (2000a) *Power and Subjectivity: Critical History and Psychology*. Online. Available HTTP: http://www.academyanalyticarts.org/rose1.htm (accessed 26 January 2011).

—— (2000b) 'Government and control', *British Journal of Criminology*, 40: 321–39.

Russell Group of Universities (2009) 'Memorandum 76', submission to Department for Innovation, Universities and Skills, *Students and University – Memoranda of Evidence*. Online. Available HTTP: http://www.publications.parliament.uk/pa/cm200809/cmselect/cmdius/memo/170/170memo0902.pdf (accessed 26 January 2011).

Schmitt, D. (2010) 'UKBA guidance on providing evidence of English language proficiency', paper presented at BAAL Testing, Evaluation and Assessment SIG conference Language Tests for Immigration: Conflicting Ideologies and Challenges, 12 November. Online. Available HTTP: http://www.beds.ac.uk/baalteasig/events/2010/ds (accessed 26 January 2011).

Sen, A. (2006) *Identity and Violence: The Illusion of Destiny*, London and New York: Allen Lane.

Stryker, S. and Burke, P.J. (2000) 'The past, present and future of an identity theory', *Social Psychology Quarterly*, 63, 4: 284–97.

UK Border Agency (2010) *The Student Immigration System: A Consultation*, UK Border Agency, Immigration Group.

Vallerand, R.J., Pelletier, L.G., Blais, M.R., Briere, N.M., Senecal, C. and Vallieries, E.F. (1992) 'The academic motivation scale: a measure of intrinsic, extrinsic, and amotivation in education', *Educational and Psychological Measurement*, 52: 1003–19.

Wagner, J. (1999). 'Aesthetic value', in M. Holbrook (ed.) *Consumer Value: A Framework for Analysis and Research*, London: Routledge.

Walker, M. (2010) 'Pedagogy for rich human being-ness in global time', in E. Unterhalter and V. Carpentier (eds) *Global Inequalities and Higher Education: Whose Interests are you Serving?*, Houndmills: Palgrave MacMillan.

Part III

Language

Chapter 12

Negotiating writing

Challenges of the first written assignment at a UK university

Carol Bailey

In the beginning I was thinking a sentence in Greek and then I was trying to translate that in English. After writing a few essays, words started coming to my mind directly in English.

(Vasiliki)

This chapter draws on the reflections of non-native-English-speaking students (NNESs) concerning their first experience of writing extended essays at a post-1992 UK university.[1] I begin by outlining some aspects of academic writing the students identified as challenging: writing at length; finding sources; reading in a foreign language; selecting relevant information; structuring a text; using an appropriate style; checking for accuracy; and observing academic writing conventions. I then argue from a critical pedagogical viewpoint that, rather than seeing the writing of NNESs as a 'problem' to be 'fixed' by admissions policies and 'support' staff, higher education institutions (HEIs) should reconsider their assessment strategies in a more inclusive light. Finally I discuss some of the inherent tensions and contradictions in critical English for academic purposes (EAP) teaching.

The students

Most of the primary data in this chapter come from students following a three-month English language foundation course designed to bring them from an English level equivalent to IELTS 5.5[2] to university entrance level (in this case IELTS 6.0 equivalent or above). Between January 2005 and May 2009, the 311 students who took the course came from Cyprus (142), mainland China (84), India (17), Spain (17), Japan (9), Poland (8), Greece (5), Pakistan (4), Taiwan (4), Hong Kong (3), Iran (3), Cameroon (3), Saudi Arabia (2), Korea (2), Bulgaria (2), Kuwait (1), France (1), Turkey (1), Algeria (1), Ghana (1) and Albania (1). Broadly speaking the students from Cyprus, Greece, Poland, Hong Kong, Ghana and Albania had completed high school education and were preparing to enter Year 1 of a UK undergraduate degree. The rest had completed two to four years of higher education in their home country and were preparing to enter postgraduate courses or Years 2–3 of an undergraduate degree.

On two of their modules (study units) students completed scaffolded essay writing tasks (1,200–2,000 words) and were asked to reflect on the process afterwards.[3] Naturally the content and language of their reflections were influenced by their English level, by what they had been taught on the course and by their consciousness that this was an assessed piece of work. Over the years several themes emerged as areas of challenge in academic writing. To illustrate these themes I have selected quotations from the reflective accounts: not on a numerical/quantitative basis but inasmuch as they appear to shed light on the issue in question. Where stated I have supplemented the reflections of the foundation students with voluntary comments from postgraduates on an advanced language and academic skills in-sessional module, collected ad hoc from emails and tutorial discussions. All quotations are used with permission and followed by an indication of the student's nationality and degree subject.

I felt it important to quote the students verbatim, including grammar and lexis 'mistakes'. It seemed only fair to let them speak for themselves, given the high degree of editorial control I had already exerted in identifying themes and selecting material from their work. Furthermore, the students' own words illustrate – far better than I can – not only their difficulties in writing but also their creativity in expressing themselves despite limited linguistic resources.

Given the small data set, it would be inadvisable to draw essentialist conclusions about national education systems on the basis of my students' comments. I have also tried to avoid generalizing from the UK academic writing purlieu to 'western' or 'Anglophone' contexts since I am told that academic writing practices in Western Europe, North America and Australia are markedly different from those of the UK. And of course, international students in the UK are not a homogeneous group. Not all the challenges described below are experienced by every international student, and most are experienced by first year home students too (Bailey and Pieterick 2008).

Writing at length

It may come as a surprise how few international students have experience of writing an extended essay prior to entering UK study. In many education systems the primary means of assessment is by end-of-course examination, comprising multiple choice and short essay questions. Even students who have completed an undergraduate dissertation in their mother tongue may have written no more than 400 words at a time in English. The process of researching, planning and writing a long essay (in a foreign language!) can therefore be daunting:

> In India there is different system of teaching and exams in schools as well as colleges for example ready made notes are available and students need to learn by heart that notes and write in exam its very easy.
>
> (Indian postgraduate: biotechnology)

The most dangerous part of this module that I hear is to write 1,200 words essay . . . The most difficult part on this assignment it was the amount of words because it was a long essay and it was my first time which I had to write such a long essay.

(Cypriot: mechanical engineering)

Finding and selecting sources

One of the first challenges of a research-based essay is finding source material. This may involve acquiring a range of new information literacy skills. Many of my Cypriot students had never been in a library before. Some Indian students had used closed-access libraries, where the borrower fills out a book request form but is not allowed to browse the shelves (Jordan 1997). One Cameroonian student on the course explained that during his HND studies all the materials had been provided by the teacher. Chinese universities have libraries and increasing access to e-resources, but from what I observed while teaching in HEIs across China in 1997–2005, there was typically one set textbook per study unit, and students were rarely required to search for extra material.

Learn center have abundant learning source for ours study. But I feel giddy when I entered into the complex learning center system sometimes.

(Chinese: ceramics)

Increasingly, resources are made digitally available. This can be problematic for students from areas with intermittent electricity supply, infrequent access to computers and limited Internet provision.

I studied Computing for three years in India, but never used a computer during my course. We had all our lessons in an IT lab but weren't allowed to touch the computers in case we damaged them. I had never used Google or any other search engine before coming here. Basic things like uploading my student photo during online enrolment took me ages to do.

(Indian postgraduate: computer science)

Selecting the most useful sources from a wide range of material may pose a challenge. As Smailes and Gannon-Leary point out (2008: 55), students who are used to working from a set textbook may lack practice in differentiating between core and peripheral material or assessing the reliability of a source.

Searching information is also a hard work, because when faced to the whole information from internet or books, I have to read and choose what I need. Most importantly, I had to judge if they are accuracy or objective and whether I could find the reference of them. So, in my opinion, finding information is the most difficult thing in writing.

(Chinese: business)

In a number of cases I observed students becoming frustrated because they could not find one source that 'answered' their essay question. For example, one business student had chosen to compare the tax system in China and the UK: 'The big problem is I should change my research topic that can't find the information in website or university article. It is only found the tax system in UK or China, not both the UK and China.'

In the following account, the student's assiduous quest for sources is complicated by her imprecise use of search terms. Spelling or grammar mistakes and limited vocabulary range may be frequent stumbling blocks for NNESs searching library and journal databases which, unlike Internet search engines, make no allowances for language and typing errors.

> My essay topic was sale price in public holiday. It was about promotion. I tried to find information in the Internet. There were 53,900,000 for 'sale price' information in the Google, 822 search results in the BBC website. However, I couldn't find anyone was useful for my topic. I changed to pay attention books. When I typed in 'strategy marketing', I found some books. However, most of books were already borrowed. I went to [a distant campus] to borrow four books about sales promotion. I used two days to read the books. I couldn't find useful information for my essay. I felt despond. How could I do? Where could I find information to support my opinion? Deadline was near, I hadn't written any letter. I felt I didn't want to do it, and not idea in my mind. At the end I wanted to abandon this topic. But it was too late . . . Homework, a lot of homework, headache was coming.
>
> (Chinese: accounting)

Reading in a foreign language

Once students have found relevant source material, they have to read it. This poses several challenges for non-native English speakers. One frequently mentioned is that of grappling with discipline-specific terminology:

> Before I came here, I just learned some academic and general words, but I knew nothing about my subject words. Because of this reason I almost cannot understand the sentences . . . For example nugget the means is a small solid lump especially of gold. This word is very strange for me . . . There are a lot of strange words in jewellery design.
>
> (Chinese: jewellery design)

A second problem for students with lower levels of English is understanding complex grammatical structures – which are unfortunately common in academic writing:

> It got very long sentence to explain something which is the meaning in the business. For instance, 'we shall also examine the main forms of business

enterprise and consider what the key financial objective of the business is likely to be.' I didn't understand at the first in English, so I translated it, used me long time. After I see. It is not really difficult, but I used the double times to read it.

(Chinese: business)

All students who mentioned reading as a challenge commented on how long it took them to understand a text, and expressed frustration that they were spending time decoding language that they would rather have spent on dealing with content. This is more of an issue for speakers of languages not cognate with English. 'If it takes an English speaker one hour to read a text in English, a French speaker will need two hours and a Chinese speaker four' (Chinese postgraduate: business; see also Jordan 1997: 50–2). Another issue is that students may need to acquire new reading strategies. The stereotype of the Asian student as 'rote learner' has been called into question (see for example Watkins *et al.* 1991), but it remains a fact that reading a set textbook from cover to cover – and in many cases memorizing it – is a primary stage in the learning process for students from many countries (Smailes and Gannon-Leary 2008: 55). This slow, almost meditative way of reading does not always work well in the UK when students are required to survey a range of material and pick out key points in a short time. 'Read English is not practised to the Chinese. I often like read every word on the every sentence, which very waste time in the exam' (Chinese: jewellery design).

Structuring a text

On the foundation course, we require students to submit an outline plan before beginning their first draft. For some of the Cypriot high-school leavers, this was a new experience: 'I am a person who prefers to write my ideas coming like brainstorm and not to prepare so much for my work.' Most students found the process beneficial – because it saved time at the draft stage – and easy, because they had done similar exercises in their previous education. Two Chinese students who were very creative in their reflective writing felt constrained by having to follow an 'academic' structure. Interestingly, despite their limited command of English they were both aware of the need to conform to a certain discourse in order to be accepted and succeed:

I didn't like to write academic article. It had their pattern. I couldn't change anything. It is boring to me, because it baffle my mind. However, I must to write. My subject study will need it.

(accounting)

Next, I think outline is the bone of an essay. If you don't want your essay is a monster, you will have to let your outline and essay structure is good enough (not a nonconventional type).

(computer aided product design)

Several postgraduates said they had received negative feedback about their essay structure from tutors on their other modules. One Indian law student was asked to rewrite an essay introduction 'to be more specific'. A Chinese education student said she lost marks for not being concise, including 'irrelevant' information and frequently quoting Chinese sages. A Syrian law student explained:

> The Arabic method of writing an essay is extremely different from the English method of writing an essay, in the Arabic method we put general introduction about the title, and then in the body, which is the core of the essay, we talk about the title in one long paragraph, and then come the conclusion. While in the English method the introduction is very important because it contains a work plan, moreover it mention points about what the body will talk about, the body is very important too it contains paragraphs, each paragraph explain the points that was mentioned in the introduction, then come the conclusion.
>
> (Syrian: law)

Cultural preferences regarding text organization are explored in the field of contrastive rhetoric (see for example Connor 2002). Such explorations can be very helpful to students, teachers and assessors of academic writing since they reveal potentially problematic differences such as those mentioned above. At the same time, care should be exercised to avoid making culturally essentialist assumptions about discourse patterns (Hyland 2006: 44) or upholding any one rhetorical model as superior to others (Kachru 1999).

Using an appropriate style

Linked to linguistic and cultural variations in academic discourse patterns are those of academic style. In some countries it is considered good practice to quote proverbs in a science assignment, or cite classical poets in an essay on business management. In the UK, as my Chinese Education postgraduate discovered, this is less acceptable.

Anglo-American academic style incorporates several features – complexity of sentence structure, formality (e.g. special academic register; avoidance of colloquialisms), objectivity and impersonality (e.g. passive voice, impersonal pronouns). The academic writer must be explicit yet at the same time (depending on the discipline) cautious, supporting every assertion with evidence, reasons and reference to work by recognized scholars (Swales and Feak 2004). Any breach of these conventions is punished by the academy's gatekeepers: journal editors, reviewers, university lecturers. This can be demoralizing for mature postgraduates, who may have a wealth of ideas, knowledge and personal experience (Ryan and Viete 2009) but will not be 'heard' unless they can find an acceptable means of expression (Canagarajah 2001: 129).

It was not formal because it is not an academic writing. It just like I was talking to somebody. So I need to correct it.

(Chinese: business)

Beside the grammar, the style is also a difficult part of my writing. The transition from informal to formal, from active to passive form, all this things seemed to be impossible.

(Bulgarian: business)

The question of appropriate style is complicated further (for native English speakers too) by the fact that many students are enrolled on mixed-discipline courses – for example public health, commercial law, social work – which require multiple genres and sometimes disparate reference systems (Schmitt 2005).

Checking for accuracy

As well as style, the need for grammatical accuracy may cause concern to NNESs – sometimes with good cause:

The composition of academic sentences was not easy as it was confusing me with the structuring sentences on my home language, what was as result non-understandable and sometime without making sense writing in English.

(Cypriot: automotive engineering)

However, often students worry unnecessarily about grammar – many lecturers (depending to an extent on the academic discipline) are prepared to 'peer through' the language mistakes (HEA 2010) to focus on content and argumentation (Jordan 1997: 46–8).

Writing is the worst part of the English language for me. I always had problems with vocabulary, punctuation and grammar. I never learnt how to write essays or any writing in English language . . . When I hand in my essay I was afraid and proud. I was really surprised when I saw my feedback . . . Although I made thousands of grammar and punctuation mistakes my essay wasn't so bad.

(Polish: biological science)

Academic writing conventions

One cause of major anxiety for students facing written assignments is the requirement to observe academic writing conventions and 'avoid plagiarism'. Some express this as a relatively new concept:

Plagiarism is a very serious problem in West, especially in the University. We have to study how to avoid plagiarism. In fact, plagiarism is not a serious problem in China, because China is a developing country. Pirate is very popular in China, such as books, music and movie. So, most people haven't concept of plagiarism. I always copy information on Internet and books without reference when I study in China.

(Chinese: business)

In contrast, Liu (2005) contests the assertion that copying others' writing is acceptable in China, citing his own educational experience, eighth-century Chinese scholars and twentieth-century Chinese composition textbooks as evidence that the concept of plagiarism has long been understood. Likewise Phan Le Ha (2006) takes issue with the notion that plagiarism arises from cultural conditioning, arguing that Vietnamese students are well aware of the concept but that referencing practices differ. Certainly the mechanics of referencing posed problems for some of my students:

The strict Harvard style reference really made me woozy. I also did it in my country, but it not so strict that a punctuation must be correct.

(Chinese: business)

Sometime, I found source on the Internet, but I can not very easy to found the article publishing date and page, it is difficult to write the reference . . . I very worry about this, because I should write academic essay when I have degree course.

(Chinese: ceramics)

Errey (2002) found that international students – contrary to their teachers' expectations – were less uncertain about the concept of intellectual ownership and the mechanics of citation than how to incorporate others' words into their own text. Writing an academic essay is an incredibly complex task. The weaving together of others' voices with one's own to create a coherent written text is challenging for native speakers and even more so for those with an incomplete grasp of the language (Schmitt 2005). One Indian business student explained that in her previous MBA studies, 'if I needed to write an essay just I used to copy and paste the whole assignment [while] modifying the certain part of my essay'. The texts she had produced for her foundation course essays were precise and coherent patchworks of other writers' words. She had read quite widely and had cited all her sources – i.e. she was not intending to cheat (Pecorari 2003). However, she was not versed in the habits of paraphrasing, quoting and stating her own position.

Paraphrasing is especially difficult for NNESs as it requires the writer to manipulate grammatical structures as well as identifying suitable synonyms. Keck (2006: 272), comparing paraphrases by native- and NNESs, found that the latter group 'used significantly more Near Copies' (i.e. textual borrowing) than their native-English-speaking peers.

For me the biggest problem was paraphrasing original tekst because my essay was about DNA and it was very hard to change vocabulary or grammar. I could not change vocabulary because it was specialist and specyfic and teksts or articles are written by author in passive so it was the most difficult point of my essay.

(Polish: biotechnology)

Several students commented on the amount of time they spent on trying to paraphrase:

I don't know how to write and I should change the sentences structure or words so that make sure no plagiarism. After three hours, I only write nearly 100 words. I worried about if I can finish my assignment on time.

(Chinese: business)

Paraphrasing someone's words was the most difficult part in the assignment, as I need to find different synonyms for some words and make sure how to use them. Another problem was facing me in my writing that I could not speed up; I spent long hours writing my essays due to limited vocabularies that I have.

(Saudi Arabian: mathematics)

Pressure of time, as well as limited linguistic resources, may lead students (inadvertently or otherwise) to commit plagiarism. (For a comprehensive discussion on writing from sources and the linguistic aspects of plagiarism, see Pecorari 2008.)

Discussion

If international students experience certain aspects of academic writing as particularly difficult, why do we insist on them? Is transformation through paraphrase the only way to demonstrate understanding of a text? Is a literature review the best way to demonstrate knowledge of a field? Why do we ask undergraduates to mimic the style of scholarly publication when so few of them plan a career in the academy?

All too often when faced with 'poor' writing by international students, academic staff argue that English language entry criteria should be raised. While this may help, as a solution it does not fully acknowledge the complexity of the issue. First, even students from countries such as India or Nigeria, where English is widely spoken and a medium of instruction, may be unfamiliar with writing at length, information literacy, UK style requirements and academic writing conventions. Second, while English language tests may provide a useful indication of students' linguistic competence, they do not necessarily predict success in academic writing. For example, in the IELTS test there is no link between the reading and writing papers. The first writing task (150 words) requires candidates to describe a visual prompt but not to explain or interpret it. Task 2 (250 words) requires candidates to draw on their own ideas and experience in an opinion-based essay type not commonly found in higher education. The length and nature of the tasks and lack of integration with the reading passages mean that a candidate may score highly on the IELTS writing test yet underperform on a 3,000-word literature-based university essay.

Another commonly proposed solution to the 'problem' of unsuccessful writing by international students is EAP and/or academic skills tuition, both before and during degree study. This can undoubtedly benefit students' academic writing, all the more so when it is embedded in the curriculum and not stigmatized as an optional 'remedial' or 'support' add-on. However, I would argue that institutions (while not neglecting academic language/literacy provision) need to move beyond an assimilation/acculturation focus on inducting international students into the locally dominant academy. Following Benesch (1993), Scollon (1994), Pennycook (1996) and Kachru (1999), I suggest that educators should adopt a more open and self-critical approach to 'foreign' rhetorical conventions. In 2008/9, international students formed 68 per cent of the full-time population on taught postgraduate courses in the UK (UKCISA 2011; based on data from the Higher Education Statistics Agency). Given such an international context, how can one justify clinging to assessment practices designed primarily with home students in mind?

One argument for preserving the status quo is that people choose to study overseas because they seek experience they could not obtain in their own country. For example, Egege and Kutulieh (2008: 74–5) contend that 'transnational/ international students enrol in Western degrees because they see them as transformative', desiring to explore 'new ways of being and doing'. Undoubtedly many students do appreciate the transformative aspects of overseas education. According to one Indian computer science postgraduate, 'Education is more practical here – I'm learning how to *do* things, not just write about them.'

> In China, if I don't understand something, the teacher will tell me the answer. It's more convenient . . . but in Britain the teachers force you to study yourself, to work things out on your own. This way you can get more experience, learn how to do things for yourself.
>
> (Chinese postgraduate: business)

However, not everyone studies overseas because they intrinsically value the education system of their host country. They may be studying abroad because the demand for higher education in their home country exceeds supply, or because they believe an overseas qualification may make them more employable, or because they hope to migrate to the country in question. And even a student whose motivation for study is transformative may feel daunted when faced, early in their course, with a 4,000–5,000 word assignment requiring them to discuss an unfamiliar topic critically.

A second frequently voiced argument against revising assessment strategies in consideration of international students is that this might involve 'lowering' or 'dumbing-down' standards. I believe that this need not be the case, and that UK law and government policy actively endorses more inclusive assessment practices. Although UK HEIs set their own assessments and validate their own programmes, since 2003 they have been required to align their awards and qualifications to the national Framework for Higher Education Qualifications (FHEQ) (QAA 2008), which provides a series of reference points (learning outcomes) for different levels of study. In addition, many degree programmes have to demonstrate adherence to professional, statutory and regulatory body requirements. The precepts and outline guidance set out in the FHEQ aspire to 'accommodate diversity and innovation'. Awarding institutions are exhorted to consider 'whether the design of the curriculum and assessments is such that *all students following the programme have the opportunity to achieve and demonstrate the intended outcomes*' (QAA 2008: 12; my italics).

A persuasive case for inclusive assessment is made in the context of disability legislation. UK law now requires institutions to make 'reasonable adjustments' to assessments, in order to 'enable disabled students to demonstrate the achievement of the learning outcomes' (QAA 2010: 8). There is no requirement to alter the learning outcomes, or the 'competence standards' that may be set by professional, statutory and regulatory bodies. There is, however, an expectation that assessment methods be flexible and that 'there may be more than one way of a student demonstrating that they have achieved a particular outcome' (ibid.). Moreover, institutions have an 'anticipatory duty', when designing programmes, to consider how assessment methods and strategies might disadvantage disabled students, and to propose alternatives. Waterfield and West (2006: section 3) are critical of the way these requirements are implemented by the majority of UK institutions, suggesting that it is limited and assimilationist. They argue for an 'inclusive approach' whereby flexible assessment methods 'capable of assessing the same learning outcomes in different ways' be made available for all, to meet the needs of a diverse student body.

In referring to disability legislation I am not suggesting that being an international student (possibly with an imperfect command of English) is equivalent to having a disability, defined by the Disability Discrimination Act 1995 as 'a physical or mental impairment which has a substantial and long-term adverse effect on [one's] ability to carry out normal day-to-day activities' (section 1). One may assume that, over time, international students can adapt to their new academic culture and improve their communication skills. I cite the disability legislation as a useful (and, in the UK, legally enforceable) precedent for varying assessment practices while keeping academic standards intact. Moreover, there is a nascent synergy between the equal opportunities and internationalization agendas (Eade and Peacock 2009). Both aspire to foster respect for others and promote inclusive approaches to education, not least in the context of assessment.

If our assessment continues to be based upon a Western template of knowledge that values Western ways of knowing and learning, all our lip service to developing interculturally competent students is meaningless. It also institutionalises discrimination against students from non-dominant backgrounds and privileges students from dominant groups.

(MacKinnon and Manathunga 2003: 132)

When students from particular cultural contexts consistently experience problems with assessment, we need to consider the role that culturally based factors may be playing and respond to these appropriately. This calls for an awareness of and respect for other assessment cultures and a realisation that our local culture is not the only one, nor necessarily the best.

(Brown and Joughin 2007: 70)

There is some evidence that certain assessment types do disadvantage certain groups of international students. For example, NNESs may under-perform in time-constrained written examinations due to lack of fluency and accuracy when writing (De Vita 2002: 221). Equally, they may under-perform in multiple choice tests that require a certain reading speed and the ability to differentiate between apparently similar lexical items (Dolan and Macias 2009: 27). I am not suggesting that institutions dispense with exams because some NNESs find them hard (though it would be interesting to consider why NNESs are not offered extra time and laptop use as dyslexic students are). There needs to be 'a balanced diet of different means of assessment within a course . . . to ensure that no particular group is favoured over any other group' (Race et al. 2005: 3).

The question, then, is not: should we change our learning outcomes to make assessments more achievable for international students?, but: how creative can we be in designing ways of demonstrating these outcomes that are meaningful, valid and give all students a fair chance of success? Institutions also need to consider to what extent lecturers, when marking work, can accept 'bad English' and different rhetorical approaches, or exercise leniency regarding patchwriting and unskilled referencing.

The past two decades have heralded a wealth of scholarship and innovation in higher education assessment design, driven by various factors including a desire for greater authenticity; making the assignments more engaging; designing out opportunities for plagiarism; dealing with large cohorts; cutting costs; responding to the widening participation agenda; improving student retention; developing transferable skills; and enhancing employability. However, an innovatively designed assessment may pose its own challenge to international students, particularly where use of unfamiliar genres is required. For example, the assessment tasks suggested by Brown et al. (1994: 20) as alternatives to academic essays include a letter to an MP, a magazine article and a committee briefing paper. Each of these has its own discourse requirements that are different from those of an academic essay, and may be very different from those of a similar text in the student's home country (journalese varies widely from country to country, as does the style of formal letters). The alternative task – designed to offer more authenticity and transferability – may burden international students with the need to master yet another discourse type (Brown and Joughin 2007: 69). Where non-standard assessments are used, it is imperative to provide explicit guidelines and models of the aims, format and assessment criteria (Waterfield and West 2006: inclusive assessment case study 6).

Conclusion

I have outlined some of the aspects of academic writing that international students may find difficult when newly arrived in the UK. In drawing on my students' written reflections and oral comments, I have selected observations about areas of challenge and left out remarks such as 'the teachers are very kind', and 'I have learned so much from this course'. My aim in focusing on the difficulties of academic writing is not to present a deficit view of international students as needing 'support', but to provide an overview of some of the issues HE providers should bear in mind when designing and validating courses. With governments decreasing state funding for higher education, institutions are increasingly looking to maximize their revenue from external sources, including international student tuition fees. As international students form an ever-growing proportion of the student population in our institutions, we can no longer expect them to 'fit in' with a system designed primarily for a home-grown student body. Moreover, it is now widely recognized that innovations made on behalf of international students will commonly benefit all (Ryan and Carroll 2005).

In my discussion of assessment practices in UK HEIs I have tried to take a critical pedagogical stance, epitomized by Pennycook (1994: 297) as 'education grounded in a desire for social change'. I hold with Pennycook that the rhetorical conventions that currently predominate in my academic sphere are not a 'canonical truth to be handed on to our students' but 'something to be negotiated, challenged and appropriated' (ibid.: 299). The possibility that certain types of assessment disadvantage certain groups of international students is an equal opportunities issue that has to be addressed.

At the same time, critical EAP pedagogy carries an inherent tension between the 'utopian vision' of education reform and the 'pragmatic realities' of our institutions and classrooms (Benesch 2001: 141). One such reality is that very few EAP teachers have any influence over assessment strategies in their institutions. Increasingly, HEIs are employing EAP professionals not on academic contracts but on academic-related or administrative scales, and/or on part-time, short-term contracts. EAP provision is often located in 'units' or 'centres' which report to student support departments and are isolated from mainstream academic provision and curriculum reviews.

A second 'pragmatic reality' and locus of tension is that no matter how EAP teachers may question the validity of local assessment practices or academic writing conventions, our students have the right to expect our assistance in mastering these so that they can succeed in their studies (Benesch 2001: 137). 'Ignoring the dominant conventions puts one in danger of losing the intended audience' (Canagarajah 2001: 129). We may hope for our students that they can challenge and transcend the 'rules', but in order to do so they must first understand them.

A third tension inherent in critical EAP pedagogy is the compelling necessity, while challenging political and cultural assumptions that underpin our education systems, to avoid portraying NNESs as defenceless victims incapable of learning, adapting or themselves critiquing different writing styles. Pennycook, discussing language use in the former British colonies, describes how English has been 'appropriated for different ends' such as political resistance, personal empowerment and liberation (1994: 260–87). Canagarajah (2001: 117) shows how 'language-minority students' from 'periphery English' communities (i.e. former colonies) 'negotiate a place for their local discourse conventions, intellectual traditions, cultural practices and the vernacular'. This 'negotiation for expression' fuels criticism and creativity in writing and gives rise to richly 'multivocal texts' (ibid.: 129).

In arguing that HEIs should reconsider their assessment strategies, I have moved away from my primary data: my students' voices. Despite frequent requests for 'less homework' and 'more fun' activities in class, none of them actually suggested that we alter the assessments. Instead, several described the huge sense of achievement and agency they experienced, having overcome the challenges of their first written assignments in the UK.

> During the time I spent in doing the [assignments] I have experienced different feelings. However, when I finished my tasks the feeling was only one, satisfaction . . . Every beginning is hard, especially for us foreigners . . . these tasks were the most difficult but they make me feel confident that I can manage with all the tasks which will be given to me in the future.
>
> (Bulgarian: law)

> After of my essay I feel excellent with myself because an essay 1,200 words was difficult target for me. But then when I finished my essay I thought that nothing is difficult, you have to just believe yourself.
>
> (Cypriot: mechanical engineering)

I would like to end as I began, with the words of Vasiliki,[4] a Greek student who progressed from the language foundation course to a three-year degree in English language and linguistics. Vasiliki found writing difficult, and was diagnosed with dyslexia part way through her degree studies. Despite this and the added challenge of being a non-native English speaker, she graduated with a sound 2.1 degree, including an A for her honours dissertation.

When I look back at all the assignments I've done since I came to the UK ... it's a huge pile ... I wonder how I ever managed to write so many thousands of words. And when I reread my essays, even the ones I wrote in my first year, I think: 'Did I write that? It's really good!'

Notes

1 'Post-1992' indicates former polytechnics and colleges of higher education that became universities following the Further and Higher Education Act 1992.
2 The International English Language Testing System is widely accepted as evidence of English language competence by HEIs in the UK, Australia, New Zealand, Canada, South Africa and Ireland.
3 The task description was as follows: 'Describe your feelings about the academic writing process we have been going through in the past ten weeks (choosing a topic, finding information, writing an essay outline, taking notes, drafting and redrafting the essay). Were you surprised by the feedback on your first draft? What did you find difficult/easy about the assignment, how much time did you spend, and what do you need to improve about your writing skills? You should write 250 words.'
4 Name used with permission.

References

Bailey, C. and Pieterick, J. (2008) 'Finding a new voice: challenges facing international and home students writing university assignments in the UK', in *Third Annual European First Year Experience Conference, May 7–9, University of Wolverhampton, UK*. Online. Available HTTP: http://wlv.openrepository.com/wlv/handle/2436/98516 (accessed 3 December 2010).

Benesch, S. (1993) 'ESL, ideology, and the politics of pragmatism', *TESOL Quarterly*, 27, 4: 705–17.

—— (2001) *Critical English for Academic Purposes: Theory, Politics and Practice*, New York: Routledge.

Brown, S. and Joughin, G. (2007) 'Assessment and international students: helping clarify puzzling processes', in E. Jones and S. Brown (eds) *Internationalising Higher Education*, Abingdon: Routledge, 57–71.

Brown, S., Rust, C. and Gibbs, G. (1994) *Strategies for Diversifying Assessment in Higher Education*, Oxford: the Oxford Centre for Staff Development.

Canagarajah, S. (2001) 'Addressing issues of power and difference in ESL academic writing', in J. Flowerdew and M. Peacock (eds) *Research Perspectives on English for Academic Purposes*, Cambridge: Cambridge University Press.

Connor, U. (2002) 'New directions in contrastive rhetoric', *TESOL Quarterly*, 36, 4: 493–510.

De Vita, G. (2002) 'Cultural equivalence in the assessment of home and international business management students: a UK exploratory study', *Studies in Higher Education*, 27, 2: 221–31.

Dolan, M. and Macias, I. (2009) *Motivating International Students: A Practical Guide to Aspects of Learning and Teaching*, Economics Network. Online. Available HTTP: http://www.economicsnetwork.ac.uk/handbook/international (accessed 3 August 2010).

Eade, K. and Peacock, N. (2009) *Internationalising Equality, Equalising Internationalisation: The Intersection Between Internationalisation and Equality and Diversity in Higher Education: Scoping Report*, London: Equality Challenge Unit (ECU). Online. Available HTTP: http://www.ecu.ac.uk/publications/files/Internationalising-equality-equalising-internationalisation-09.pdf/view (accessed 28 November 2010).

Egege, S. and Kutulieh, S. (2008) 'Dimming down difference . . .', in L. Dunn and M. Wallace (eds) *Teaching in Transnational Higher Education: Enhancing Learning for Offshore International Students*, New York: Routledge, 67–76.

Errey, L. (2002) 'Plagiarism: something fishy . . . or just a fish out of water?', *Teaching Forum*, 50: 17–20.

HEA (2010) 'Assessment and feedback', *Teaching International Students Project*, Higher Education Academy. Online. Available HTTP: http://www.heacademy.ac.uk/ourwork/teachingandlearning/internationalisation/studentlifecycle (accessed 3 July 2010).

Hyland, K. (2006) *English for Academic Purposes: An Advanced Resource Book*, Abingdon: Routledge.

Jordan, R.R. (1997) *English for Academic Purposes: A Guide and Resource Book for Teachers*, Cambridge: Cambridge University Press.

Kachru, Y. (1999) 'Culture, context and writing', in E. Hinkel (ed.) *Culture in Second Language Teaching and Learning*, Cambridge: Cambridge University Press.

Keck, C. (2006) 'The use of paraphrase in summary writing: a comparison of L1 and L2 writers', *Journal of Second Language Writing*, 15: 261–78.

Liu, D. (2005) 'Plagiarism in ESOL students: is cultural conditioning truly the major culprit?', *English Language Teaching Journal*, 59, 3: 234–41.

MacKinnon, D. and Manathunga, C. (2003) 'Going global with assessment: what to do when the dominant culture's literacy drives assessment', *Higher Education Research and Development*, 22, 2: 131–44.

Pecorari, D. (2003) 'Good and original: plagiarism and patchwriting in academic second-language writing', *Journal of Second Language Writing*, 12: 317–45.

—— (2008) *Academic Writing and Plagiarism: A Linguistic Analysis*, London: Continuum.

Pennycook, A. (1994) *The Cultural Politics of English as an International Language*, London: Longman.

—— (1996) 'Borrowing others' words: text, ownership, memory, and plagiarism', *TESOL Quarterly*, 30, 2: 201–30.

Phan Le Ha (2006) 'Plagiarism and overseas students: stereotypes again?', *English Language Teaching Journal*, 60, 1: 375–81.

QAA (Quality Assurance Agency for Higher Education) (2008) *The Framework for Higher Education Qualifications in England, Wales and Northern Ireland*. Online. Available HTTP: http://www.qaa.ac.uk/Publications/InformationAndGuidance/Documents/FHEQ08.pdf (accessed 8 August 2011).

—— (2010) *Code of Practice for the Assurance of Academic Quality and Standards in Higher Education. Section 3: Disabled Students*. Online. Available HTTP: http://www.qaa.ac.uk/academicinfrastructure/codeOfPractice/section3/Section3Disabilities2010.pdf (accessed 15 September 2010).

Race, P., Brown, S. and Smith, B. (2005) *500 Tips on Assessment*, 2nd edn, Abingdon: RoutledgeFalmer.

Ryan, J. and Carroll, J. (2005) '"Canaries in the coalmine": international students in Western universities', in J. Carroll and J. Ryan (eds) *Teaching International Students: Improving Learning for All*, Abingdon: Routledge, 3–10.

Ryan, J. and Viete, R. (2009) 'Respectful interactions: learning with international students in the English-speaking academy', *Teaching in Higher Education*, 14, 3: 303–14.

Schmitt, D. (2005) 'Writing in the international classroom', in J. Carroll and J. Ryan (eds) *Teaching International Students: Improving Learning for All*, Abingdon: Routledge, 63–74.

Scollon, R. (1994) 'As a matter of fact: the changing ideology of authorship and responsibility in discourse', *World Englishes*, 13, 1: 33–46.

Smailes, J. and Gannon-Leary, P. (2008) 'Have we got it right? A case study on international student views of inclusive teaching and learning at Northumbria', *International Journal of Management Education*, 7, 1: 51–60.

Swales, J.M. and Feak, C.B. (2004) *Academic Writing for Graduate Students: Essential Tasks and Skills*, 2nd edn, Ann Arbor, MI: University of Michigan Press.

UKCISA (2011) *Higher Education Statistics', UK Council for International Student Affairs*. Online. Available HTTP: http://www.ukcisa.org.uk/about/statistics_he.php (accessed 21 April 2011).

Waterfield, J. and West, B. (eds) (2006) *Inclusive Assessment in Higher Education: A Resource for Change*, University of Plymouth SPACE Project (Staff–Student Partnership for Assessment Change and Evaluation). Online. Available HTTP: http//:www.plymouth.ac.uk (accessed 20 September 2010).

Watkins, D., Reghi, M. and Astilla, E. (1991). 'The-Asian-learner-as-a-rote-learner stereotype: myth or reality?', *Educational Psychology*, 11, 1: 21–34.

Chapter 13

Ways with writing

International students' perspectives on responding to academic writing requirements in UK higher education

Weronika Górska

Introduction

In recent years in the UK, higher education issues related to academic writing support have attracted much attention from both practitioners and researchers, and subsequently writing support provision has become one of the very vivid areas of research in UK academia. In many ways, the research has focused on the understanding of the nature of academic writing as well as needs and expectations held by key stakeholders, i.e. students who are required to write various academic texts for assessment and academics who assign and then evaluate these texts. This chapter brings into the debate the voices of international students by presenting their perspectives on the support they receive, the academic requirements they have to meet and their own engagement in learning to write academically approved texts. The international students in this chapter are students who come either from overseas or from European Union countries and who aspire to pursue their masters degrees in UK universities. The discussion draws on findings from a study that investigated the academic writing development of international students on an International Pre-Masters Programme (IPP) at one of the highly sought-after universities in central London. The research was conducted in the academic year of 2009/10. The students who participated in the research were of various levels of English language proficiency; usually between 5.5 and 6.0 IELTS score. The interview data provided by these students indicate that currently prevailing writing support, focused on surface text features and grammatical accuracy, helps them to understand basic differences between writing in different cultural contexts but does not provide sufficient guidance while writing for academic disciplines at university in the UK. Interviews with students further revealed that while composing their assignments, students engaged in discipline-specific literacy activities and created social networks that helped them to participate critically in their chosen field of study, and consequently allowed them to respond successfully to writing requirements. As such, the students' accounts raise questions about the assumptions underpinning 1) academic writing support in UK higher education, and 2) international students' needs as far as responding to academic writing requirements are concerned. Learning from students' experience can help not only improve academic writing support, but most of all present international students as active agents in their efforts to excel in academic writing in English.

International students at UK universities and institutional writing support

The United Kingdom is one of the most popular destinations on the contemporary map of student mobility. In the academic years of 2008/9 and 2009/10 the UK attracted 13 per cent of all international students at tertiary level (Project Atlas 2009). International students choosing to study in UK universities are usually motivated not only academically but also professionally. On the academic level, they opt to pursue their degrees in the UK because of the prestigious status of English being 'the world's predominant language of research and scholarship' (Hyland 2006: 24) and the high quality of 'western university education' (Harris 1997: 32). On the professional level, international students are attracted to UK universities by worldwide recognition of UK degrees, which are essential in the contemporary globalized employment market.

Entering UK higher education, international students become participants in a new learning environment, which is often very different to that which they had previously known. Because in the UK writing constitutes a major form of university assessment, international students' ability to respond to writing requirements becomes of paramount importance to their academic success. For that reason the inability to write academic texts puts international students in danger of failing their courses, and may lead to interruption of studies or, more gravely, to their abandoning or being dropped from their programmes (Ganobcsik-Williams 2006; Lillis and Scott 2007). Viewed from this perspective academic writing is rightly regarded as a 'high stake' activity (Jones *et al.* 1999). This activity in itself is more than just putting words onto paper. Academic writing involves the ability to communicate ideas following the epistemological frameworks and disciplinary conventions of a given subject or a field of knowledge. To be successful in academic writing students need to engage in 'ways of thinking, acting, valuing and speaking' (Boughey 2000: 3) that are characteristic of a given academic discipline and at the same time often different from everyday communication, or from academic discourses that students may be familiar with from the education received in their countries of origin or at earlier stages of their academic career. A common practice, therefore, present in almost all UK higher education institutions, is to assist students who need to improve their writing in general or who need guidance with particular academic assignments. Universities offer a range of programmes and courses available to students both before they undertake their academic degrees and while they are already studying at university. The offer for students who seek to improve their academic writing prior to enrolling for their academic programmes usually includes pre-sessional English for academic purposes (EAP) courses run during the summer as well as year-long foundation programmes, in which writing constitutes a significant component. For those of the students who need to improve their writing while already pursuing their degrees, UK universities run in-sessional programmes usually comprised of courses focused on different aspects of academic writing. Table 13.1 exemplifies options that at present are most commonly available.

The writing courses and programmes outlined in Table 13.1 are usually run by university support units outside of academic departments, most commonly in English language centres. They are prepared and taught by English language tutors holding a degree in TESOL or an ELT professional qualification. Even though there is a wide array of academic writing courses on offer, the courses tend to be fairly similar in content. Their key focus is on 1) surface features of text structure, such as 'introductions', 'body', 'conclusions', 2) discrete elements of language and academic style, such as formal vocabulary, hedging or reporting verbs, and 3) referencing styles and plagiarism. This currently prevailing model of writing support is rooted in the EAP tradition where explicit focus is placed on formal accuracy and as such on teaching discrete elements of genres (mainly text

Table 13.1 Academic writing support for international students in higher education (UK)

	Programmes/ courses	Content	Duration
Before undertaking degree studies	Pre-sessional EAP courses	Essay writing Elements of academic style Use of sources/referencing	4 to 12 weeks
	Pre-undergraduate foundation programmes	Basic academic genres: e.g. essay, report Grammar/vocabulary Elements of academic style Use of sources/referencing	6 to 9 months
	Pre-masters foundation programmes	Basic academic genres: e.g. essay, report, critique, research project (depending on a university) Grammar/vocabulary Elements of academic style Use of sources/referencing	6 to 9 months
While pursuing degree studies	In-sessional writing courses	Essay/report writing Dissertation/thesis writing Elements of academic style Use of sources/referencing	Up to 10 weeks
	Writing workshops	As above	From 1 to several consecutive sessions
	1:1 drop-in sessions	Depending on individual needs	Usually 1 session

structure), sentence structure, academic vocabulary and citation styles (Lillis 2001; Wingate 2006). In general, this approach assumes that a) surface text level, grammatical correctness and familiarity with referencing systems are key elements in academic writing, and that b) genres and disciplinary conventions can be taught separately from the subject content and then applied to any academic discipline. While learning to write, students 'undertake exercises which draw their attention to linguistic patterns and distinctions in written language, and their writing [in these courses] is assessed according to how accurately these patterns have been produced' (Ivanic 2004: 227). This dominant model of support is often criticized as insufficient by researchers in academic writing (Ivanic and Lea 2006; Lea and Street 1998; Lillis and Scott 2007). It is argued that academic writing is inscribed in disciplinary knowledge and cannot be taught or practised separately from it. It is also pointed out that the EAP approach 'assumes transparency in relation to language, and transmission in relation to pedagogy' (Lillis 2006: 32) which fails to take into consideration that the meaning carried by language depends on social context – in the case of academic writing, on a particular academic discipline – and that it cannot be unproblematically transferred from one academic field to another.

In this context, key questions arise: 1) what do international students do in order to bridge the gap between subject specific requirements and general writing provision, 2) what literacy practices do they engage in while responding to academic writing requirements, and finally 3) what, if anything, can be learnt from their experience? With these questions being central to this chapter, the following sections will report on research, conducted by the author, that investigated the academic writing development of international students on an IPP. The sections below will outline the theoretical foundations of the research project, data collection procedures, writing support offered on the IPP and the writing requirements of that programme. Most attention will be given to presenting students' perspectives on learning how to write academic texts and responding to writing requirements in their chosen fields of study.

Researching international students' experience

In the understanding of academic writing the research presented in this chapter took into consideration the criticism of current support provision, outlined in the previous section. Extending beyond the EAP model, the study drew on an academic literacies approach which views academic writing as a socially situated practice focused on meaning making (Lea and Street 1998) and therefore 'works as critique by serving as an oppositional frame to conventional approaches to students writing' (Lillis 2006: 32). Brian Street, whose research into academic writing directly contributed to the development of the academic literacies approach, explains:

> An academic literacies approach views the institutions in which academic practices take place as constituted in and as sites of discourse and power (Lea

and Street, 1998). It sees the literacy demands of the curriculum as involving a variety of communicative practices, including genres, fields, and disciplines. From the student point of view a dominant feature of academic literacy practices is the requirement to switch practices between one setting and another, to deploy a repertoire of linguistic practices appropriate to each setting, and to handle the social meanings and identities that each evokes.

(Street 2004: 15)

The academic literacies approach, problematizing the view of student writing as a uniform skill, highlights the disciplinary nature of academic writing, and sees it as discourses situated in the social context of the academy rather than surface text features, both in terms of structure and language. For these reasons, in the study presented here, adopting an academic literacies approach opens a critical space for exploring what students do in order to respond to academic writing requirements when the support options seem not to assist them in an efficient way, as discussed earlier. In other words, by defining academic writing on the level of epistemology and power relations and explaining that academic disciplines often follow different writing conventions, thereby requiring a different repertoire of linguistic practices, the academic literacies approach is particularly helpful in understanding what students engage in while negotiating their responses to academic writing requirements in their academic programmes.

The academic literacies approach, apart from providing a theoretical foundation for the study, also influenced the choice of methodology and data collection procedures. The academic literacies approach, drawing on the social study of language and literacy, has brought a key research method of these fields – ethnography – to the study of academic writing which previously was dominated by various methods of textual analysis and would draw on various traditions of rhetoric, genre analysis or linguistic frameworks (Hyland 2003, 2006; Juzwik *et al.* 2006; Kroll 2003). The use of ethnography allows for:

> observation of practices surrounding the production of text – rather than focusing solely on written texts – as well as participants' perspectives on the texts and practices. This ethnographic framing of the study of students writing connects strongly with . . . practitioners' interest . . . in exploring and making sense of students' perspectives on academic writing, including challenging 'taken for granted' conventions that they are expected to write within.

(Lillis and Scott 2007: 11)

As gaining insights into students' perspectives is one of the main aims of the research presented here, the study employed an ethnographic perspective in the data collection. Adopting such an ethnographic perspective allowed engagement with students while they attempted to grapple with academic writing at a UK university.

The following sections will present the IPP, describe the participants and outline how the data were collected and analysed.

IPP: writing requirements and support

The IPP lasts over nine months (from October to June) and is offered by the university English language centre to international students who completed their first degrees in their home countries and who would like to continue their higher education in the UK. This programme is aimed at enabling a successful transition from undergraduate to graduate programmes and at the same time from a non-UK to a UK university educational system. For these reasons the IPP provides students not only with academic writing support by language specialists, but it also gives students an opportunity to study discipline-specific subjects taught by university lecturers. The discipline subjects include a compulsory general foundation module on topics relevant to British culture and society, and a selective module where students choose one out of three MA preparatory courses; the choice includes a course in law, politics and business management. The programme objectives, taken from the IPP Handbook, are shown in Box 13.1.

Academic writing constitutes one of the key components of the programme, and it has a significant bearing (approximately 62.5 per cent) towards the final grade for the course (see the appendix for a detailed breakdown).

In order to prepare for the written assessment, students were offered an intensive writing module (1.5 hour sessions, three times a week) taught by language specialists. Each writing session was to be focused on a different aspect, i.e., writing; writing/reading; writing/grammar/vocabulary. The course outline for

---

Box 13.1 IPP

The programme is designed to provide a structured pathway into postgraduate programmes related to the fields of arts, humanities, social sciences, business and law for international students of high potential.

The full-time three-term programme aims to:

- support you in gaining entry to some of the best postgraduate degree programmes in arts, humanities, social sciences, including management related degrees and law;
- improve your understanding of and ability to use academic English appropriately and effectively at postgraduate level;
- provide you with a range of study, English and communication skills to help you succeed in your postgraduate study in the UK;
- introduce you to the British educational system and the traditional lecture/seminar/tutorial format;
- provide you with a specially designed course related to the academic field in which you intend to specialize.

the writing classes was descriptive, not prescriptive; therefore, writing tutors were able to adjust the content of the classes in order to better respond to students' needs. Both classroom observations and the interview data indicate that most of the sessions were devoted to surface text features and use of language in academic writing, and that reading was the most marginalized part, focused on study skills such as skimming and scanning. In writing classes the only assessed piece of work was a critique in term two (1,500 words), which contributed 12.5 per cent towards the final grade for the IPP.

The majority of assessed writing, constituting 50 per cent towards the final grade, comes from end of term essays and end of year exams written for a compulsory foundation module as well as for MA preparatory modules in the students' chosen disciplines. For these subjects students were required to produce an essay each term. These essays were progressively longer each term: 1,000 words in term one; 1,250 words in term two and 1,750 words in term three. The assignments in term one were formative and in terms two and three summative and as such only these contributed to the final course grade. The assignments were assessed by the lecturers teaching given modules using the following criteria: relevance, critical analysis, clear organization/structure, use of sources, understanding the material, clarity of expression/grammar/syntax/spelling, academic conventions. The subject lecturers would distribute the essay topics to the students, and would offer a brief discussion of these topics. They would assume that it was not their role to offer any more assistance with academic writing. In an interview one of the subject lecturers justified this by saying that 'this is how university traditionally works, and that the students receive help in [the] writing component of the foundation programme' (Andrew). In the interviews the writing tutors confirmed that there is little communication between them and subject lecturers and often voiced opinions that the assumption is that the students should be able to transfer what they learn in writing classes to the writing in the subject modules. Some of the tutors expressed their reservations regarding the efficiency of such provision, but at the same time stated that this is what the university currently offers.

Student participants

Twenty participants volunteered to take part in this research: twelve international students from countries in Europe, South America and South-East Asia, four writing tutors, three subject tutors and one programme coordinator. The international students all had degrees from their home countries and sometimes a history of successful professional careers in their fields. All of the students enrolled for the IPP as they wanted to enhance their chance of being offered a place on an MA programme at a UK university of their choice. In most of the cases, even though the IPP is not a prerequisite but due to language level they would not be admitted, instead of preparing to re-take an English language proficiency exam, usually either IELTS or TEOFL, they chose to study on the pre-masters programme as they saw this as an opportunity not only to improve their English language competence but also to study foundation subjects in their chosen disciplines and gain general familiarity with the English HE system.

Data collection and analysis

The data collected during this study included ethnographic observations of writing classes and in-depth interviews with those involved in teaching on the IPP and with students studying on the programme. The data were collected during three terms of the academic year 2009/10, and each term the collection procedures followed the same pattern represented in Figure 13.1.

Each term started with the observation of the writing classes, towards the end of the term the interviews with students and tutors would take place, and usually at the beginning of the next term students' written work would be collected. The interviews were around the production of the assignments, focusing on students' application of generic writing classes to writing in the disciplines, the support from the subject tutors received by the students before or while writing, and the students' own engagement in responding to the disciplinary requirements of academic writing. The interviews were transcribed and themes were coded. The content analysis suggested prevailing themes, and these themes will be discussed later in the chapter.

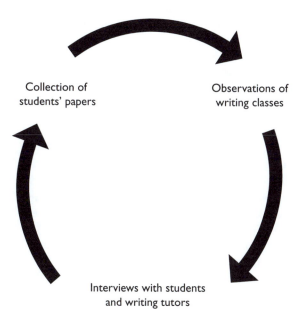

Collection of
students' papers

Observations of
writing classes

Interviews with students
and writing tutors

Figure 13.1 Data collection.

Students' accounts: from institutional support to students' ways with writing

This section presents the themes that were most prevalent in students' interviews. All names given below have been changed, and the students' own voices are used to illustrate issues that emerged from their experience of learning how to write academically approved texts and how to use this knowledge while responding to the requirements of their subject modules on the IPP.

Writing classes are 'good for me'

In the interviews one of the clear themes was students' high appreciation of writing classes. Students many times underlined that received guidance on writing academic papers in English was 'the most valuable thing' (Genji). My informants talked in particular about becoming familiar with the academic conventions of an essay and a critique, as well as improving their written language ability and learning differences between university writing in the UK and in higher education institutions in their home countries.

With reference to essay writing, students stated that the classes were 'helpful on structure: introduction, body, conclusion and reference' (Farisa).

> Peter [writing tutor] told me everything. All I know is because of Peter . . . It's like that you have to have a beginning, a middle and an end, but in the beginning, in the middle and the end, actually you say the same things. Like in the beginning you introduce your idea and what you're going to say and what's your position and where you're going to get, and then the devises . . . like giving examples . . . to like make it stronger your point like . . . And then put something like, 'In conclusion' . . . And in the conclusion you state what your essay's about, you know, yeah, you just state it all over again and again and again . . . That's it!
>
> (Maria Teresa)

Exploring the text structure, students also learnt how to write a thesis statement, topic sentence and a well-structured paragraph. Moreover, they also became familiar with how to compile a bibliography and use sources in writing:

> Sue [writing tutor] gave us a hand-out of different kinds of bibliography, how can we write different kinds of sources, how can we like sorted the . . . how can we sort that into bibliography like with different letters . . . And if we see from internet, how can we write down in bibliography . . . And the hand-out is like for us like writing bible.
>
> (Chyou)

Apart from learning basic elements of essay structure, students learned how to write an academic critique:

> Yes, I think I also wanted to say a critique because I remember very clearly Sue gave us a lot of materials about critique and how to write a critique from the first part to summary something, and then to critique and give us the structures to structure we choose. I think very useful for me.
>
> (Mee)

Another important section of the writing course was learning language features, for example the use of prepositions or passive voice and features of academic discourse, such as hedging:

> We should say our opinions, but also use this hedging language which is very important I think because nothing is 100 per cent true so it's nice to say that they 'tend to be . . .' like this kind of language.
>
> (Agnes)

Moreover, students also learnt expressions commonly used in academic writing.

> I learned from Peter's class [academic writing class], I learned in the introduction we have to indicate our position of our essay, something like, 'This paper will examine, will focus on which aspect' . . . Then like show the readers, the order in our main body like the first sentence to open . . . to start a paragraph, like 'The main point in this paragraph is'.
>
> (Guan-yin)

The wide array of phrases quoted by students in the interviews include 'it would be' or 'it is known that' or 'it is acknowledged that' (Farisa). Students were highly appreciative of this language input because they felt that their English language competence was not sufficient to express themselves as precisely as they wanted: 'because [of] my English problem so I can't explain very' (Genji).

While talking about the benefits of the writing classes, students often drew comparisons between what they were learning about academic writing in the UK and what they learned from writing at universities in their home countries.

> Chinese writing is much more different from English writing because Chinese writing's like very indirect, very . . . how to say, you should like hide your emotion, you cannot show your opinions so straightly. But for English just you should let all your readers know what you are writing about. So that's difficult for me to adjust to from Chinese writing to English writing.
>
> (Chyou)

Students from South America discussed the 'linear' structure and how 'weird' it seems to repeat the same information in various part of the essay.

Another area of difference refers to the use of sources and providing supporting evidence.

> If I want to write something like assignment essay then needs evidence always, okay, it's evidence from books or journals or it's really academic . . . In my country we don't need it; we just wrote down what I think or what is the purpose to write my essay or . . . yeah, just to like give my opinion but this country's essay, they need always evidence.
>
> (Yang)

> The critique was really, really good for me because it taught me how to use my critical thinking or to think about things or not to believe 100 per cent what the author says, because in Hungary that was my problem, like when I read a book, okay, I agreed. But in the UK it's really important to express your opinion and you are free not to agree, and that's very good in my opinion.
>
> (Agnes)

'Worried about' writing an essay

Although writing classes were highly praised, in the interviews students voiced their views about the limitations of these classes. In particular they expressed anxiety about how to use the knowledge from writing classes to write in their subject modules. When discussing how they wrote subject essays they commented, 'Sue tried give information for everyone but it was general about essay' (Ana).

> So [writing] tutors they help us but Business Management or something like this one they don't know about it very much . . . They checked some grammar or structure or some ideas but not specific.
>
> (Yang)

> I worried about it [an essay for the optional module] because I think Law essay is different from CTS, the critique and other essays . . . it's hard for me to get information from Peter's class and our [subject] teacher, I think he didn't give us information about how to write essays too. So for this one I really . . . I am not sure if it's a good one.
>
> (Genji)

Subject tutors: 'they cannot help us'

In the interviews students often stated that subject module lecturers did not offer much support regarding writing:

> They taught us about the lecture but not about writing. So I don't think I got some support from them.
>
> (Yang)

If help came, it was a result of poorly written assignments:

> Yeah, they gave us the topic, but okay, they didn't say anything about how we should structure the essays, and actually today we are going to have politics module lecture and seminar and the teacher said, Roberto, that okay we are going to look at the structure of a political essay as well and, I mean, okay, but we should . . . in my opinion we should have done this at the beginning of the term.
>
> (Agnes)

Sometimes it was suggested to students to come and ask for help, but many of them would not take this opportunity and preferred to work by themselves:

> She just mention that maybe if we ask her individually she could answer us but I didn't try. It was just that I did by myself, just did it myself.
>
> (Yang)

Some students chose not to ask, as in Yang's example, as 'in my home country we do not ask', but they would still welcome more explanation: 'they [subject lecturers] should let us know'.

Some other students chose to ask but were not fully satisfied with the answers:

> Adam say little things . . . 'I was disappointed and I wanted some kind of support because I thought it's impossible for me because I'm studying English five month, not more . . . Of course I asked something Adam and he told me only, you know, by two or three sentences. It was short . . . In general they give advice but not in particular questions. Actually I asked him before I started writing; he explained in some general ideas but it was good, it was good for me but maybe not enough.
>
> (Ana)

Sometimes students say that 'they [subject tutors] avoid to give you an answer' (Maria Teresa) as they think that they would guide them too much.

The institutional help was not fully useful. As writing classes were not easily 'transferable' to other contexts, in the interviews the students often discussed literacy activities they tried to resort to in order to successfully respond to the requirements of writing in their chosen modules.

Friends and classmates – discussing writing

When discussing how they were working on their essays, one of the characteristic features of this process was looking for the opinions of others on their writing. Students often showed drafts to their friends or classmates. Students employ new technology:

With my classmate we use reviews, MSN Messenger, Hotmail messenger, so we usually chat on MSN . . . So we send our file of our assignment and then we check each other's.

(Yang)

There seem to be two main reasons why students were looking for feedback from friends. The first of these reasons is to gain some insight: 'if you could understand, if it was answering the question, if you could see my position' (Maria Teresa).

When it was ready I show it to my friend here. She's Hungarian. She's not in my [writing] class. But she's from my subject, she does politics module. And she read it and I asked her to give me like some feedback.

(Maria Teresa)

Yes, I will ask my house mates [who take the same option module], is there any problem with my essay. They will give me some suggestion and I will follow some suggestion to correct my essay . . . We share the experience.

(Lee)

The friends or classmates would not be randomly chosen. Conversely, in choosing them, the students wanted somebody who was writing an essay in the same module.

Actually what is really important that . . . yeah, when you have somebody like your friends who know something about the topic then you can discuss it. And that's why in my opinion I got A for my critique because there was a girl, Greek and a Turkish girl, and they disagreed in many things (laughter) because she doesn't like the European Union but I am more favouring the European Union. And then I discovered new ideas through her, so that's really important.

(Agnes)

Another reason to seek friends' help was to obtain some help with language. Being aware of their language problems ('some mother tongue in (their) essay(s)' (Lee)), they felt it important to discuss language details with others:

I ask my classmates to correct my grammar mistakes. I think it's helpful because when I write I don't know what's wrong with my grammar so I can't help. I can't know my grammar mistake even if it's very simple but other people will.

(Genji)

In these examples, students sought to gain access to their community of practice, to the discourses of these communities; they wanted to be understood by those who attended the same modules and were writing within the same subject area. This is a significant departure from generic support.

Reading: structure and language of the disciplines

In the interview data, students highlighted the connection between reading and writing. In their opinion, 'reading is key' (Agnes), and drives the whole process of composing a text:

> Yes, the reading and writing skills, but I think the most useful is the reading skill . . . But I can't describe how I get this skill, but after this term [the first term], I think my reading skill has improved so much.
>
> (Lee)

> First I choose the topic, which one interesting for me. And then I go back to listen to the lecture, I listen to the recording on the website and see the slides . . . And find some book list to find a book and read . . . maybe in the book, I mean the index I can choose which part is interesting for me or useful for my essay and I read that part.
>
> (Mee)

Lee, whenever he talked about his writing process, described carefully the process of looking for ideas, evaluating the sources, reading, going back to the readings, giving the topic up if he did not have enough ideas. The structure depended on the ideas:

> Firstly, get the topic, secondly think about it, thirdly find the books, articles and some information on the website or from the library and then, based according to the information I have got, I will think about the topic again and organise the information, and divide the information into different aspects . . . Because if I have different aspects, that means I have a structure it's easy for me to write down the idea.
>
> (Lee)

Ana said that 'it's not enough only to do exercises on writing'; in her interviews she underlined the importance of engagement with reading:

> First of all I think, next I read. By the reading I underline what I write. Next I collect in one place. Next I read what I have in general and my opinions also . . . it's like to build a house or something like this. It is my strategy.
>
> (Ana)

Reading helped her to build the structure of her text. The same was reported by other students:

Actually that was a kind of problem not just for me in my opinion but also for other students because we were talking about this, do you know how you could structure your essay and actually what you want to write in your essay and it was our problem that we didn't really know and we had to read about it. But it was a kind of process, reading about these topics and it took lots of time, but after that it was much easier when we knew how we wanted to structure or what we wanted to write about.

(Agnes)

Apart from ideas and structure, while reading students were sensitive to the language used in academic texts. Ana would collect vocabulary lists from the readings, and other students used similar strategies:

So what I did was to buy a little book written by Benedictus, the Pope, which is a great theologist . . . it is very easy to read. It's simple . . . It was about the life of the Apostles, you know . . . I remember that for example I learned the word 'believers' because I put the word in the draft . . . Believers like 'brotherhood' . . . I needed words linked with religious life . . . I learned the word, he use it a lot, 'And so' 'And then' and I had never heard that word from the teachers. And I said, 'Oh, well, he's a book writer', so I used it in the assignment, in both assignments.

(Beatrice)

Learning from students' experience

The experience of the students participating in this study, as presented in the interview data, strongly indicates at least two points that can be discussed with reference to writing support provision for international students in the UK higher education. The first point refers to the usefulness of generic writing support, and the second one refers to students' needs and the possibility of rethinking the content and structure of the writing courses currently offered.

In UK higher education, the last decade has seen a substantial amount of research on writing support at university and as a result, the generic support currently offered has been extensively criticized in the research literature. A key critique of this approach, presented earlier in this chapter, states that academic writing is taught without taking into consideration both the epistemological frameworks of given disciplines and the discourses characteristic to writing in given academic fields. In the study presented in this chapter, evidence from the students' interviews on the one hand supports this critique, but on the other hand it strongly suggests that generic writing support offers international students a desirable introduction to important concepts related to academic writing. As seen in glimpses of the students' experience, they view academic writing classes focused on surface text features and linguistic accuracy as 'good for them', and they say that they learnt 'so much' from these classes. It is essential, however, to notice that students give their positive evaluation not so much with reference to the adequacy of generic writing support for writing in their academic disciplines, but when a) drawing comparisons between writing in the UK and writing in their home countries, and b) discussing their learning of English language for written communication. Based on this finding, it can be stated that generic academic writing support is useful in certain contexts, such as a general introduction to academic writing at UK universities, but it is insufficient in preparing students for writing in academic disciplines. This finding is important in that it demonstrates the benefits of the support currently offered to international students, but at the same time it highlights its essential drawbacks. The academic literacies approach helps to understand this situation by employing the distinction between autonomous and ideological models of literacy (Street 1984). By doing so, the academic literacies approach problematizes the perspective on academic writing as atomized, transferable skills and foregrounds a social perspective where socio-cultural context plays a vital role:

> At a theoretical level . . . contrasting notions of autonomous and ideological positions on literacy in general provided a useful heuristic for opening up a critical exploration of the specific literacy demands and practices associated with academia. Rather than the dominant position on literacy as autonomous – whereby literacy is viewed as a single and universal phenomenon with assumed cognitive as well as economic benefits – . . . [an academic literacies approach draws on] an ideological model of literacy – whereby the focus is on acknowledging the socio-culturally embedded nature of literacy practices and the associated power differentials in any literacy related activity (Street 1984, 2004, 2005).
>
> (Lillis and Scott 2007: 11)

Generic writing support, offering useful introductory awareness of academic writing, does not prove to be equally helpful as the only support to writing at university where discipline specific discourses and issues of power and identity play a vital role. This means that students' needs in terms of being prepared for writing in their subject courses are not fully catered for by the support provision. The next paragraph discusses this point in more detail.

In the IPP, 50 per cent of the final grade comes from the assessment of student writing in their subject modules. Even though students were offered three 1.5 hour sessions a week of generic writing classes, the student interviews clearly indicate that writing in the disciplines involved more than knowing how to structure an essay or write with grammatical correctness and accuracy. Insights from student interviews present a rich account of the students' critical engagement in responding to academic writing requirements. This critical engagement involves negotiating writing requirements with subject tutors, negotiating ideas within an academic community, and negotiating text structure and disciplinary discourses through critical and analytical reading. On the basis of comments made about generic writing support, one may come to the conclusion that international students require only a general introduction to academic writing and once this is provided they should be able to transfer, without much problem, the generic knowledge into writing in their disciplines. The students' engagement in a variety of literacy activities, as has emerged from the interviews, seems to indicate that their needs are directly linked to an explicit understanding of the disciplinary conventions of writing in their academic fields. They seek to understand these conventions by engaging in dialogue with subject tutors, then by discussing their ideas with other students writing in the same discipline, and finally by critical reading. Students often resort to these practices many times in a process of writing. In order to respond to their needs more adequately, a revision of institutional support provision would be highly recommended. A starting point in this challenging work could be listening to students' experience and learning from how they negotiate both writing requirements and support received as well as how they actively engage in attempting to write academic texts at UK universities.

Conclusions

In the UK academic writing support has recently gained prominence in both various pedagogical initiatives and research in higher education. This chapter has sought to contribute to this body of work by bringing to it the voices of international students. By presenting students' perspectives on what is involved in responding to academic writing requirements, this chapter has aimed at making these voices more audible to researchers, practitioners and a broader audience. The international students in the study reported here shared their journey through institutional support, disciplinary writing requirements and their own attempts to negotiate and understand 'what is going on' with academic writing. Learning from them brings new perspectives on the support they receive but also, and more importantly, on students' needs as far as the instruction on and support with academic writing is concerned. In the light of the interview data, the limits of the support offered, and the boundaries the students have to push at without much-needed support, are highlighted. It is hoped that students' ways with writing will 'stimulate a further reflection' (Leki 2001: 26) and that instead of offering limited support, writing support informed by students' needs can be designed and implemented.

References

Boughey, C. (2000) 'Multiple metaphors in an understanding of academic literacy', *Teachers and Teaching: Theory and Practice*, 6, 3: 279–90.

Ganobcsik-Williams, L. (ed.) (2006) *Teaching Academic Writing in UK Higher Education: Theories, Practices and Models*, Houndmills: Palgrave MacMillan.

Harris, R. (1997) 'Overseas students in the United Kingdom university system', in D. McNamara and R. Harris (eds) *Overseas Students in Higher Education: Issues in Teaching and Learning*, London and New York: Routledge.

Hyland, K. (2003) *Second Language Writing*, New York: Harper & Row Publishers.

—— (2006) *English for Academic Purposes: An Advanced Resource Book*, London: Routledge.

Ivanic, R. (2004) 'Discourses of writing and learning to write', *Language and Education*, 18, 3: 220–45.

Ivanic, R. and Lea, M.R. (2006) 'New contexts, new challenges: the teaching of writing in UK higher education', in L. Ganobcsik-Williams (ed.) *Teaching Academic Writing in UK Higher Education: Theories, Practices and Models*, Houndmills: Palgrave MacMillan.

Jones, C., Turner, J. and Street, B.V. (eds) (1999) *Students Writing in the University: Cultural and Epistemological Issues*, Amsterdam: Benjamins.

Juzwik, M., Curcic, S., Wolbers, K., Moxley, K.D., Dimling, L.M. and Shankland, R.K. (2006) 'Writing into the 21st century: an overview of research on writing 1999 to 2004', *Written Communication*, 23, 4: 451–76.

Kroll, B. (ed.) (2003) *Exploring the Dynamics of Second Language Writing*, Cambridge: Cambridge University Press.

Lea, M.R. and Street, B.V. (1998) 'Student writing in higher education: an academic literacies approach', *Studies in Higher Education*, 23, 2: 157–72.

Leki, I. (2001) 'Hearing voices: L2 students' experiences in L2 writing courses', in T.J. Silva and P.K. Matsuda (eds) *On Second Language Writing*, Mahwah: Lawrence Erlbaum Associates, 17–28.

Lillis, T. (2001) *Student Writing: Access, Regulation, Desire*, London and New York: Routledge.

—— (2006) 'Moving towards an "academic literacies" pedagogy: dialogues of participation', in L. Ganobcsik-Williams (ed.) *Teaching Academic Writing in UK Higher Education: Theories, Practices and Models*, Houndmills: Palgrave MacMillan, 30–45.

—— and Scott, M. (2007) 'Defining academic literacies research: issues of epistemology, ideology and strategy', *Journal of Applied Linguistics*, 4: 5–32.

Project Atlas (2009) *Country Profiles*. Online. Available HTTP: http://www.atlas. iienetwork.org/?p=48027 (accessed 11 June 2009).

Street, B.V. (1984) *Literacy in Theory and Practice*, Cambridge: Cambridge University Press.

—— (2004) 'Academic literacies and the "new orders": implications for research and practice in students writing in higher education', *LATISS: Learning and Teaching in the Social Sciences*, 1, 1: 9–20.

—— (ed.) (2005) *Literacies across Educational Contexts: Mediating Learning and Teaching*, Philadelphia: Caslon Press.

Wingate, U. (2006) 'Doing away with study skills', *Teaching in Higher Education*, 11, 4: 457–69.

Appendix

Table 13.2 Summary of breakdown and calculation of assessment (bold sections refer to academic writing)

Module/skill assessed	Term	Coursework	Coursework value	Final exam	Coursework plus exam	Module total	Programme total (calculation of final mark)
Academic study skills/ subject knowledge							
Option module	1	Formative assignment	0%				
	2	Assignment	20%				
	3	Assignment	30%	**50%**	**+50%**	**=100%**	100%	**25%**
Culture, theory and society	1	Formative assignment	0%				
	2	Assignment	20%				
	3	Assignment	30%	**50%**	**+50%**	**=100%**	100%	**25%**
Academic English for foundation students							
Reading	1–3	Formative reading tasks	0%				
	2	Assessed reading task	5%	**5%**	**+20%**	**=25%**	100%	**50%**
Writing	1–3	Formative writing tasks	0%				
	2	Critique	15%	**15%**	**+10%**	**=25%**		
Listening	1–3	Formative listening tasks	0%				
	2	Assessed listening task	5%	**5%**	**+20%**	**=25%**		
Speaking	1	Formative oral presentation	0%				
	2	Oral presentation	10%				
	3	Oral presentation	15%	**25%**	-	**=25%**		

Part IV

Home students abroad

Chapter 14

Great expectations

The impact of friendship groups on the intercultural learning of Australian students abroad

Wendy Green

The promotion of study abroad, or 'horizontal mobility', as a culturally and academically enriching experience, voluntarily undertaken (Rivza and Teichler 2007), has been spearheaded by the European Union, as part of the Bologna process. More recently however, universities and governments in Anglophone countries – historically the net importers of international students – have also recognized the importance of boosting the mobility of domestic students. In the US, study abroad is gaining considerable support and public funding through the Simon Study Abroad Act (2009). Likewise in Australia, the establishment of the National Roundtable on Outbound Mobility in 2006 signalled the Commonwealth Government's commitment to boosting horizontal mobility – a commitment that is mirrored in the policies of many Australian universities (Olsen 2008). Perhaps most remarkable are the changes in some Asian countries. Historically net exporters of 'vertically mobile' students (Rivza and Teichler 2007), who move, of necessity from developing countries to economically, educationally advanced ones, China (Marginson and van der Wende 2007) and Singapore (NUS 2009), for example, are now in a position to promote horizontal mobility, due to their substantial investment in higher education.

This 'revolution' in study abroad is not only numerical, but also philosophical (Lewin 2009). In Australia, as elsewhere, there are high expectations that study abroad will bring national benefits of long-term economic, diplomatic and social benefits on the one hand and richer, more tolerant perspectives for individual participants on the other (McInnis *et al.* 2004). Indeed, the current 'democratization' of horizontal mobility is motivated by the desire to nurture the development of global citizens – graduates who are not only able to work successfully in a global marketplace, but also willing to work towards 'solving the most pressing problems of global significance' (Lewin 2009: xiv). For this reason, study abroad is now seen as one important component of an internationalized curriculum.

It is tempting to assume that the benefits of study abroad are self-evident. Perhaps this explains why serious research on the subject is in its infancy. In 1998, Clyne and Rizvi observed that the literature on study abroad fell into two categories: the rhetorical or the cynical. A review of the current literature suggests little has changed. Rhetorically, study abroad promises to be professionally and personally transformative. Cynics, on the other hand, deride study abroad as elitist 'fun' – the equivalent of the Grand Tour undertaken by nineteenth-century aristocrats – involving the uncritical 'acquisition' of 'culture' (Lewin 2009: xiv–xv).

In the face of such extravagant claims, for and against, it is highly likely that study abroad students and the institutions that send and receive them harbour unrealistically positive or negative expectations of the experience. Because few theoretically informed, empirical studies have investigated the study abroad experience, assumptions about its benefits remain largely unexamined (Tarrant and Sessions 2008). This chapter addresses an identified need for qualitative, student-centred research in this area (Byram and Feng 2006), by exploring the study abroad experience from the perspectives of ten exchange students from an Australian university.

Exploring the myths: what we do and don't know about study abroad

To date, research on the experiences of international students has focused on the vertically mobile (VM). These studies, often characterized by a remedial approach, have identified a range of issues, including language and academic difficulties (Cooper 2009; Rizvi 2005; Sovic 2009), housing (Sovic 2009) and an overall negative experience on campus (Brown 2009; Cooper 2009). Less easily documented, but crucially important, is the potential for intercultural learning on university campuses. Involving more than cognitive knowledge, more than a 'constellation of separate skills', intercultural learning occurs when 'a person construes his/her identity in dialogue and through negotiation with other individuals as well as the environment' (Jokikokko 2009). Self-awareness and self-acceptance are fundamental to this process (Sanderson 2008).

Numerous studies of the VM student experience suggest that the tremendous potential for intercultural learning on university campuses remains virtually untapped. While university marketing campaigns raise the expectations of prospective international students, with their images of welcoming, cosmopolitan campuses, many VM students are frustrated by the lack of interaction with local students (Summers and Volet 2008; UKCISA 2004). Indeed, the absence of host-national friendships constitutes 'a lasting source of disillusionment and disenchantment' (Brown 2009: 440) for many international students. On the other hand, lively interaction between co-national students is frequently observed.

Although some interpret this phenomenon as 'ghettoisation' (Brown 2009: 440), it may not be (entirely) negative from the students' perspective. In their pioneering study of the function of friendships among (VM) international students, Bochner and colleagues (1977) concluded that of the three types of bonds the students formed, their co-national network was the most significant. It was through this that they affirmed their culture of origin and values from home. Of secondary importance was the network of host-nationals, which acted more instrumentally to facilitate academic and cultural learning, and finally there was the network of other international students whose function was recreational. While some may sneer at co-cultural bonds, Bochner and colleagues (1977: 292) concluded that institutions should recognize their value, foster them and where possible encourage them to become more open to host- and inter-national groups. The positive link between co-national friendship and coping ability has been affirmed by more recent research (Wiseman 1997), but the finding has also been taken to the extreme, with the suggestion that international students be encouraged to 'form links with co-nationals in the host country' rather than with local students because 'they remain in the country for a relatively short time' (McKinlay *et al.* 1996: 392). By far the most widely held contemporary view is that it is host-national bonds which must be fostered, given their instrumental value for VM students in terms of academic and language learning, as well as their sense of satisfaction (Brown 2009; Sovic 2009).

The relatively little research available on the experiences of horizontally mobile (HM) students raises similar concerns about the quality of interaction with host-nationals, and subsequently their intercultural learning. Studies of Irish students in Japan (Pearson-Evans 2006), German students in English-speaking countries (Ehrenreich 2006) and American students in Australia (Luck and Reberger 2007) found marked variations between the experiences of the participants, from those who remained virtually uninterested and untouched by cultural difference or had their prejudices reinforced, to those who found the experience deeply transformative. According to Burgoon (1978) and others (McLeod and Wainwright 2009; Pitts 2006), international students' prior expectations, whether they are met or unmet, shape the way they are able to reconstrue cross-cultural experiences. Study abroad students in particular can have unrealistic expectations, but if their early disappointments are followed by successful cross-cultural encounters over time, they generally experience increased self-confidence, changed self-perception and, finally, a changed worldview. However, for some, such expectancy violation leaves unresolved tensions and leads to increased ethnocentrism (Luck and Reberger 2007; Pitts 2006).

In her extensive review of the literature on the experience of students and teachers abroad, Schuerholz-Lehr (2007) concluded that the lack of a shared nomenclature is one impediment to further research in this area. In the study discussed below, Rizvi's term 'uses' of education is employed rather than the more common reference to 'learning outcomes', to signify a philosophical and methodological perspective, derived from post-structuralist theories of identity, culture and literacy, which emphasizes students' agency. The term refers to the processes

> through which international students struggle to make sense of their experiences in [a foreign country]; the ways in which they assess their past and imagine their future; and the ways in which they feel positioned and actively locate themselves within dominant [political and cultural] narratives.
>
> (Rizvi 2005: 81)

Likewise, the term 'intercultural learning' – rather than 'adjustment', or 'competency' – has been chosen in this study, in order to signify a lifelong, emotionally charged process of negotiation with other individuals within a socio-cultural context (Jokikokko 2009).

Taking a closer look: the experiences of ten Australian students

Methodology

The study discussed here took the 'narrative turn' evident in the social sciences (Riessman 2008) since the 1980s, in order to explore the student experience of study abroad. Ten undergraduate students were recruited from the pool of students who studied abroad for one semester during 2008–9. They were attending a large research-intensive Australian university that has recently begun to actively promote study abroad. Because considerable commitment was required from participants, voluntary participation was sought. Nevertheless, the ten students recruited mirrored the typical profile of Australian study abroad students (Daly and Barker 2005), in that the majority (in this case, nine out of ten) were female, all came from what could be considered as middle to upper class backgrounds, with tertiary educated parents; they ranged in age from 19 to 24; most (eight) had travelled overseas previously; most (eight) had attended private schools; they had a strong preference for the USA/Canada (five went to North America, though one of these went to Montreal, and the others went to the Czech Republic, Eire and Denmark); and their sojourn was financed by their own part-time work, their family and university scholarships. The students were spread across the university's seven faculties, and were studying in the following disciplines: engineering, commerce, psychology, arts/humanities, law, science and architecture. As is the practice at this university, all students were near the end of their final degree and one student was in her final semester.

Narrative research methodology shaped this study in terms of its conception, design and methods. Conceptually, the individual student's experiential world was understood not as 'factual', but as a meaningful shape emerging from the selected retelling of inner and outer experiences (Clandinin and Connelly 2000). Data were collected through pre- and post-sojourn 'narrative interviews' (Jokkikoko 2009: 147) lasting 60 to 90 minutes and regular, often lengthy email correspondence to me, the researcher, while away. All interviews were taped and transcribed, with the consent of the participants. Students were encouraged to think of their emails to me as journal entries, and to write freely about whatever interested or concerned them. Over time, the emails from most students became less formal, more personal and more frequent. I responded briefly to these emails, as an interested and non-judgemental 'listener', generally within 48 hours.

It must be acknowledged that the data collection in this study, from a 'single point' (the home campus), is problematic, because it cannot 'capture the reciprocal and dynamic nature of intercultural relational development' (Ujitani and Volet 2008: 279). This limitation is discussed below in relation to implications.

Analysis of the data was inductive and iterative. Beginning with a list of potential themes drawn from the literature, I read recursively, back and forth between the transcripts, the literature and emerging themes until a 'best fit' was achieved (Polkinghorne 1995: 12). Inspired by Polkinghorne's (1995) approach to 'paradigmatic analysis', to 'honour the overall shape of narrative' (Chase 2005: 663), this process produces 'taxonomies of types of stories, characters, or settings', rather than a simple thematic analysis. By comparing similarities and differences between stories, paradigmatic analysis enables researchers to 'emphasise patterns in the storied selves' (Chase 2005: 657). The participants were given the opportunity to comment on a draft of this paper, and their feedback has been incorporated into the final version.

One of the most arresting and salient story types to emerge from the narrative data concerned friendship. That will therefore be the focus of the analysis here. Interestingly, none of the students mentioned difficulties in adjusting to the different teaching and learning environments they encountered. This could be an effect of the students' maturity (they had all completed at last half of their degree programmes prior to departure) and/or their confidence and previous success as students (only academically successful students are accepted into the programme).

Making sense of the findings

In a nutshell, all ten narratives concerned expectations of friendship that were unmet. How the students dealt with the ensuing shock and reappraised their expectations ultimately shaped the way they were able to use their experience. In this sense, the ten narratives mirror work done first by Burgoon (1978) on expectancy violation. All ten students made good use of their experiences, gaining insight about themselves, their culture(s), their country and the world. However, their reflections on their unmet expectations and the ways they reappraised and adjusted them shed new light on our understanding of this kind of study experience.

The findings from this study are illustrated, developed and discussed below, under three subheadings that represent three distinct phases found in all ten narratives: expectations prior to departure, experience on exchange, and post-exchange reflections. In quoting students below, pseudonyms have been used and care has been taken to protect their identities.

Expectations before departure

During the pre-departure interviews, all ten students said they expected to befriend the local students. They saw this as essential, as one of the most important reasons for going on exchange; they all spoke about it early in the interview and continued to return to the issue throughout. They believed that they would need to be proactive if they were to make friends with host country nationals; all had thought about the challenges in this regard and had developed appropriate strategies to address them. Commonly, these strategies included the following: choosing accommodation with host country students, where possible; joining sporting and other clubs on campus; working on campus; and taking part in buddy or mentoring programmes.

All students had also reflected on their own capacity to make friends and adapt to new situations. The eldest, Jane, was particularly self-aware. Mindful of her previous difficulties and her ambivalence about short-term relationships, she said: 'I think I'm only there for six months, what's the point? . . . This is the problem with me. I'm not very good at making friends. But that's another part of why I want to go.' On the other hand, most of the students over-estimated their 'natural' ability to make friends. 'I don't have any trouble talking to people' was a refrain heard many times throughout the first interviews. Although most of the students had some previous experience as international travellers, the majority of them appeared to be naive about the challenges of cross-cultural communication. They tended to base their expectations on stereotypes. Generalizing from one or two encounters was also common. According to Jack: 'Canadians are similar to Australians . . . I've met two . . . They are so easy to get along with.'

As Luck and Reberger (2007) found with US students visiting Australia, the four students going to Anglophone North America expected to find few cultural differences. Of the remaining students just two expressed doubt about their ability to communicate effectively while away – the only two who had developed some proficiency in the languages of their host countries. Most surprising were those going to non-Anglophone countries (where English was nevertheless offered as a language of instruction) who had not attempted to learn the language of their host country, and had not considered the impact this might have on their ability to form meaningful relationships. One thought she'd 'pick it up' and one thought it wouldn't matter. Samantha explained her approach this way:

> I thought about going to a Czech class while I was over there, but that'd mean learning the polite, formal Czech and I don't want that. I don't want to learn how to write an essay in Czech. I just want to learn how to converse. Because if I spoke in proper English every day, proper polite – that'd be like ooh you're a little odd.

However, one would have to question how much of this apparent naiveté was a rationalization, some reassuring self-talk, as only one of the students had her application approved in time to allow for language classes. The remainder said they had their destination confirmed just weeks before their departure.

In contrast to their positive, albeit naive expectations about friendships with host nationals, very few students had considered the possibility of friendships with compatriots. Of the three who mentioned the topic in their interview, two were disparaging: it would be 'cheating', a sign of weakness and something to be avoided. On hearing that she had been placed in accommodation with another Australian student, Alice said: 'Given a choice I would have liked to have lived with a Czech person. I really don't want to live with someone from Australia. I mean the point of going overseas is to meet other people.' For Samantha, avoiding fellow Australians would be a mark of maturity and resilience; it would be what distinguished this exchange experience from the one she did at school: 'I was in a group from my school so I always had that little backup . . . So I'm really interested to see what it's like when I go over there and I don't have my liaison and I don't have my friends.'

Most students were equally disparaging about the value of friendships with other internationals. Five did not mention it; four felt it was something to be avoided. Warned in the seminars offered by the Student Exchange Office that 'it is too easy' to meet other international students, they saw it as a 'soft option'.

The reality: friendships on exchange

Contrary to expectations, most of the students never made meaningful contact with host-national students throughout their stay. Instead they forged friendships with international students, and several also made friends with co-nationals.

In line with studies on VM students, 'the image of an alienating and indifferent host' (Brown 2009: 444) was particularly strong in the students' emails (also see Sovic 2009). Early on, eight students reported numerous negative or perplexing encounters with host-nationals (the two anomalies will be discussed in the next sub-section). For seven this characterized their experience on campus throughout their stay (though they all eventually had meaningful encounters, to varying degrees, with non-student locals). Initially, just as Pitts (2006) found in her study of exchange students, such expectancy violation on campus led to self-blame, a deep sense of failure, confusion and self-doubt. From Samantha's perspective, 'they [local students] stare through you. I'm like, what's happening? I felt like a freak.' The students struggled to understand the host-national staff and students' apparent lack of interest in them and their home country. Jane wrote: 'No one asks about Australia. It's weird, there's so little interest. But I guess it's the attitude here – "we're awesome, everyone else is fairly average".' The students resigned themselves to this apparent lack of interest; comments like 'You try but in the end you just get sick of being ignored' became increasingly common. But, for some, their inability to befriend host-nationals also provoked anger, particularly when they felt used by those local students wanting help with English assignments. As Samantha put it:

> It's hard because everyone emails me with their papers to edit. It can be 10 pages, really badly written too, real crap . . . And then, nothing, they don't want to know you. Like, they just use you . . . If anyone else sends me a paper now, I'll be like, you know, we're not that close.

Such sentiment brings to mind Bochner and colleagues' (1977) finding that shows that relationships between host and international students are typically instrumental in nature. With English being the language of instruction at all host institutions featured in this study, the Australian students, as native English speakers, might have been particularly vulnerable to such instrumental behaviour.

Initially, the eight students who had difficulties deeply resented the way they felt 'herded' together with other international students by the policies and practices of their host institutions. As Samantha put it, the internationals walk around in 'a bubble' separated from the local, host country students. For Mysha, being corralled into international student groups brought a concomitant sense of loss, of being excluded from the local culture: 'It annoys me, even though I'm living in Montreal I'm not really connected with the culture. I don't know anything about the local music, bands, film.'

Sooner or later, however, the students moved from frustration to acceptance of the situation, finally embracing the possibilities it offered. As Emma concluded:

> At the start I was thinking . . . I wish, I wish I was living with Irish students, but in hindsight, it worked out really well, because the [international students], we made friends, we wanted to travel . . . I will definitely go to their countries which are kind of, all over the place. I'll definitely stay with them.

Indeed, most felt that international friendships were critical to their development of a more cosmopolitan identity. As Samantha wrote:

> I was kind of hoping that I would make friends with a lot of Czech people because I really wanted to experience Czech culture . . . but I think it was really cool to hang out with like the Erasmus kids and Europeans because like I really fitted in . . . like I've become really cosmopolitan.

Interestingly, the nascent 'cosmopolitan' identity being forged by Samantha and others in this international milieu differs from the kind of 'instrumentalist' or 'strategic cosmopolitan imaginary' identity Rizvi (2005: 91) found in his study of international students in Australia. Samantha's reflections seem closer to Rizvi's ideal of a 'new cosmopolitanism [that is] self aware, critical of its own positioning, of its own potential collusion' (90). For example:

> If I were describing Australians before I left, I'd say, yeah, we're all right. Maybe a bit racist. But then I did this course on European policies towards ethnic minorities. My lecturer, who was Canadian, was really interested in Australia. You know, he was like okay, what's Australia's stance on immigration, and I would try to tell him. You know [I realized] we try to keep everyone out. Like, dam, we are racist. It was an eye-opener for me. Actually we're really not as multicultural as we think we are, not at all actually.

Such initially confronting or confusing encounters can play a critical role in 'perspective transformation'; i.e. the 'process of becoming critically aware of how and why our assumptions have come to guide the way we perceive, understand and feel about the world' (Jokikokko 2009: 143).

For several students, their relationships with fellow Australians also turned out to be significant, because they enabled them to form, and make sense of, international friendships. Just as Bochner and colleagues found in relation to VM students, these students found their co-national bonds helped them maintain self-esteem and 'rehearse their national identity' (1977: 279). For example, Mysha found meeting up with Australians 'good, because they are going through the same thing as you. You feel comfortable . . . they know what you're talking about.' Over time, such friendships functioned not only to provide empathy, but also to support their efforts to reach out to host-nationals off-campus. In contrast to the stereotype of co-nationals forming ghettos, these students found their compatriots were the key to their eventual success in meeting locals. As Emma put it:

> I've traveled a lot with [Australian friends]. I went with [Australian friend X] to Belfast, and her mum's best friend had us for the night. So it's another source of Irish family contact, and she treated us like her kids and that was lovely. You know the good thing about X is we can just set off on trips . . . I've learned a lot about Irish culture and politics that way. But I wouldn't have done this on my own.

Students' post-exchange reflections

It is clear from the narratives that the two students who experienced little difficulty in befriending local, international and co-national students were partially enabled to do so by the policies and practices of their host institutions. On reflection, they attributed their ability to make such friends to a range of factors including wide interest in cultural diversity (modelled by teaching staff), accommodation designed to bring internationals and host nationals together, small classes at their host university, a strong campus culture, spaces to meet students and staff, good (enough) English language proficiency among all students and an effective 'buddy' programme (one that does not separate international students from new host students).

Bridie's abbreviated reflection illustrates this perfectly:

> The small classes helped. Even the lecturers knew my name . . . They made a big effort . . . Then it was like, they [students] all flocked over and wanted to talk to us . . . Uni life brought us together. They had a gym, a student's room with a pool table, ping-pong table, plasma screen, and there was a cafeteria. That's where a lot of people mingled too. They all work during their summer holidays, and then they quit their jobs when uni starts . . . Not

like here, where we multitask all the time . . . There was this buddy programme where all first year students or new students were matched up with an older student. I think it also helped that I shared accommodation with four girls who came from different parts of Canada. It's the sort of university where even the Canadians aren't very local; they've come from everywhere. So I guess they were coming in, needing to make new friends too. We also hung around with people from America, quite a few people from Africa, and also a few from Asia as well. Everyone's English was pretty good . . . I'm so proud of myself. It was a big leap . . . I made good friends . . . from everywhere. It became much more than acquaintances, it's mateship.

While this combination of factors is probably unique to North American college life, the remaining eight students felt their host institutions could do far more to facilitate relationships with host-nationals. In their post-exchange interviews, they highlighted the following factors that they believed had contributed to their institutionalized segregation.

1   *Accommodation and on-campus spaces.* Echoing Engle and Engle's (2003) perception about the importance of housing arrangements, students in this study identified segregated accommodation as one of their greatest sources of frustration. According to Mysha:

> [The host university] made it so easy to meet other exchange students in our faculty [through the] international student network, and impossible to meet local students. There was absolutely no way that an exchange student was ever going to get a dorm room [with local students] because they were just overflowing with their own permanent students. They said go find your own apartments and stuff. So pretty much all my friends were exchange students. We clumped together.

For some, it was the university's failure to provide on-campus spaces for students to meet informally that made it difficult to interact with host-nationals. Elizabeth found: 'There's nowhere to sort of loiter on campus. The local students did a lot of socializing in [night]clubs, but at uni it's not like you can go and sit and talk.'

2   *Poorly run 'buddy' programmes.* Most of the students welcomed the buddy systems organized by their host institutions, as a means of obtaining instrumental knowledge (Bochner *et al.* 1977), about the transport system, for example, early in their sojourn. Emma was not so fortunate; her account clearly outlines what institutions should not do!

> Well, it was just kind of randomly organized . . . just here you go, two Irish students are going to be your buddies. I think the buddies were forced into it. So the whole programme was a failure and there was nothing, no follow up or anything. They can definitely improve on that

system, getting people that want to be there and telling us what they're doing, why they're doing it.

3   *Attitudes of teaching staff.* In stark contrast to Bridie's experience of interested teaching staff, whose inclusive practices she felt modelled behaviour for students, most students experienced varying levels of antipathy from host-national academics. The lack of interest already highlighted by Jane was a common experience, but some felt it went further. Samantha said:

> Even the lecturers are hostile. One came up to me, and said, what are you doing here? He said it quite harshly. Why did you come here? He made me feel like an alien, as if I had a tail or something. He was standing over me, pointing. It was a weird, weird thing.

4   *Age differences between study abroad and local students.* Because it can be challenging to find courses at the host institution that are accepted as credit-bearing courses at home, many of the students in this study felt they had no choice but to take courses well below or above their level. For some, this meant taking first-year courses, for others, it meant postgraduate ones. While they coped academically, they found the age differences placed additional barriers to interacting with host-nationals. Again, Emma found:

> As friendly as the Irish students are, they're also – well I was in first year classes – so they were younger to start with. They come with their high school friends . . . So, yeah, the Irish students were younger and they were in their little cliques.

In contrast, Monique found in her postgraduate course:

> I think it was mainly just the fact that the course was a lot of work and people didn't really have time, so they didn't really have the inclination to seek out new friendships with random people and they have established friendship networks.

This issue, also highlighted by Sovic (2009) in relation to international students in the UK, can be understood as an effect of 'micro-cultures'. Sharing a micro-culture, such as age, religion, sexual orientation, etc., as a means of establishing empathy can be 'an essential' prerequisite for a 'genuine encounter' with the other (Jokikokko 2009: 153).

Reflecting on the difficulties of breaking into established cliques of busy host students, the participants realized that they became more sympathetic towards the other's point of view over time. They recognized the reluctance to befriend strangers as a universal issue; indeed they came to see themselves reflected in this behaviour. As Emma said: 'It was kind of like when I first [started university]. I had a lot of friends. We had our own cliques. I guess it was similar to that.' In a similar vein, Alice reflected:

> The Czech students had been together in classes for years. They all knew each other really well. But I was new. They were all nice, but . . . it's really hard to fit into a well established group . . . I realized I'd done the same thing at home with international students.

Identifying with the other in this way proved to be transformative, and all students who returned to university found themselves seeking out and enjoying interactions with international students.

Implications

It is often assumed that the value of an international learning experience can be measured according to the level of immersion in the host culture (Engle and Engle 2003). This is an assumption all students in this study initially shared, yet most of them struggled and failed to befriend local students at their host institutions. Sadly, most of the students initially experienced this as a personal failure, but ultimately made good 'use' (Rizvi 2005: 81) of their overseas experience, by becoming more reflective and cosmopolitan. In the face of confusion, self-doubt and anger at having their expectations of befriending local students frustrated, they came to recognize the value of friendships more readily available – with other international students and compatriots. These two friendship groups were not mutually exclusive. On the contrary, strong co-national bonds bolstered their confidence as they sought friendships with internationals and ultimately host-nationals outside of the university. For all students, the combination of the friendship groups proved to be transformative. This finding calls into question the strong focus on promoting host-national friendships in the current research, and reasserts Bochner and colleagues' (1977) original finding regarding the critical importance of co-national bonds. In contrast to that research, however, this study underscores the critical role played by other inter-national students and staff. It was through their challenging, sometimes painful inter-national encounters, that they made new meaning of and for themselves as citizens in a rapidly globalizing world.

Of course, one needs to be cautious about applying the findings from this study to vertically mobile students, those who study away from home for their entire degree programme. Spending three or more years at a university should provide more opportunities to develop friendships with host-nationals on campus than the HM students in this study had. Moreover, the consequences of not befriending host-nationals have been shown to be far more severe, with negative impacts on academic performance as well as emotional well-being (Brown 2009; Cooper 2009; Sovic, 2009). Nevertheless, when considered alongside the extant literature on both VM and HM students, this study raises some urgent questions regarding each university's responsibility as an institution that is home to some and host to others. Analysis of the narrative data suggests that the challenges most students faced in befriending local students stemmed from institutional, rather than from personal, shortcomings. Admittedly, data collection from a 'single point' in this study presents limitations, because it cannot 'capture the reciprocal and dynamic nature' of intercultural learning (Ujitani and Volet 2008: 279). The students' violated expectations may well have distorted their perceptions of the others' motivations (Brown 2009). Even so, the ten students in this study were perceptive, socially adept and highly motivated to establish host-national friendships, and in fact many did – outside of the university.

If the benefit of studying abroad is to be measured on the basis of levels of immersion in the host culture, universities that send and receive students need to do more to support this intention. While students' (intercultural) learning cannot be dictated in advance by organizations or teaching staff, it does need to be designed or planned for (Wenger 1998). Institutions could expand the possibilities for intercultural learning by processing student applications in a timely manner. This would enable their outgoing students to find suitable accommodation (that which is likely to enhance host–national contact); establish connections with co-national exchange students; and learn something of the language and culture of the country of destination pre-departure. It could also be argued that the university has some responsibility for helping students establish more realistic expectations prior to departure. Finally, in line with others (e.g. Cooper 2009), this study shows the value of supporting students' critical reflection – in this case, via interviews and email exchange with the researcher.

Regarding the role of universities as hosts to incoming international students, this study reiterates extant findings that they need, first, to develop accommodation and other spaces that enhance contact between local and international students; second, to develop well-designed buddy systems that consider students' micro-cultures such as age and interests (Jokikokko 2009: 153), in order to better support all incoming students (domestic and international) through the critical transition stage; and third, to support the internationalization of the academic self (Sanderson 2008), so that staff are able to teach inclusively and model ways of valuing diversity for their students. In taking these measures, universities would at the same time address the most disturbing implication of all in this study: the apparent lack of interest, even antagonism, that host-national students in so many universities display towards their cultural others.

References

Bochner, S., McLeod, B.M. and Lin, A. (1977) 'Friendship patterns of overseas students: a functional model', *International Journal of Psychology*, 12, 4: 277–94.

Brown, L. (2009) 'A failure of communication on the cross-cultural campus', *Journal of Studies in International Education*, 13, 4: 439–54.

Burgoon, J.K. (1978) 'A communication model of personal space violations: explication and an initial test', *Human Communication Research*, 4: 129–42.

Byram, M. and Feng, A. (eds) (2006) *Living and Studying Abroad: Research and Practice*, Clevedon, Buffalo & Toronto: Multilingual Matters.

Chase, C. (2005) 'Narrative inquiry: Multiple lenses, approaches, voices', in N. Denzin and Y. Lincoln (eds) *The Sage Handbook of Qualitative Research*, Thousand Oaks: Sage Publications.

Clandinin, D.J. and Connelly, F.M. (2000) *Narrative Inquiry: Experience and Story in Qualitative Research*, San Francisco: Jossey-Bass.

Clyne, F. and Rivzi, F. (1998) 'Outcomes of student exchange', in D. Davis and A. Olsen (eds) *Outcomes of International Education: Research Findings*, Refereed Proceedings from 12th Annual Australian International Education Conference, Canberra: ACT.

Cooper, V.A. (2009) 'Inter-cultural student interaction in post-graduate business and information technology programs: the potentialities of global study tours', *Higher Education Research and Development*, 28, 6: 557–70.

Daly, A. and Barker, M. (2005) 'Australian and New Zealand university students in international exchange programs', *Journal of Studies in International Education*, 9, 1: 26–41.

Ehrenreich, S. (2006) 'The assistant experience in retrospect and its educational and professional significance in teachers' biographies', in M. Byram and A. Feng (eds) *Living and Studying Abroad: Research and Practice*, Clevedon, Buffalo & Toronto: Multilingual Matters.

Engle, L. and Engle, J. (2003) 'Study abroad levels: toward a classification of program types', *Frontiers: The Interdisciplinary Journal of Study Abroad*, 9: 1–20.

Jokikokko, K. (2009) 'The role of significant others in the intercultural learning of teachers', *Journal of Research in International Education*, 8, 2: 142–63.

Lewin, R. (ed.) (2009) *The Handbook of Practice and Research in Study Abroad: Higher Education and the Quest for Global Citizenship*, New York and London: Routledge.

Luck, M. and Reberger, H. (2007) 'Australia, the 51st state: student learning and intercultural development', *Proceedings of the 2007 ISANA International Conference, 'Student Success in International Education'*, Adelaide, Australia, 27–30 November.

Marginson, S. and van der Wende, M. (2007) *Globalisation and Higher Education*, Education working paper no. 8, Paris: Organisation for Economic Co-operation and Development (OECD).

McInnis, C., Coates, C., Hooper, C., Jensz, F. and Vu, T. (2004) *Study Abroad and Study Exchange Systems in Industrial Countries*, Canberra: Department of Education, Science & Training (DEST).

McKinlay, N.J., Pattison, H.M. and Gross, H. (1996) 'An exploratory investigation of the effects of a cultural orientation programme on the psychological well being of international university students', *Higher Education*, 31, 3: 379–95.

McLeod, M. and Wainwright, P. (2009) 'Researching the study abroad experience', *Journal of Studies in International Education*, 13,1: 66–71.

NUS (National University of Singapore) (2009) *Spirit of the Explorer: NUS Annual Report, 2009*. Online. Available HTTP: http://www.nus.edu.sg/annualreport/index.html (accessed 10 September 2010).

Olsen, A. (2008) 'International mobility of Australian university students: 2005', *Journal of Studies in International Education*, 12, 4: 364–74.

Pearson-Evans, A. (2006) 'Recording the journey: diaries of Irish students in Japan', in M. Byram and A. Feng (eds) *Living and Studying Abroad: Research and Practice*, Clevedon, Buffalo and Toronto: Multilingual Matters.

Pitts, M. (2006) 'The role of everyday talk in sojourner adjustment: an ethnography of communication among US sojourners', *Proceedings from the 56th Annual International Communication Association Conference*, Dresden.

Polkinghorne, D.E. (1995) 'Narrative configuration in qualitative analysis', *Qualitative Studies in Education*, 8, 1: 5–23.

Riessman, C.K. (2008) *Narrative Methods for the Human Sciences*, California and London: Sage Publications.

Rivza, B. and Teichler, U. (2007) 'The changing role of student mobility', *Higher Education Policy*, 20: 457–75.

Rizvi, F. (2005) 'International education and the production of cosmopolitan identities', in A. Arimato, F. Huang, K. Yokoyama and D. Hiroshima (eds), *Globalization and Higher Education*, Hiroshima: Research Institute of Higher Education.

Sanderson, G. (2008) 'A foundation for the internationalization of the academic self in higher education', *Journal of Studies in International Education*, 122, 3: 276–307.

Schuerholz-Lehr, S. (2007) 'Teaching for global literacy in higher education: how prepared are the educators?', *Journal of Studies in International Education*, 11, 2: 180–204.

Sovic, S. (2009) 'Hi-bye friends and the herd instinct: international and home students in the creative arts', *Higher Education*, 58: 747–61.

Summers, M. and Volet, S. (2008) 'Students' attitudes towards culturally mixed groups on international campuses: impact of participation in diverse and non-diverse groups', *Studies in Higher Education*, 33, 4: 357–70.

Tarrant, M. and Sessions, L. (2008) 'Promoting global citizenship: educational travel and study abroad in the South Pacific', in *Proceedings from the ISANA International Education Association 19th International Conference*, Auckland, 2–5 December. Online. Available HTTP: http://proceedings.com.au/isana2008/ (accessed 10 September 2010).

Ujitani, E. and Volet, S. (2008) 'Socio-emotional challenges in international education: insight into reciprocal understanding and intercultural relational development', *Journal of Research in International Education*, 7, 3: 279–303.

UKCISA (2004) 'Broadening our horizons: international students in UK universities and colleges'. Online. Available HTTP: http://www.ukcisa.org.uk/about/pubs_research.php (accessed 10 May 2009).

Wenger, E. (1998) *Communities of Practice: Learning Meaning and Identity*, Cambridge: Cambridge University Press.

Wiseman, H. (1997) 'Far away from home: the loneliness experience of overseas students', *Journal of Social and Clinical Psychology*, 16: 277–98.

Chapter 15

'Going the other way'

The motivations and experiences of UK learners as 'international students' in higher education

Brendan Bartram

Introduction

Most literature and research studies on 'international students' tend to be uni-directional – in other words, they focus on non-native-English-speaking students entering higher education institutions (HEIs) in Anglophone countries (a few of many examples include Thorstensson (2001), who examined the experiences of Asian students in the USA; Zhang and Brunton (2007), who focused on Chinese students in New Zealand; and Tian and Lowe (2009), who looked at Chinese students in the UK). This chapter aims to address this imbalance by scrutinizing the perspectives of UK students who – in apparently growing numbers after a long period of decline (British Council 2008) – decide to study abroad for part of their degree. An analysis of existing research looking at issues faced by English-speaking students when studying overseas is followed by a discussion of survey data collected through an online questionnaire. This was completed by over 150 students, enrolled at five HEIs in different parts of the UK, who had all spent at least one semester studying at universities in different parts of the world. The following research questions formed the focus of the enquiry:

- What factors motivate UK students to study abroad?
- How do UK students describe their experiences of overseas study?

The chapter aims to provide a critical examination of the students' motivations and experiences as they endeavour to make the transition to 'international student' in what are for most unfamiliar educational and socio-cultural environments. An attempt will also be made to investigate the extent of 'experiential commonality' between UK and other groups of international students. In this respect, it is important to acknowledge from the outset that differences in the length and nature of sojourn may be significant (most UK students studying abroad for part of their UK-based degree, compared with most 'international students' electing to enrol full-time at overseas HEIs for degree duration). This issue will be examined later in the chapter and in the conclusion, in an effort to account for any key differences, while considering potential implications for UK HEIs.

Literature review

As suggested above, little research attention has been directed at this particular dimension of horizontal mobility (Rivza and Teichler 2007) – the perspectives of English-speaking students who travel abroad for the purposes of study. Olsen (2008: 364) refers to our scant knowledge of such 'movement in the other direction – that is the international mobility of Australian university students', and though speaking clearly about the Australian context (and echoed by Green in this same volume), his remarks apply equally to the UK and US situations. The reasons for this under-represented perspective are perhaps simply numerical – it is well known that students from other countries represent relatively large contingents on university campuses throughout the English-speaking world. Daly and Barker (2005) discuss, for example, how less than 1 per cent of American, Australian and New Zealand students spend time studying abroad, yet more than a fifth of the Australian university population comes from other countries. In the UK last year, UCAS (2010) reported that around 6 per cent (104,000) of undergraduates came from overseas. As a larger presence, then, it would seem logical that more attention has focused on the experiences of these students. However, it would certainly be true to say that relatively more UK students study abroad than students from other English-speaking countries (Sussex Centre for Migration Research (SCMR) 2004), perhaps because closer geographical proximity to other European countries presents more affordable possibilities. The European Union's ERASMUS exchange scheme has been particularly influential in promoting study abroad activity, and yet British involvement had been rather limited in recent years. Coleman (2009: 114) reveals how 'British participation in the ERASMUS student exchange scheme peaked in 1994–1995, before entering a steady decline which has only recently been halted'. This of course raises questions about the reasons behind low participation, and in his subsequent discussion, Coleman highlights a damaging amalgam of factors ranging from casual British xenophobia and Europhobic mass media, to political and commercial insularity, which combine to negate an interest in 'the cultural other' in general, and in foreign language learning in particular. Some of these factors are reflected in one of the few British studies to look specifically at the mobility of UK students, carried out by the SCMR (2004: 7). They identified four key deterrents to studying abroad:

- inadequate foreign language skills;
- financial barriers;
- institutional barriers (lack of promotional efforts and information, etc);
- negative student attitudes and dispositions.

These issues are of course somewhat beyond the scope of this chapter, and as such will not be discussed further, though emphasis in other studies on the reasons for low mobility rates does serve to underscore the value of exploring the motivations of those UK students who *do* decide to study abroad.

Motivations to study abroad

Many researchers have examined the reasons why students decide to study at HEIs abroad. Guruz (2007) discusses a range of intrinsic and extrinsic factors including lack of opportunity at home, perceptions of better teaching and academic standards, a desire for exposure to new cultures, opportunities to gain what are considered to be more prestigious qualifications, the chance to network internationally, and improved residency prospects. Jackling (2007) cites this last point as the main motivation of the international students who participated in her Australian study. Similar motives are identified by Beaver and Tuck (1998) in New Zealand and in a more recent UK survey by IPSOS Mori/Unite (2006). This survey suggested that career enhancement was the primary motivation of international students choosing the UK as a study destination. Of the few studies looking specifically at English-speaking students, Clyne and Rizvi (1998) offer a similar blend of personal, cultural and career-related motives among Australian students. The desire to travel, experience other cultures and develop skills that would enhance their employability were the most frequently cited reasons. Similar factors are echoed in Findlay and King's (2010) study of mobile UK students, though their study revealed that the desire to attend a 'world class university' was the main motivation for many (88.7 per cent) to study outside the country: 'failure to get into universities such as Oxford and Cambridge stimulated some students to look abroad' (2010: 29).

This may, however, reflect the fact that their sample was based entirely on 'diploma-mobile' students – i.e. the relatively small number of UK students who study abroad for the entirety of their degree, and, as the authors acknowledge, are disproportionately drawn from higher income, professional and managerial homes. As such their motivations may not be representative of the greater number of British students who study abroad for just part of their degree – credit-mobile students and voluntary movers (SCMR, 2004) – and who constitute the sample discussed here. All the same, it would appear that social class plays an important part in moulding student mobility choices in the UK, and even the SCMR survey, whose sample is made up of a broader demographic mix, concedes that mobile UK students are 'more likely to be younger, female, white and from families in the higher social classes' (ibid.: 7). Given the expenses often involved in study abroad, however, it is perhaps not unreasonable to suggest that this situation is reflective more generally of students from other countries who elect to study overseas.

Though the students in Findlay and King's study may have been primarily driven by a quest for elitist and career credentials, the authors found that 'the desire simply to be different . . . often in the guise of seeking adventure' (2010: 30) was also a much mentioned motive. Returning to the SCMR survey of UK credit-mobile and voluntary movers, student motivations reflect this personal dimension more prominently, and the authors comment on a range of largely 'personal drivers' relating to a desire for personal, social and cultural development.

Student experience

There is a wealth of literature examining the lived experiences of international students during their time abroad, and again, most of this is from the perspective of non-native speakers of English entering HE in the Anglophone world. Various studies have explored their experiences of and strategies for dealing with adjustment, many showing that this process of transition is often accompanied by certain challenges. Anderson *et al.* argue that:

> The most common challenges faced by international students are psychological in nature. International students often face homesickness, loneliness, depression, stress, anxiety, alienation, isolation, and the loss of identity, status and self-value after they come to a new country.
>
> (Anderson *et al.* 2009: 19)

Others would challenge the focus on individual psychological issues here, identifying challenges that relate more to socio-cultural adjustment (Bartram 2007), overt and indirect forms of discrimination in the host country (Lee and Rice 2007; Tian and Lowe 2009) and the demands of adjusting to new academic environments with different expectations, conventions, styles of teaching and learning, assessment regimes, etc. (Gu *et al.* 2010). Some commentators have been critical of such literature because they believe the focus on problems and needs casts international students as victims within a deficit model that does little justice to the notions of student agency and resilience. These issues reflect the dynamic nature of current debates surrounding international students, and the scope of this chapter does not allow for a more extended discussion. Whichever position one takes, it is perhaps less contentious to suggest that differently balanced amalgams of some of the above issues will variously colour the experiences of many international students, and the extent to which such challenges are successfully negotiated will depend on a variety of factors. Anderson *et al.* (2009) identify these as individual personality, language proficiency, previous experience, available support and self-efficacy. Gu *et al.* (2010), who challenge the linear psychological model of adaptation, offer a sophisticated analysis of the ways in which international students at the UK HEIs in their survey manage a complex set of shifting factors implicated in their personal development and positive experiences. For McLeod and Wainwright, who looked at the experiences of American students studying abroad, successfully negotiating difficult transitions similarly emerged as an important part of the students' self-development:

> The students in our focus groups repeatedly suggested that the violation of expectancies and the feeling of being forced to take risks were a centrally important and necessary, albeit painful, part of their positive learning experience.
>
> (McLeod and Wainwright 2009: 69)

In terms of research examining the experiences of UK students abroad, the picture that emerges is a largely positive one, marked by relatively few challenges. The SCMR survey (2004: 7) revealed that 'mobile students generally felt very positively about their foreign experiences. 95 per cent thought it had enhanced their personal development, and 90 per cent felt that it was relevant to the development of an international career. Strict academic benefits were stressed less often.' These positive findings are impressive, especially when considering the sample size of over 1,400 students, and are reinforced throughout the report. The authors go on to suggest that 'mobile students struggled to identify any major problems with their time abroad' (ibid.: 37), though three issues were noted by some: financial difficulties (mentioned by 22 per cent, and much mentioned in the general literature); difficulties making friends and interacting with local students (again, a much observed phenomenon among international students – see Summers and Volet 2008); and absence from a partner.

The SCMR findings are corroborated by Findlay and King's survey. They identify finance as a concern for half of the UK undergraduates they interviewed, but the students' positive experiences are again clearly allied to a sense of personal enrichment and intercultural learning:

> The overwhelming experience of UK undergraduates . . . was very positive. Most valued were academic benefits and career enhancement, but also important was how the way that living abroad contributed to personal development and to thinking about the country of origin.
>
> (Findlay and King 2010: 36)

Alred and Byram (2006: 211) come to similar conclusions in their research on British students who spent a year studying in France. The authors describe how the students' time abroad was perceived to have made a significant contribution to their personal development. The students they interviewed felt their year out was 'a major episode in their lives, affecting self-understanding and outlook on life. Many also reported marked changes in self-perception, personal development and maturity.' Again, such experiences are of course described elsewhere in the literature on international students (see Gu *et al.* 2010, for example, who discuss issues of transformative experience and intercultural development among overseas students in the UK). All the same, it is interesting to note at this stage the extent to which the few studies that exist of UK students abroad underline such positive experiences. This degree of positivity would appear unmatched by the more general literature on international students. It also contrasts with Bartram's smaller-scale study (2008), which revealed more negatively textured UK experiences, as students struggled to adjust socially, culturally and academically. Another key difference with this study relates not just to sample size – the UK students Bartram interviewed were all from lower socio-economic groupings, and though caution must be exercised in any interpretations here, questions arise as to the extent to which issues of potentially greater social and cultural capital are implicated in the more positive experiences of the more middle class samples included in the two large-scale UK studies discussed above.

Research design

The current study is based on data generated by an online questionnaire. The questionnaire itself consisted of two types of questions – a set designed to establish key background features (home and host universities, gender, age, etc.) and ten open-ended questions inviting the students to comment on their reasons for studying abroad, their experiences and perceived support needs. In order to access a wider range of student views, discussions were held with colleagues working in the international departments of ten UK universities. After fully briefing them on the nature and intentions of the research, and providing assurances of student and institutional anonymity, five agreed to participate in the study and distribute an electronic questionnaire link to students who had engaged in study abroad over the last five years. Of the five participating HEIs, two were located in the North of England, two in the Midlands and one in the South. Two of these were older universities, established in the 1800s; the other three were former polytechnics that achieved university status in 1992.

The link was sent to over 1,000 students but responses were received from a total of only 159 individuals. Although this is a somewhat disappointing rate of return, it is hoped that the cross-institutional nature of the survey and the reasonably large sample it generated will go some way towards supporting credible impressions, despite the self-selective nature of the sample and the accompanying potential for selectivity effects. Of the 159 participants, around half had spent two semesters abroad, 15 per cent one semester and nearly one-third three semesters. The vast majority of these students (96 per cent) studied abroad during the second or third year of their degree. Over 90 per cent were aged 18–25 (85 per cent were 20 or 21 when studying overseas), and 81 per cent were female (cf. the SCMR survey above, 2004). They had attended a total of 45 institutions in 15 different countries in Europe, North America, South America and the Far East, and were studying a broad range of degrees. These include courses in education, geography, engineering, business studies, modern languages, law, European studies, economics, natural sciences and biology. Of these, 96 per cent had studied or were studying at undergraduate level.

The thematic analysis of the student responses was based on coding using the research questions listed at the start of the chapter. In cases of overlap, segments of data were multiply coded as and where appropriate. This broad approach served to regroup the data into the key areas of interest underpinning the enquiry, and was followed by a more detailed vertical analysis of responses in order to identify sub-themes and patterns within the two categories. Findings relating to each question will now be examined in turn. It should be noted that although the total sample consisted of 159 students, not all participants chose to answer each question, hence response totals are often below 159.

Findings: motivations to study abroad

When analysing the reasons students gave for studying abroad, four clear categories emerged. Table 15.1 shows the number of responses within each category.

Clearly, many students' decisions appeared motivated by a range of personal drivers, as noted in the other UK studies above. The following examples illustrate typical comments in this first category:

> I wanted to put myself outside of my comfort zone and challenge myself personally and become more independent.

> To broaden my perspectives and attitudes, learn the language and get life experience.

Many comments related to a desire for socio-cultural enrichment and connection:

> I wanted to experience a different culture and way of life other than British. Such experience is priceless and teaches you that extra you simply cannot get from reading in a library.

> A unique experience, to not only travel to, but become part of a country even if only for a semester. I wasn't just a tourist trying to see the culture, I was living and learning in a different culture.

For some, the appeal related to fulfilling a sense of adventure – 'the glamour of studying and living in another country' or just to 'do something different/stand out from the crowd' while enjoying 'novel experiences, climate and food'. The smallest number of responses revealed instrumental motivations relating to academic and career aspirations:

> I wanted the TESOL qualification and to move to Canada later on to work.

> Enhancing the value of my degree, giving me extra skills which would add to my employability.

Table 15.1 Study abroad: motivations

	Number of responses volunteered
Motivation related to personal development	60 (42%)
Motivation related to socio-cultural factors	46 (32%)
Motivation related to a sense of adventure	21 (15%)
Motivation related to qualifications and career	17 (12%)
Those who felt motivations largely fulfilled	145 (94%)
Those who felt motivations largely unfulfilled	9 (6%)

Experience abroad

When asked to comment on what they had enjoyed most about their time abroad, the students' comments revealed a set of experiences that related to the categories identified above, with some clear differences in emphasis, however. The social dimension of their experiences attracted the largest number of responses (66, i.e. 52 per cent):

> We all socialized as much as we could. I loved the friends I made as they were people I would probably never meet or make friends with in England.

> Meeting new people, the different experiences they could share.

This was followed by 21 comments (17 per cent) that related to improved cultural understandings and insights:

> Helped language skills, learnt loads about new culture, lifestyle and cultural differences, reflections on your own culture too . . . definitely changes ways of looking at things.

> I actually learnt as much about my own culture as that of the host country . . .

Sixteen (13 per cent) further comments highlighted the students' sense of personal growth and development:

> My time abroad definitely allowed me to experience something completely outside of what I am used to. It broadened my horizons academically but most importantly I feel personally.

> I feel like not only am I more independent but I did a lot of growing up.

> It has made me a stronger and braver person.

Only 15 responses (12 per cent) related to positive academic experiences. Some students simply expressed their enjoyment of teaching and learning overseas (e.g. 'I loved my lectures which were extremely interesting and inspired me to work hard', 'loved learning about a different legal system') but others provided more detail. Some comments revealed a sense of fulfilment that was related to their developing language learning skills:

> It was brilliant learning how to write lab reports in French and understand classes.

While some appreciated what they felt was a lesser workload, others enjoyed a wider choice of modules and an experience they perceived to be more academically demanding, 'taught by more expert and competent lecturers'. Two students from post-1992 UK HEIs commented specifically on 'the more traditional approach to learning' as something that added positively to their experience abroad, revealing perhaps a disjuncture between their own learning preferences and more facilitative teaching styles at their home institution.

Finally, nine comments (7 per cent) reflected students' enjoyment of travel opportunities:

> Being on mainland Europe, the ability to travel to France, Belgium, etc from Holland was a lot easier than in England, and as travel was one of my main reasons, I enjoyed this thoroughly.

Their negative experiences are categorized in Table 15.2. At first sight, it is surprising that social issues draw frequent negative comment, especially when considering the positive social points above. However, this is perhaps less contradictory than would seem. As one student explained:

> I enjoyed least what I enjoyed most, being abroad! It's hard to be away from home and it teaches you a lot about yourself, your strengths and weaknesses. But at least I was only a 50min plane journey away from home when I had pangs of homesickness, not in Japan!

In fact many of the comments on negative social experiences related to occasional bouts of homesickness or transitional difficulties that were soon overcome, and it is therefore important to consider these comments against this background.

The practical problems related chiefly to perceived financial and accommodation difficulties, as noted elsewhere. Negative academic experiences, however, appeared more frequent and persistent in nature, and related mostly to language difficulties and a perceived lack of support and guidance:

> Some lecturers won't make the effort to understand you're not learning in your mother tongue.

> The French don't understand that this is not normal for you and that you find their systems confusing. I didn't get information about deadlines, but

Table 15.2 Negative student experiences

Negative experiences	Numbers of responses
Academic issues	56 (44%)
Social dimension	46 (36%)
Practical matters	26 (20%)

there were lots of confusing emails about how we would be assessed which made the academic experience less positive than it could have been.

Several students at European HEIs commented negatively on greater attendance requirements and heavier workloads:

I had to do a lot more work than at my home university so I felt I didn't get to experience the country and the culture as much as I could have.

And while some students above clearly enjoyed what they perceived to be a more traditional approach to learning and teaching, more voiced criticisms of courses felt to 'lack structure and direction' and teaching seen as 'old-fashioned, boring and uninspiring', suggestive once again of teaching and learning disjunctures.

In view of the common difficulty of social integration noted in the general literature on international students, the students were asked to comment specifically on their experiences of getting to know home students. Of the 105 students who answered this question, a rather divided impression emerged; 53 had experienced no difficulties compared to 52 who found this aspect rather problematic. The students explained their positive and negative experiences in this regard by drawing on a broadly similar set of factors: living arrangements (among or separated from local students); the extent to which staff organized social events; language competence; personal attributes of the local students; the UK students' own personalities (outgoing/shy). The overriding perception of those who had trouble here resonates quite strongly with comments made more generally in the literature – the common difficulty sojourners have penetrating established social networks in and outside university:

It's difficult – class sizes are big. You can meet a person one week then never see them again. They are all friendly but I've sometimes felt in group work I am just slowing everyone down and I feel bad for making their work harder. However, I was made welcome and took part in an integration weekend run by the students. But it's just hard trying to break into pre-established friendship groups.

Though some students found it difficult integrating with local students, a huge compensation for many was the ease with which socializing with other (often EU) students took place. For some, this was seen as a necessary social coping strategy ('the locals aren't interested in us, so the exchange students had to stick together whether we liked it or not'). For others, it was a social convenience that in some ways militated against greater integration with domestic students:

It's just so easy to fall into the trap of only socialising with other Erasmus students, and then it's just hard to escape from the Erasmus bubble.

Discussion and conclusions

A number of conclusions arise from the study. First, it should be noted that an attempt to examine the asymmetricality of the students' motivations and experiences yielded no significant differences – an analysis of the findings in relation to a number of individual and contextual factors (e.g. age, gender, study abroad year, length of sojourn, subject studied, institution attended, etc.) consistently showed broadly similar patterns. This may reflect the relative homogeneity of the sample, particularly in terms of the first four factors above, as outlined in the design section, but it is worth acknowledging that a more heterogeneous sample (particularly with regard to greater numbers of male/postgraduate/degree-mobile students) could well reveal a far more differentiated picture of experiences. The under-representation of some of these types of students in the sample here clearly makes it difficult to draw meaningful conclusions based on some of these relationships.

In terms of the motivation to study abroad, it would appear that those taking part in the survey are driven by a high degree of self-determination, and that their primary motives are intrinsic – those moved by essentially instrumental concerns appear rather few, as issues related to career, academic and qualification benefits are mentioned far less frequently than issues relating to social and personal development and the quest for adventure. This marks something of a contrast with the more general literature on international students. Though the studies discussed earlier showed a range of motivations, instrumental concerns (cf. the IPSOS Mori/Unite survey, 2006) often appear to figure more prominently among the motivations of 'other' international students. As suggested in the introduction, this may relate in part to length of sojourn – diploma-mobile students may naturally be more focused on qualification and career than shorter-term credit-mobile and voluntary movers. This could explain the motivational alignment between the UK students in Findlay and King's study (2010) and the overseas students surveyed in the IPSOS Mori poll in the UK. On the other hand, in a globalizing world increasingly dominated by Anglo-Saxon economics and the commodified utility of the English language, UK students are arguably rather differently positioned. Located in the economic and linguistic heartlands of the new (neo-liberal) global order, study abroad for them is not dominated by the utilitarian quest for improved English language competence and credentialist advancement; as such, it may be that intrinsic motives are able to occupy the motivational space left vacant by instrumental fulfilment and perceived positional advantage.

In terms of their experience abroad, there is perhaps overall a greater alignment with international students discussed in the general literature – many students experience the same social and academic adjustment challenges, the same financial and practical problems, and some also the same commonly noted integrational difficulties. Despite the challenges, however, it is noticeable that the participants' descriptions of their experiences are predominantly positive. It is equally striking that their experiences are largely conceived of in terms of social, cultural and personal development. This is no doubt a reflection of their motivations, and it could also explain why their academic experiences received the largest number of negative comments – they position themselves primarily as social actors and occasionally as educational tourists, concerned with personal agency. As such, academic issues appear (on the whole) removed from their primary motives for embarking on study abroad. This degree of distance from their motivational focus and 'sojourner identity' perhaps raises the stakes for this area of experience, amplifying any perceived deficiencies and disjunctures in the process. Since many of the issues highlighted relate to academic delivery, support and guidance, however, this may indeed be an area that HEIs could usefully direct more attention to in terms of preparing students prior to and during their sojourns.

Reflecting more generally on the findings, it is worth mentioning that few, if any, of the students participating show signs of ethnocentricity and other negative factors that are suggested by Coleman (2009) to explain low UK student mobility rates. This may of course be a function of selectivity effects in this research study, but it is heartening to see evidence here corroborating the positive experiences highlighted in the other UK studies discussed. Though there has been no explicit focus on intercultural development in this study, it is equally encouraging to see that many students' comments reveal examples of increased intercultural learning and transformative shifts in self-identity. These positive gains and experiences arguably justify a need for the greater promotion of mobility opportunities for UK students – the SMCR survey showed that less than one-third of UK HEIs have a plan for mobility. It could surely be argued that this lack of strategic initiative is an equally significant factor implicated in low UK mobility rates and constitutes something of an educational disservice to UK students. Given evidence above that mobile UK students are more likely to be from higher social groupings, this disservice gains a rather unsettling dimension – surely it is time for UK HEIs to go beyond espousing the rhetoric of global citizenship and commit more convincingly to greater efforts to address the imbalance in UK student outflows.

References

Alred, G. and Byram, M. (2006) 'British students in France: ten years on', in M. Byram and A. Feng (eds) *Living and Studying Abroad: Research and Practice*, Clevedon: Multilingual Matters.

Anderson, G., Carmichael, K.Y., Harper, T.J. and Huang, T. (2009) 'International students at four-year institutions: developmental needs, issues and strategies', in S.R. Harper and S.J. Quaye (eds) *Student Engagement in Higher Education*, New York: Routledge.

Bartram, B. (2007) 'The socio-cultural needs of international students in higher education: a comparison of staff and student views', *Journal of Studies in International Education*, 11: 205–14.

—— (2008) 'Supporting international students in higher education: constructions, cultures and clashes', *Teaching in Higher Education*, 13, 6: 657–68.

Beaver, B. and Tuck, B. (1998) 'The adjustment of overseas students at a tertiary institution in New Zealand', *New Zealand Journal of Educational Studies*, 2: 167–79.

British Council (2008) 'Number of UK students choosing to study abroad with Erasmus continues to rise', press release, 6 November.

Clyne, F. and Rizvi, F. (1998) 'Outcomes of student exchange', in D. Davis and A. Olsen (eds) *Outcomes of International Education*, Sydney: IDP Education Australia.

Coleman, J.A. (2009) 'Why the British do not learn languages: myths and motivations in the United Kingdom', *Language Learning Journal*, 37, 1: 111–27.

Daly, A.J. and Barker, M.C. (2005) 'Australian and New Zealand University students' participation in international exchange programs', *Journal of Studies in International Education*, 9, 1: 26–41.

Findlay, A.M. and King, R. (2010) *Motivation and Experience of UK Students Studying Abroad, Research Paper Number 8*, London: Department for Business Innovation and Skills.

Gu, Q, Schweisfurth, M. and Day, C. (2010) 'Learning and growing in a "foreign" context: intercultural experiences of international students', *Compare*, 40, 1: 7–23.

Guruz, K. (2007) *Higher Education and International Student Mobility in the Global Knowledge Economy*, Albany: New York State University Press.

IPSOS Mori/Unite (2006) *The International Student Experience Report*. Online. Available HTTP: http://www.ipsos-mori.com/assets/docs/archive/polls/unite-international.pdf (accessed 15 May 2010).

Jackling, B. (2007) 'The lure of permanent residency and the aspirations and expectations of international students studying accounting in Australia', *People and Place*, 15, 3: 31–41.

Lee, J.J. and Rice, C. (2007) 'Welcome to America? International student perceptions of discrimination and neo-racism', *Higher Education*, 53: 381–409.

McLeod, M. and Wainwright, P. (2009) 'Researching the study abroad experience', *Journal of Studies in International Education*, 13, 1: 66–71.

Olsen, A. (2008) 'International mobility of Australian university students: 2005', *Journal of Studies in International Education*, 12, 4: 364–74.

Rivza, B. and Teichler, U. (2007) 'The changing role of student mobility', *Higher Education Policy*, 20: 457–75.

SCMR (Sussex Centre for Migration Research) (2004) *International Student Mobility*, Bristol: Higher Education Funding Council for England.

Summers, M. and Volet, S. (2008) 'Students' attitudes towards culturally mixed groups on international campuses', *Studies in Higher Education*, 33, 4: 357–70.

Thorstensson, L. (2001) 'This business of internationalization: the academic experiences of 6 Asian MBA international students at the University of Minnesota's Carlson School of Management', *Journal of Studies in International Education*, 5: 317–40.

Tian, M. and Lowe, J. (2009) 'Existentialist internationalisation and the Chinese student experience in English universities', *Compare*, 39, 5: 659–76.

UCAS (2010) 'Find out more about studying in the UK'. Online. Available HTTP: http://www.ucas.ac.uk/students/wheretostart/nonukstudents/ (accessed 29 June 2010).

Zhang, Z. and Brunton, M. (2007) 'Differences in living and learning: Chinese international students in New Zealand', *Journal of Studies in International Education*, 11, 2: 124–40.

Index

Note: Page numbers followed by 'f' refer to figures and followed by 't' refer to tables.